CLAMP

10

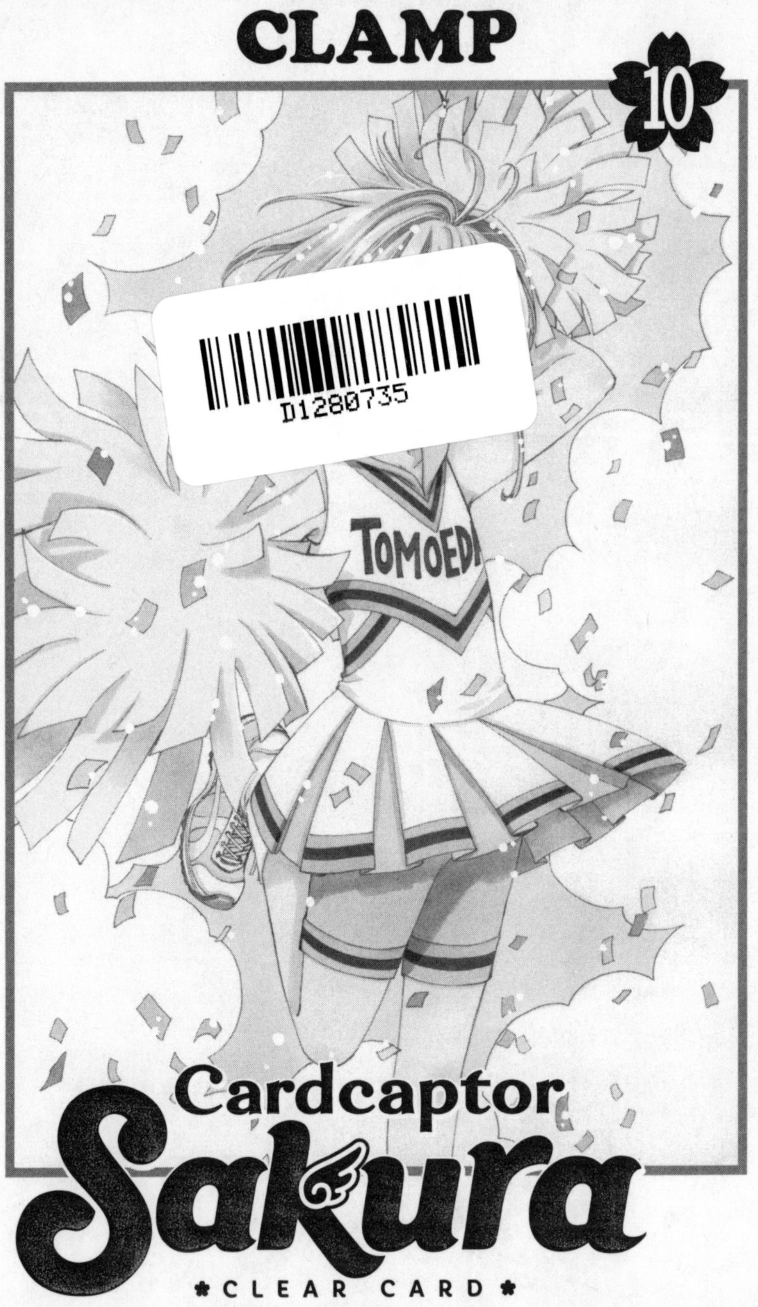

Cardcaptor Sakura

CLEAR CARD

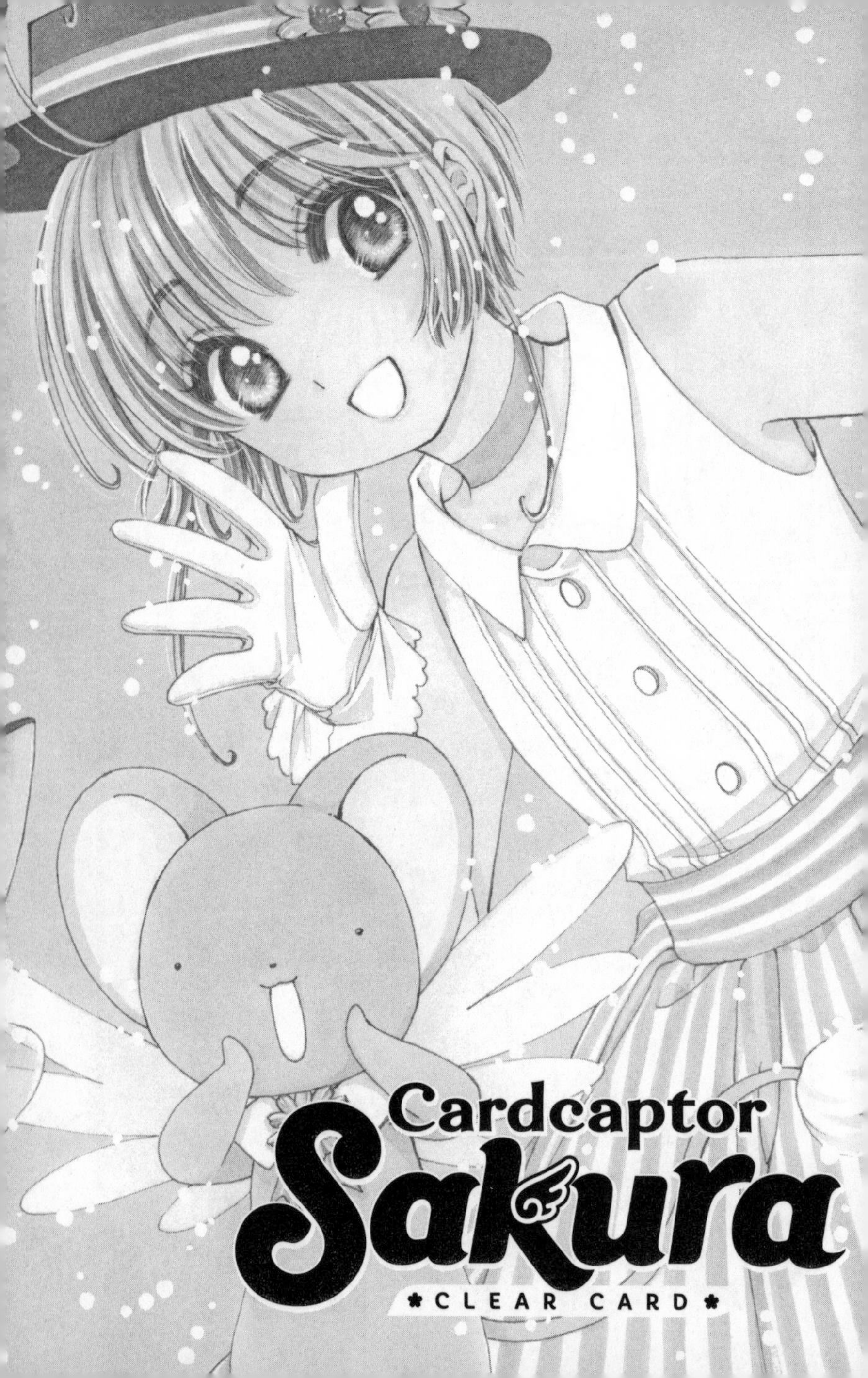
Cardcaptor
Sakura
CLEAR CARD

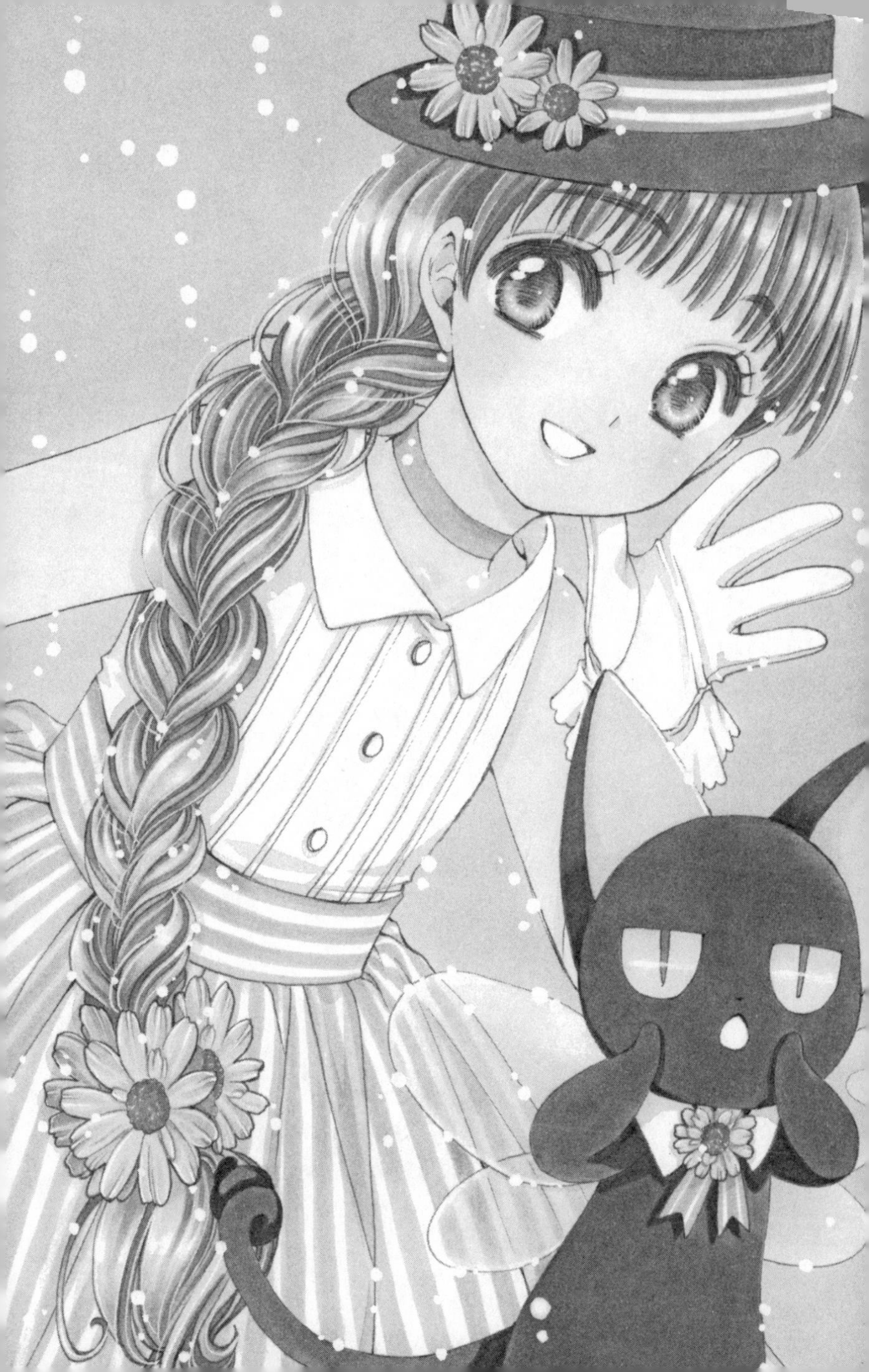

Cardcaptor Sakura
CLEAR CARD

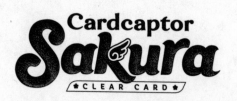

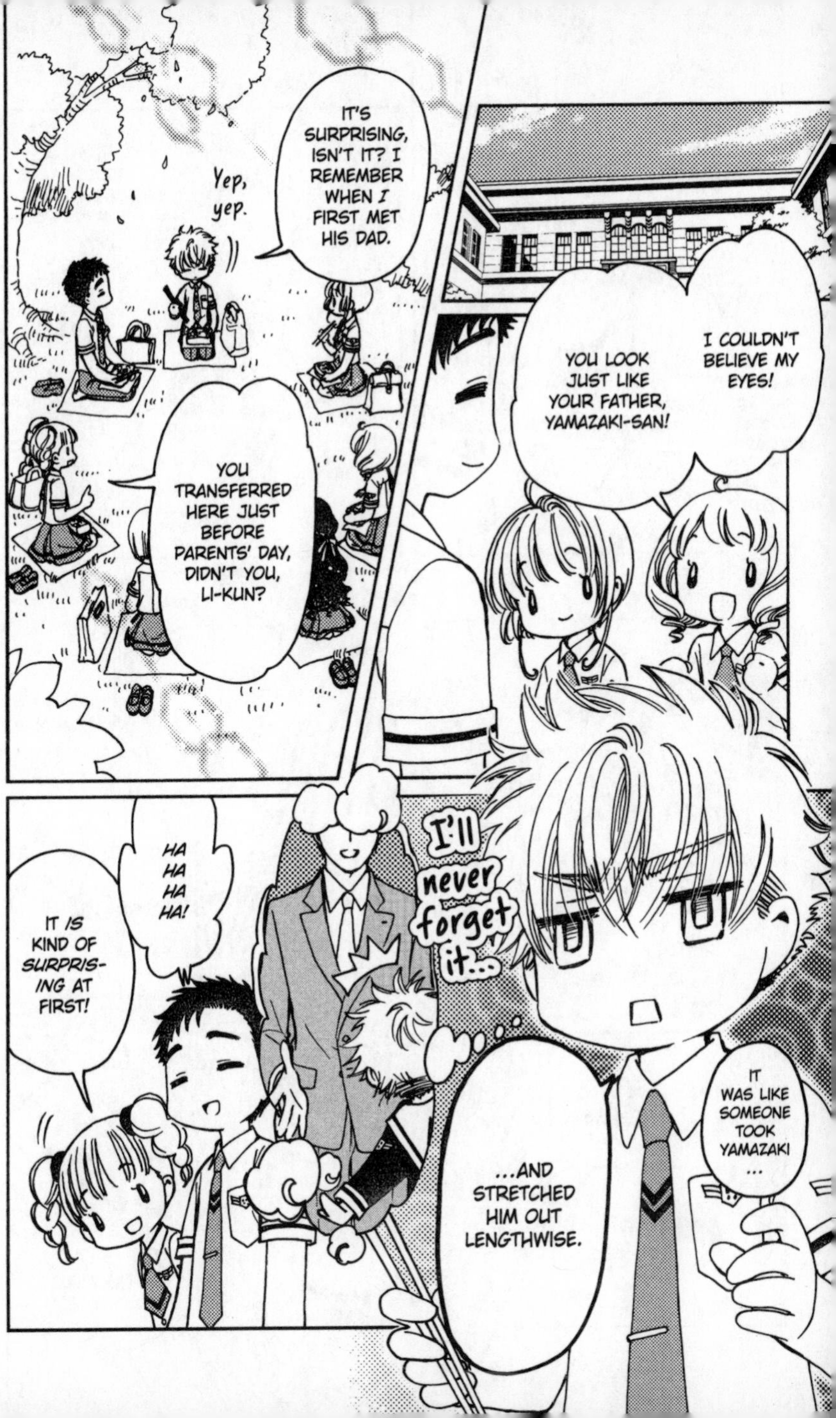
I COULDN'T BELIEVE MY EYES!
YOU LOOK JUST LIKE YOUR FATHER, YAMAZAKI-SAN!
IT'S SURPRISING, ISN'T IT? I REMEMBER WHEN I FIRST MET HIS DAD.
Yep, yep.
YOU TRANSFERRED HERE JUST BEFORE PARENTS' DAY, DIDN'T YOU, LI-KUN?
IT WAS LIKE SOMEONE TOOK YAMAZAKI ...
...AND STRETCHED HIM OUT LENGTHWISE.
I'll never forget it...
HA HA HA HA!
IT IS KIND OF SURPRIS-ING AT FIRST!

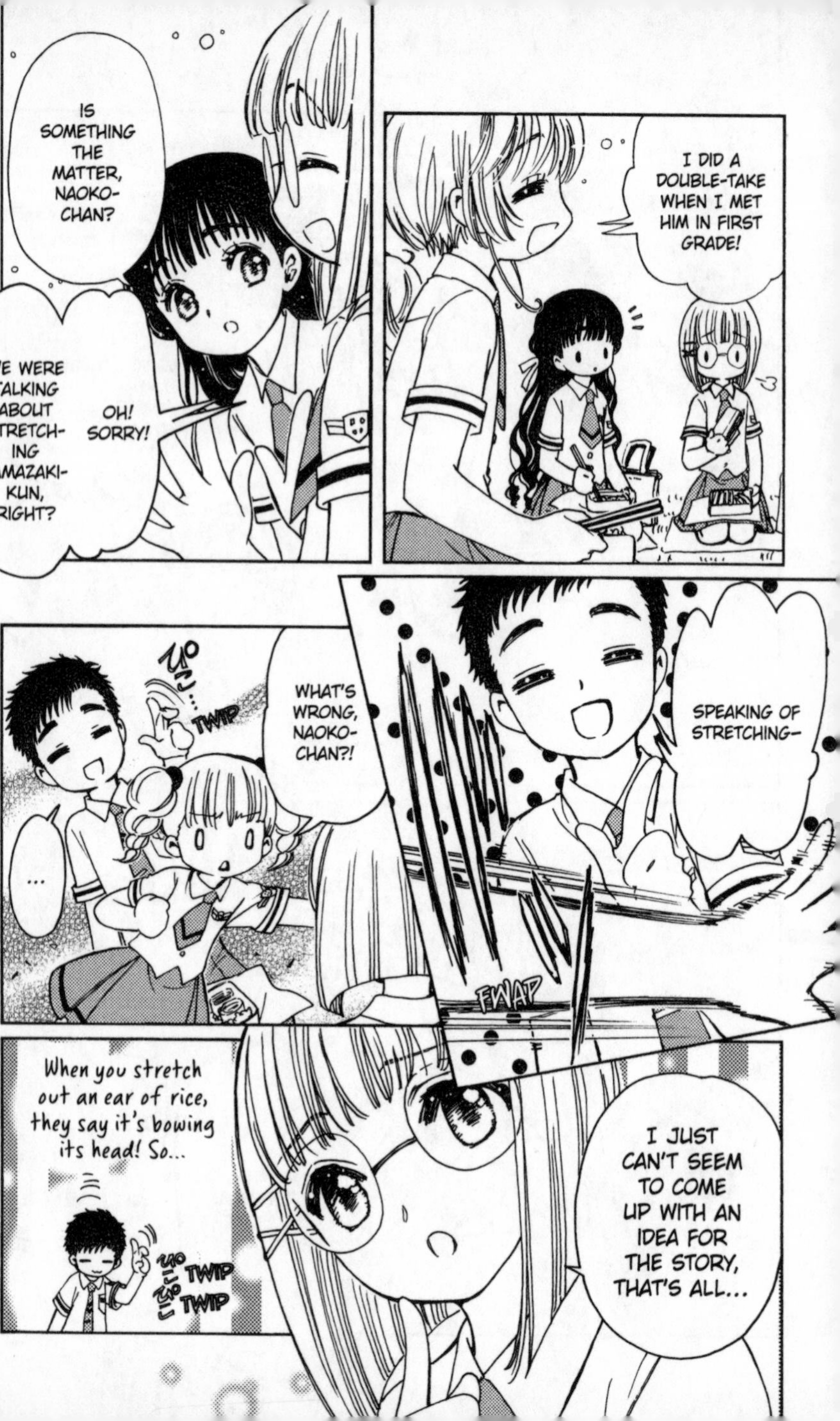
I DID A DOUBLE-TAKE WHEN I MET HIM IN FIRST GRADE!
IS SOMETHING THE MATTER, NAOKO-CHAN?
OH! SORRY!
WE WERE TALKING ABOUT STRETCHING YAMAZAKI-KUN, RIGHT?
SPEAKING OF STRETCHING–
FWAP
WHAT'S WRONG, NAOKO-CHAN?!
TWIP
...
I JUST CAN'T SEEM TO COME UP WITH AN IDEA FOR THE STORY, THAT'S ALL...
When you stretch out an ear of rice, they say it's bowing its head! So...
TWIP
TWIP

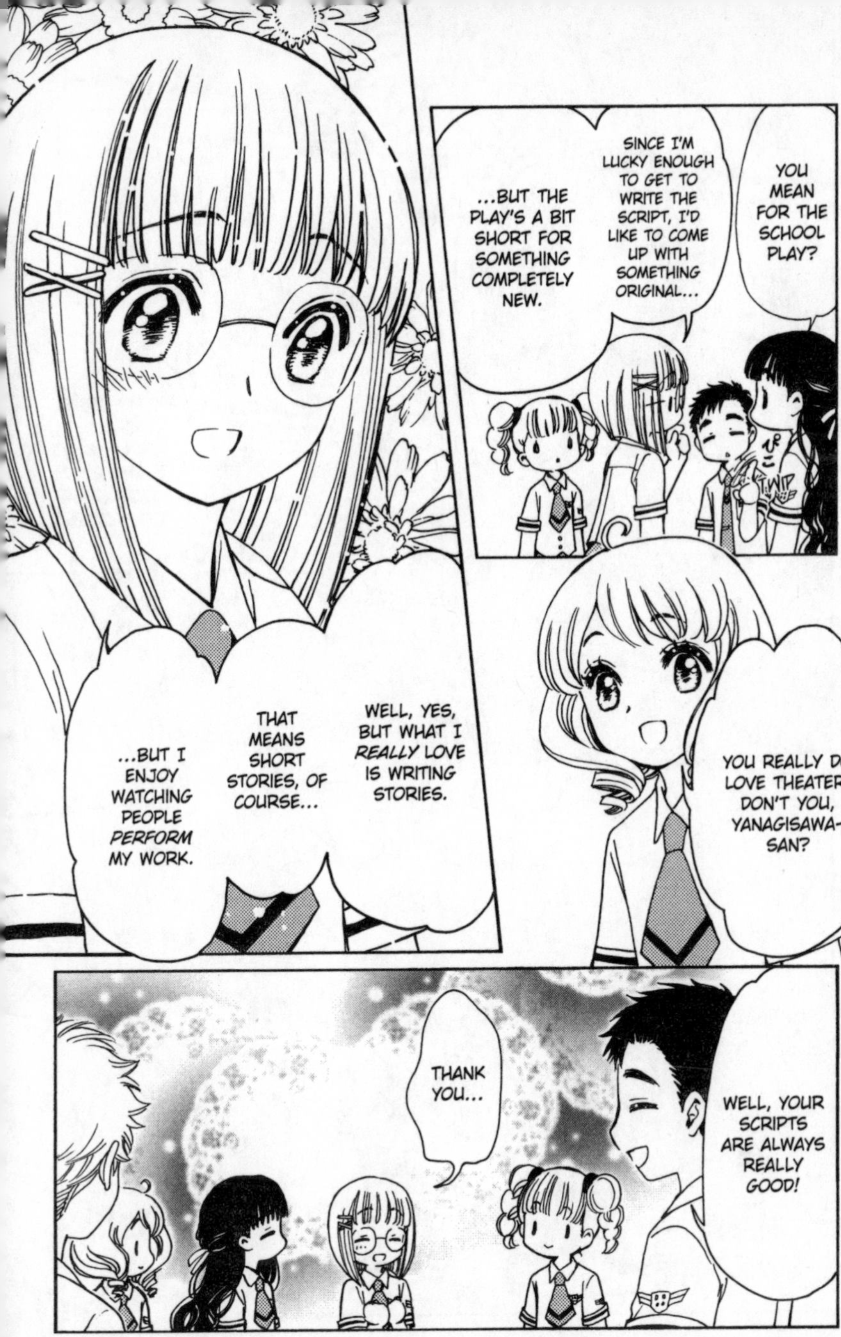
YOU MEAN FOR THE SCHOOL PLAY?
SINCE I'M LUCKY ENOUGH TO GET TO WRITE THE SCRIPT, I'D LIKE TO COME UP WITH SOMETHING ORIGINAL...
...BUT THE PLAY'S A BIT SHORT FOR SOMETHING COMPLETELY NEW.
YOU REALLY DO LOVE THEATER, DON'T YOU, YANAGISAWA-SAN?
WELL, YES, BUT WHAT I *REALLY* LOVE IS WRITING STORIES.
THAT MEANS SHORT STORIES, OF COURSE...
...BUT I ENJOY WATCHING PEOPLE *PERFORM* MY WORK.
WELL, YOUR SCRIPTS ARE ALWAYS REALLY GOOD!
THANK YOU...

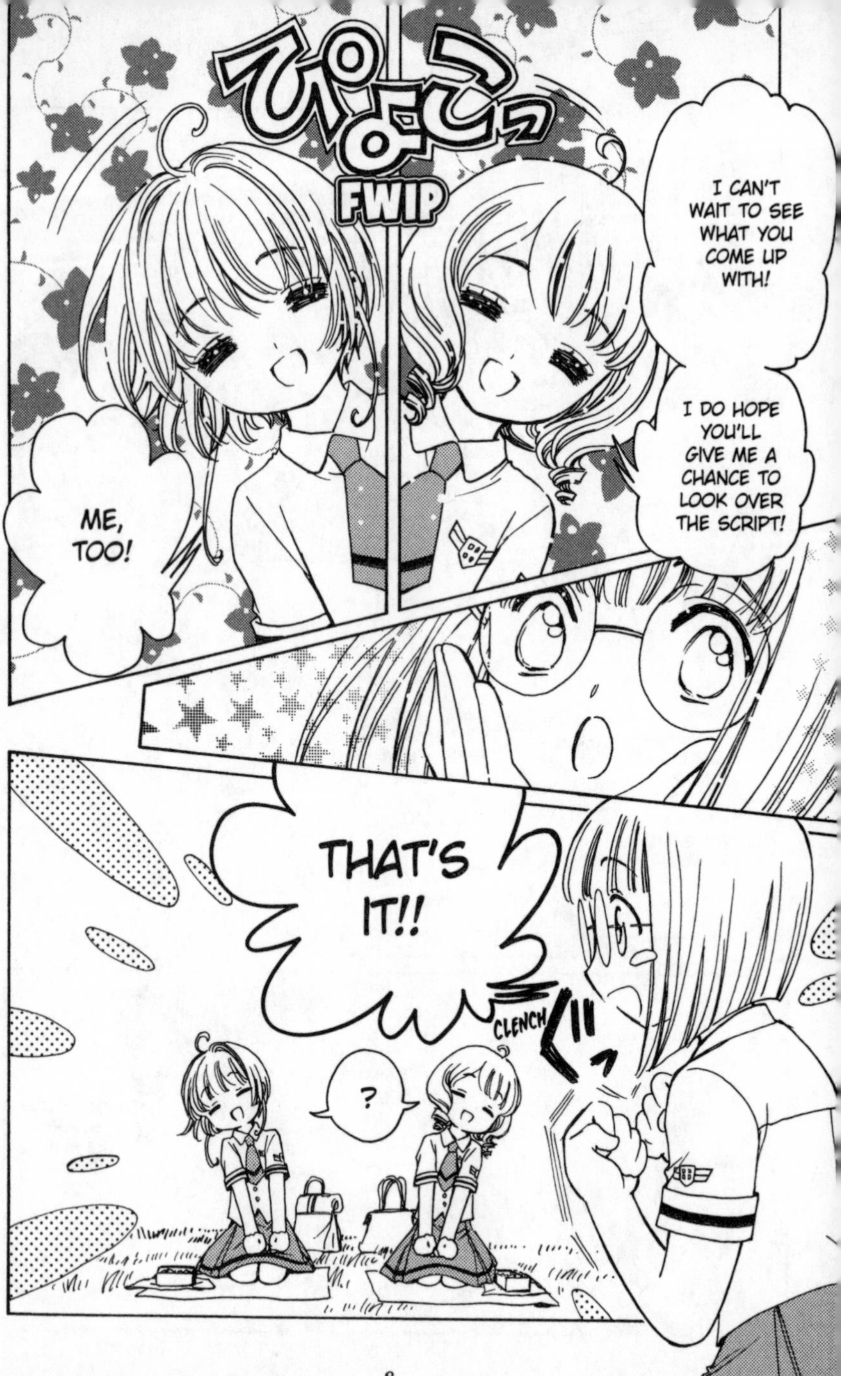
I CAN'T WAIT TO SEE WHAT YOU COME UP WITH!
I DO HOPE YOU'LL GIVE ME A CHANCE TO LOOK OVER THE SCRIPT!
ぴょこっ
FWIP
ME, TOO!
THAT'S IT!!
CLENCH
?

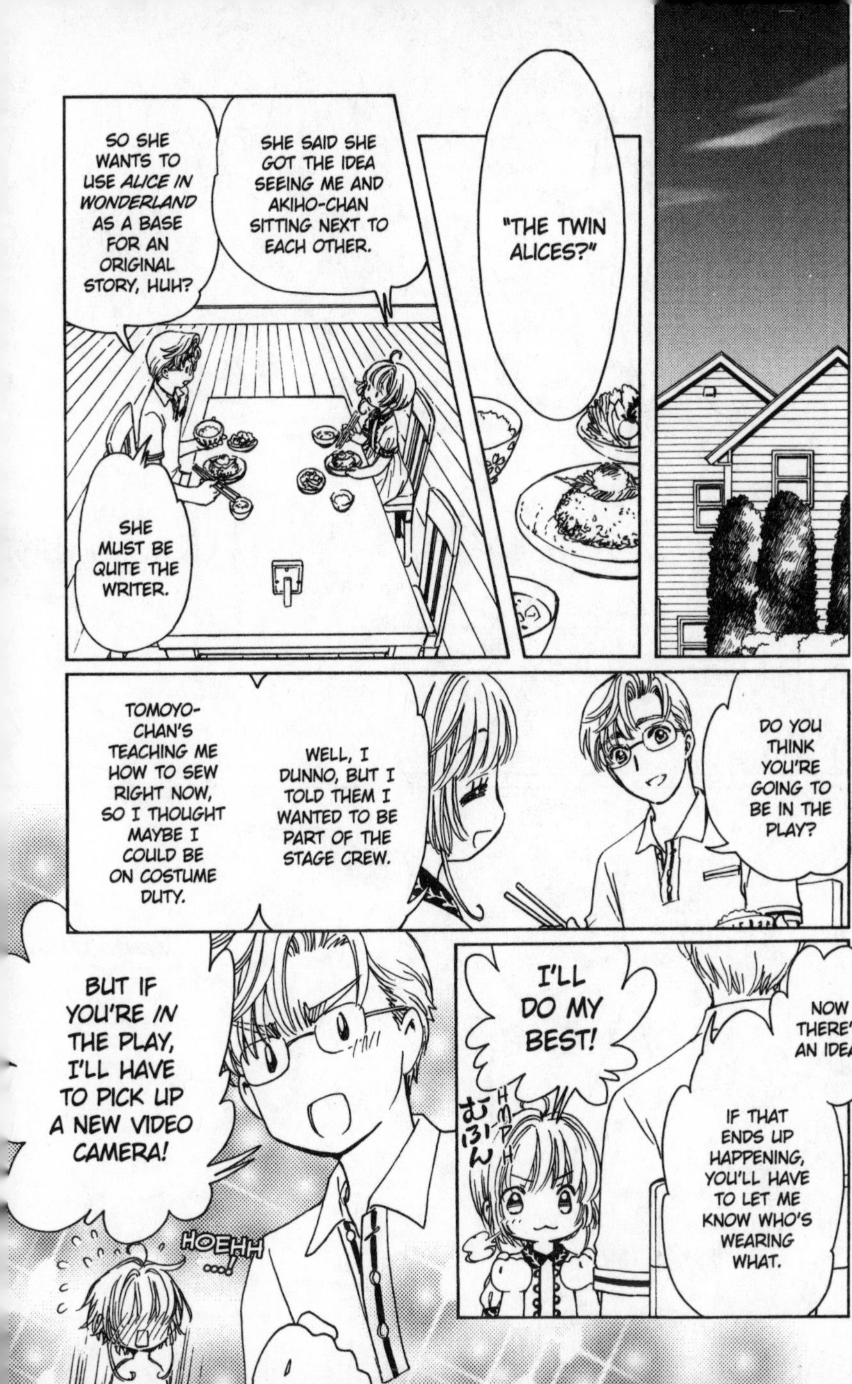
"THE TWIN ALICES?"
SHE SAID SHE GOT THE IDEA SEEING ME AND AKIHO-CHAN SITTING NEXT TO EACH OTHER.
SO SHE WANTS TO USE *ALICE IN WONDERLAND* AS A BASE FOR AN ORIGINAL STORY, HUH?
SHE MUST BE QUITE THE WRITER.
DO YOU THINK YOU'RE GOING TO BE IN THE PLAY?
WELL, I DUNNO, BUT I TOLD THEM I WANTED TO BE PART OF THE STAGE CREW.
TOMOYO-CHAN'S TEACHING ME HOW TO SEW RIGHT NOW, SO I THOUGHT MAYBE I COULD BE ON COSTUME DUTY.
NOW THERE'S AN IDEA!
IF THAT ENDS UP HAPPENING, YOU'LL HAVE TO LET ME KNOW WHO'S WEARING WHAT.
I'LL DO MY BEST!
HMPH
むふん
BUT IF YOU'RE *IN* THE PLAY, I'LL HAVE TO PICK UP A NEW VIDEO CAMERA!
HOEHH...!

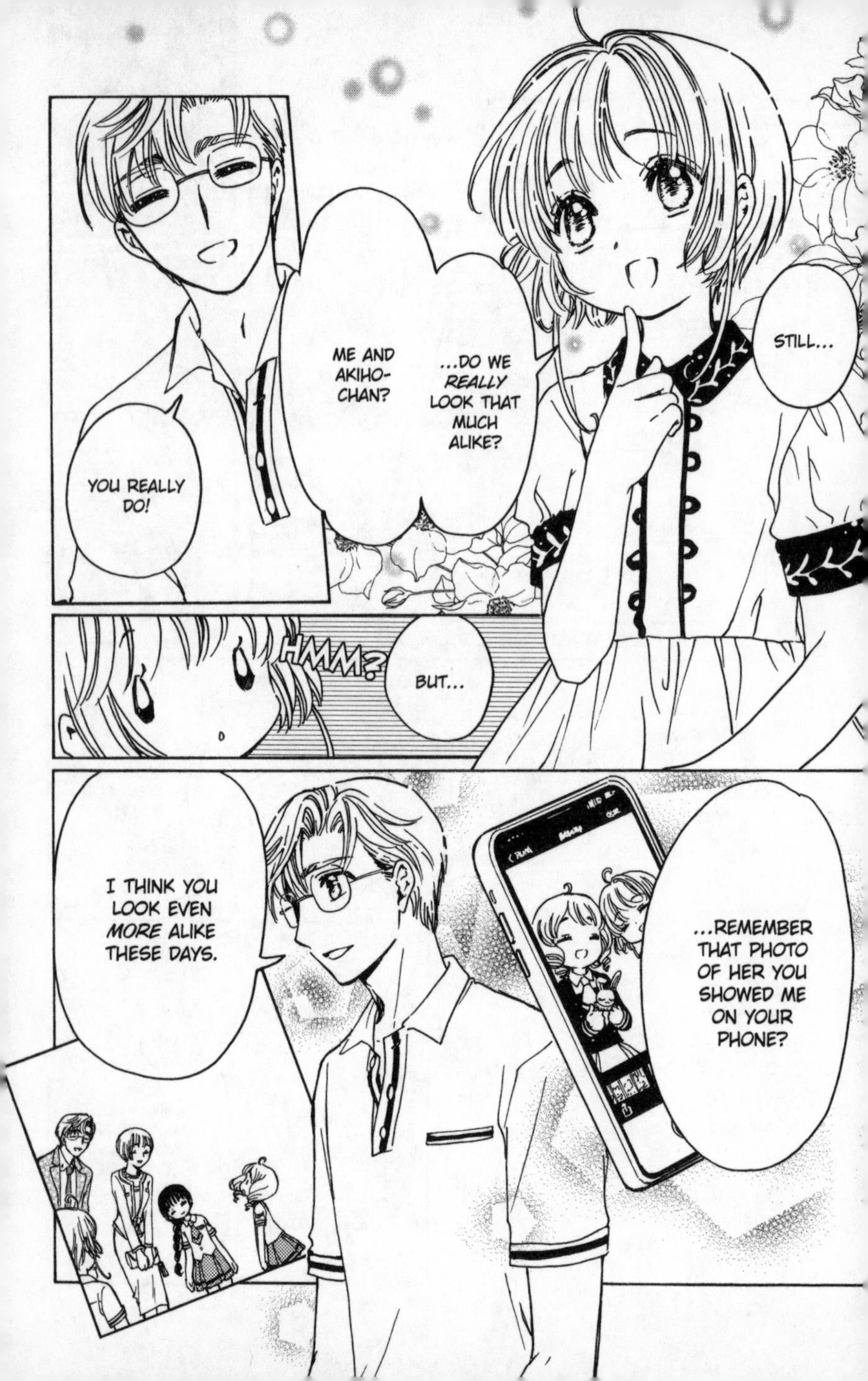
STILL...
ME AND AKIHO-CHAN?
...DO WE *REALLY* LOOK THAT MUCH ALIKE?
BUT...
YOU REALLY DO!
HMM?
...REMEMBER THAT PHOTO OF HER YOU SHOWED ME ON YOUR PHONE?
I THINK YOU LOOK EVEN *MORE* ALIKE THESE DAYS.

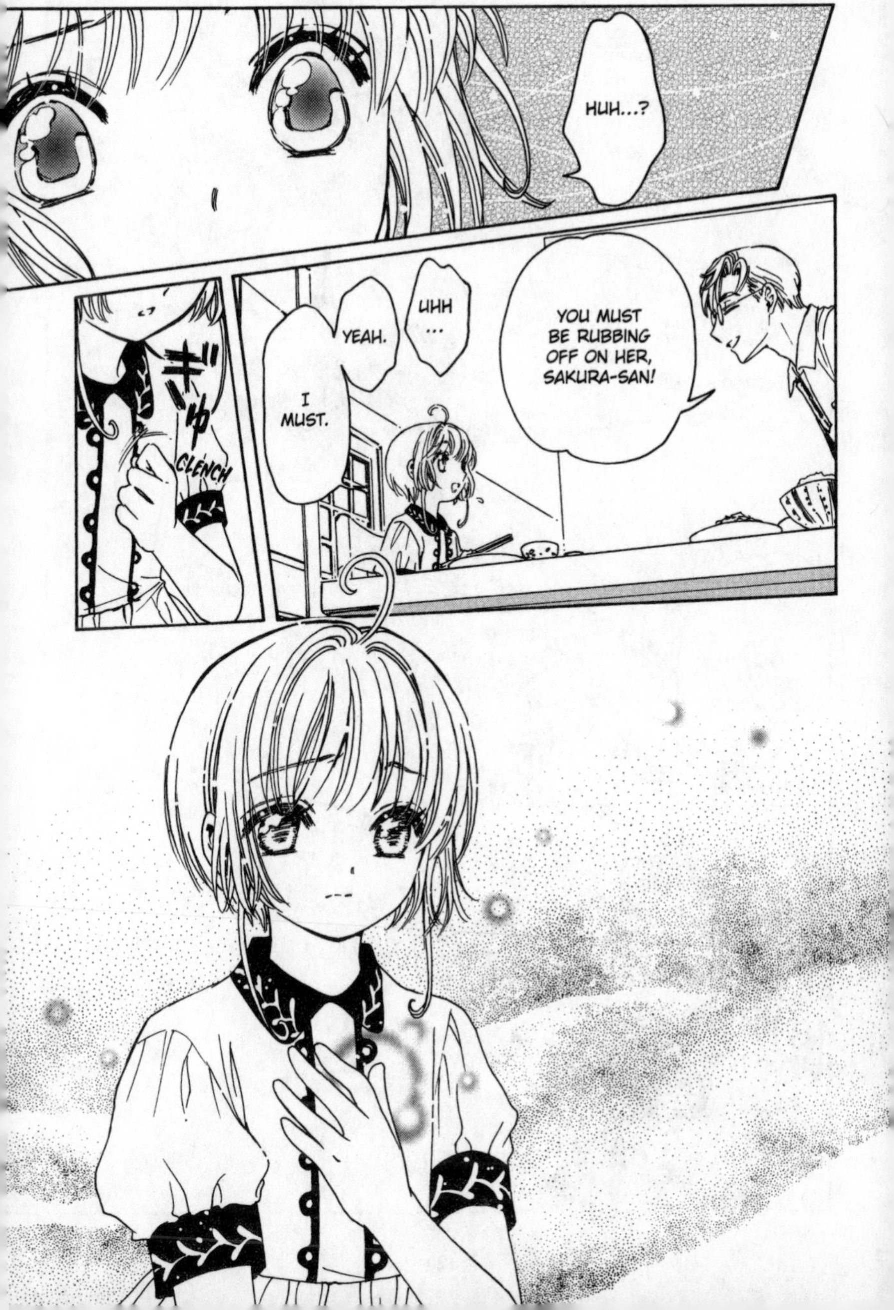
HUH...?
YOU MUST BE RUBBING OFF ON HER, SAKURA-SAN!
UHH ...
YEAH.
I MUST.
ギュ
CLENCH

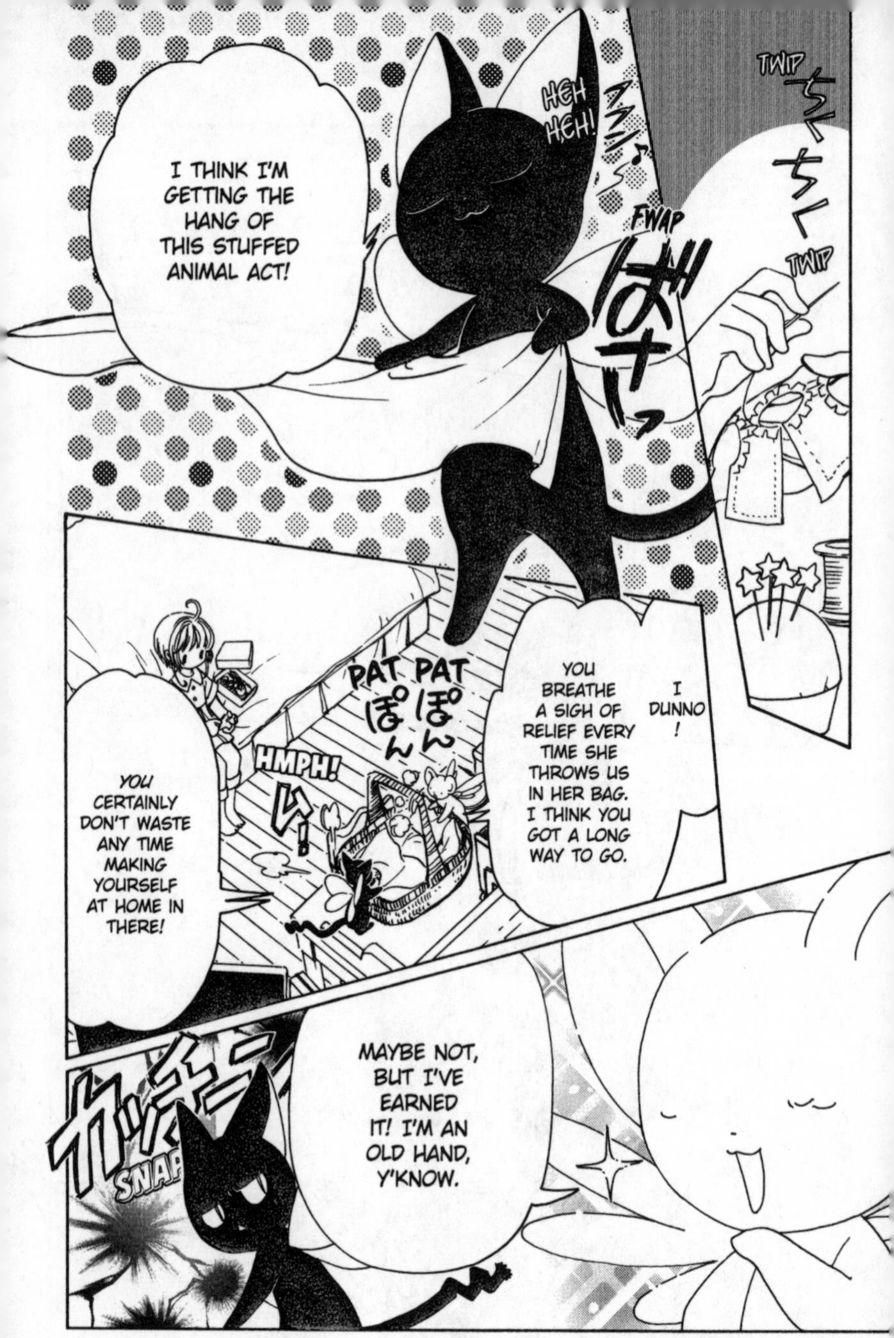

TWIP ちくちく TWIP
HEH HEH! ふふふ♪
FWAP ぱさーっ
I THINK I'M GETTING THE HANG OF THIS STUFFED ANIMAL ACT!
I DUNNO!
YOU BREATHE A SIGH OF RELIEF EVERY TIME SHE THROWS US IN HER BAG. I THINK YOU GOT A LONG WAY TO GO.
PAT PAT ぽんぽん
HMPH! ぷい!
YOU CERTAINLY DON'T WASTE ANY TIME MAKING YOURSELF AT HOME IN THERE!
MAYBE NOT, BUT I'VE EARNED IT! I'M AN OLD HAND, Y'KNOW.
SNAP カッチー

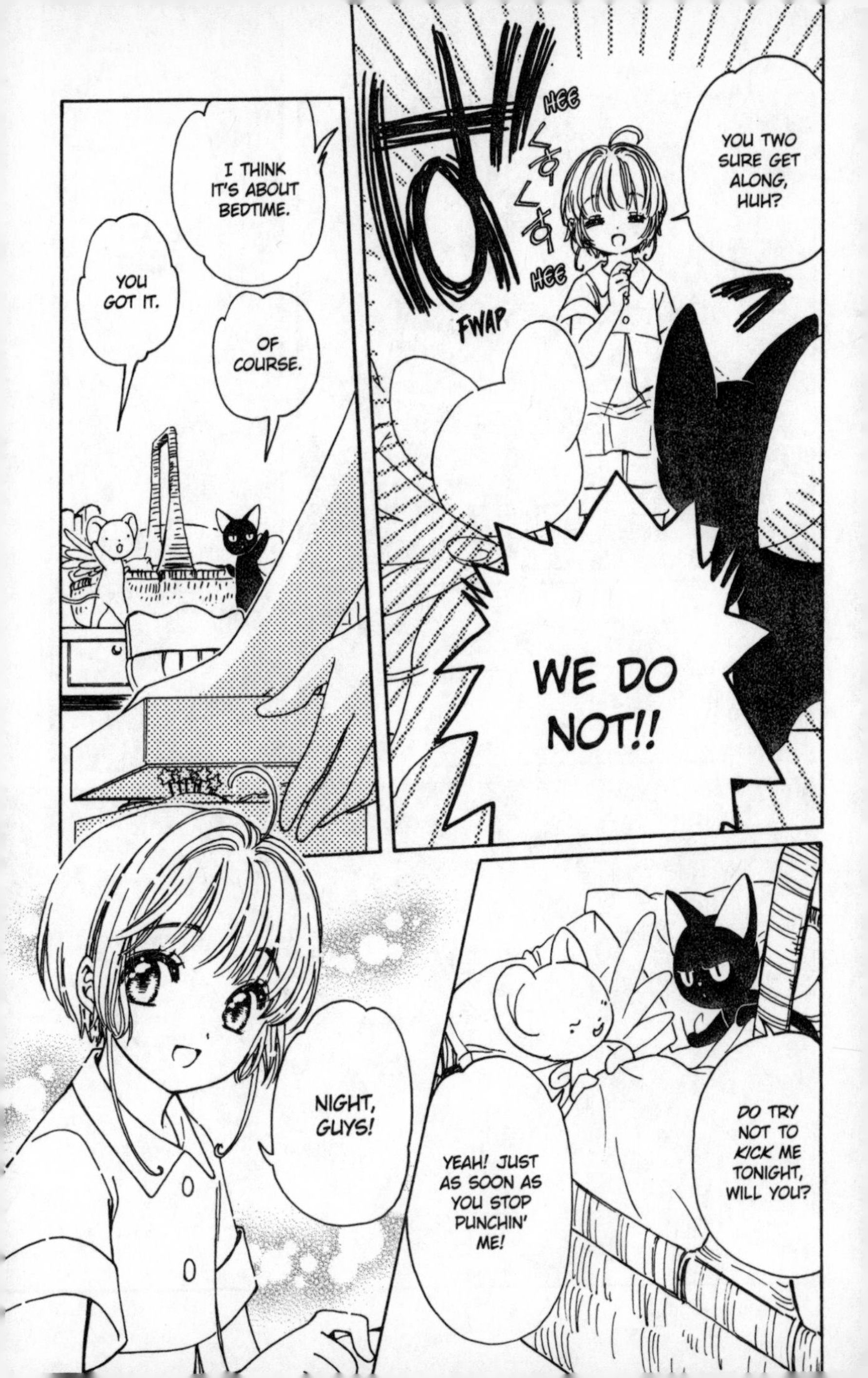
YOU TWO SURE GET ALONG, HUH?
HEE
HEE
FWAP
WE DO NOT!!
I THINK IT'S ABOUT BEDTIME.
OF COURSE.
YOU GOT IT.
DO TRY NOT TO *KICK* ME TONIGHT, WILL YOU?
YEAH! JUST AS SOON AS YOU STOP PUNCHIN' ME!
NIGHT, GUYS!

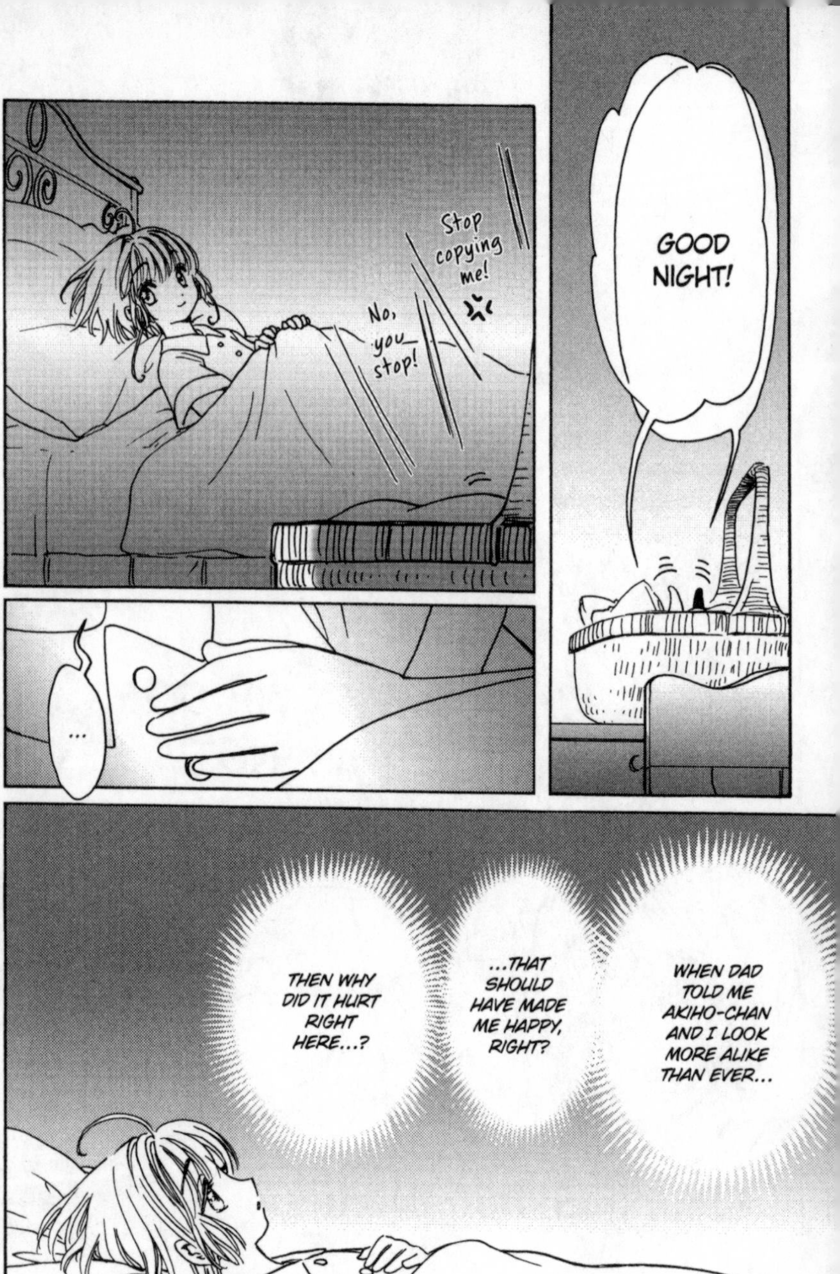
GOOD NIGHT!
Stop copying me!
No, you stop!
...
WHEN DAD TOLD ME AKIHO-CHAN AND I LOOK MORE ALIKE THAN EVER...
...THAT SHOULD HAVE MADE ME HAPPY, RIGHT?
THEN WHY DID IT HURT RIGHT HERE...?

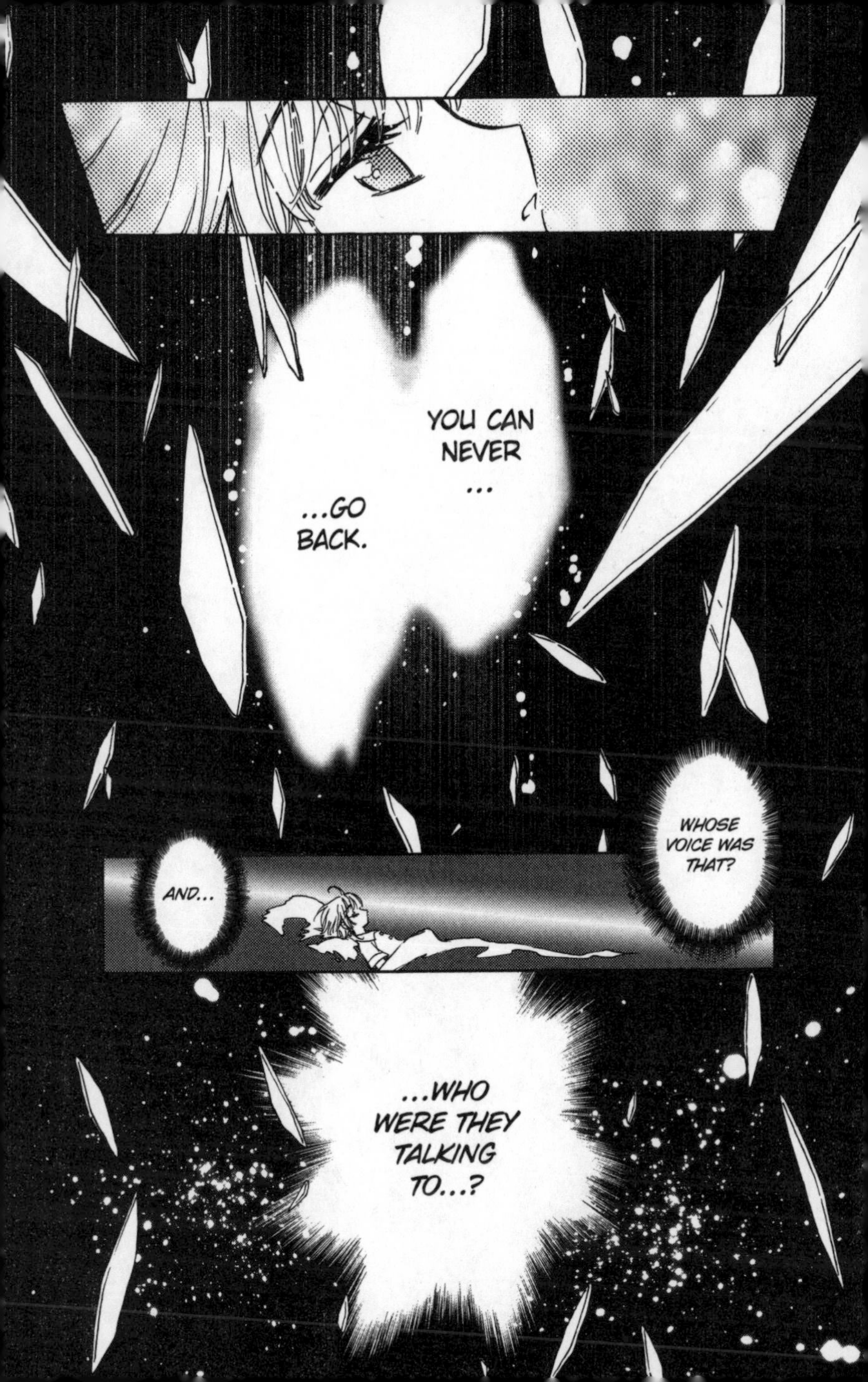
YOU CAN NEVER ...
...GO BACK.
WHOSE VOICE WAS THAT?
AND...
...WHO WERE THEY TALKING TO...?

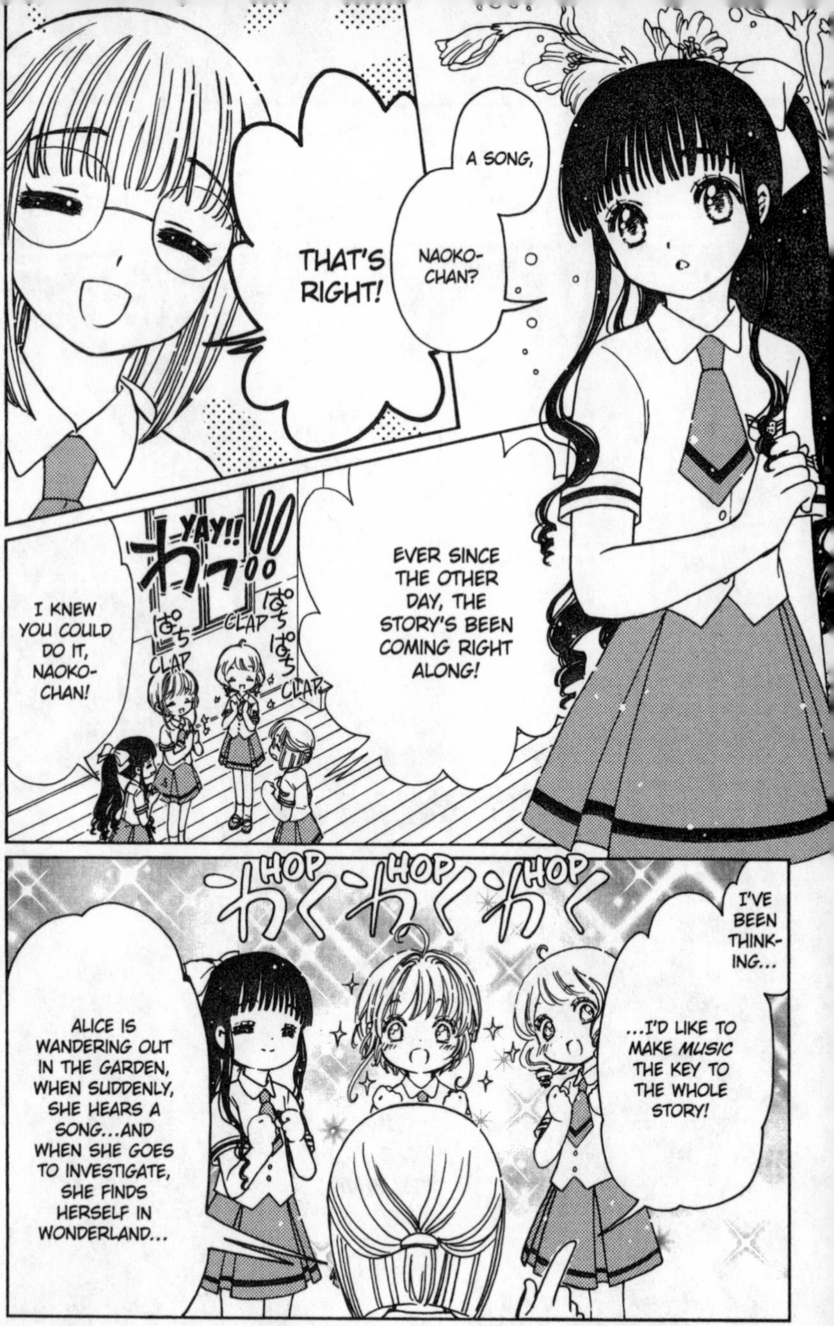

A SONG,
NAOKO-CHAN?
THAT'S RIGHT!
EVER SINCE THE OTHER DAY, THE STORY'S BEEN COMING RIGHT ALONG!
わっ
YAY!!
ぱちぱち
CLAP CLAP CLAP
I KNEW YOU COULD DO IT, NAOKO-CHAN!
わくわくわく
HOP HOP HOP
I'VE BEEN THINKING...
...I'D LIKE TO MAKE *MUSIC* THE KEY TO THE WHOLE STORY!
ALICE IS WANDERING OUT IN THE GARDEN, WHEN SUDDENLY, SHE HEARS A SONG...AND WHEN SHE GOES TO INVESTIGATE, SHE FINDS HERSELF IN WONDERLAND...

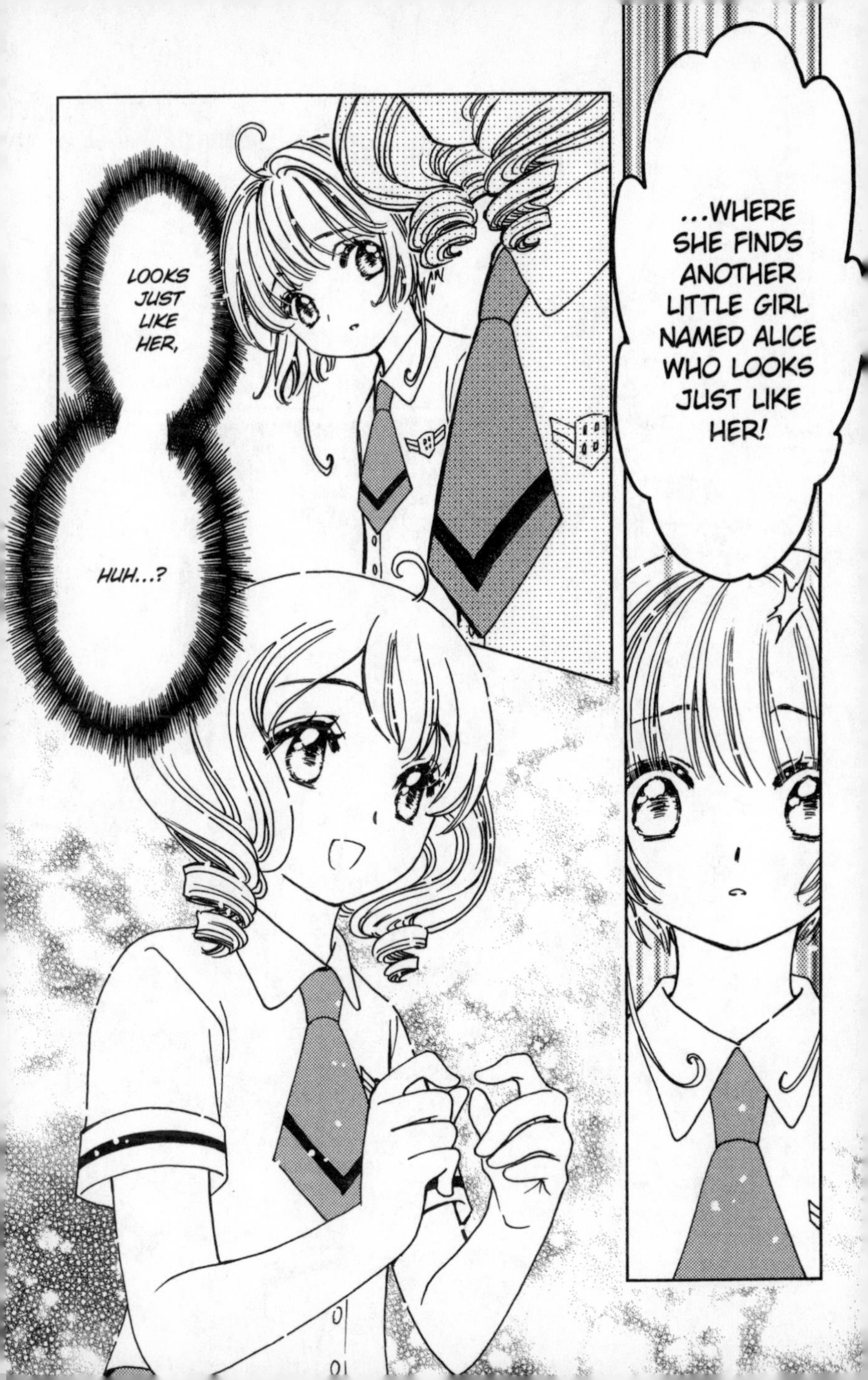
...WHERE SHE FINDS ANOTHER LITTLE GIRL NAMED ALICE WHO LOOKS JUST LIKE HER!
LOOKS JUST LIKE HER,
HUH...?

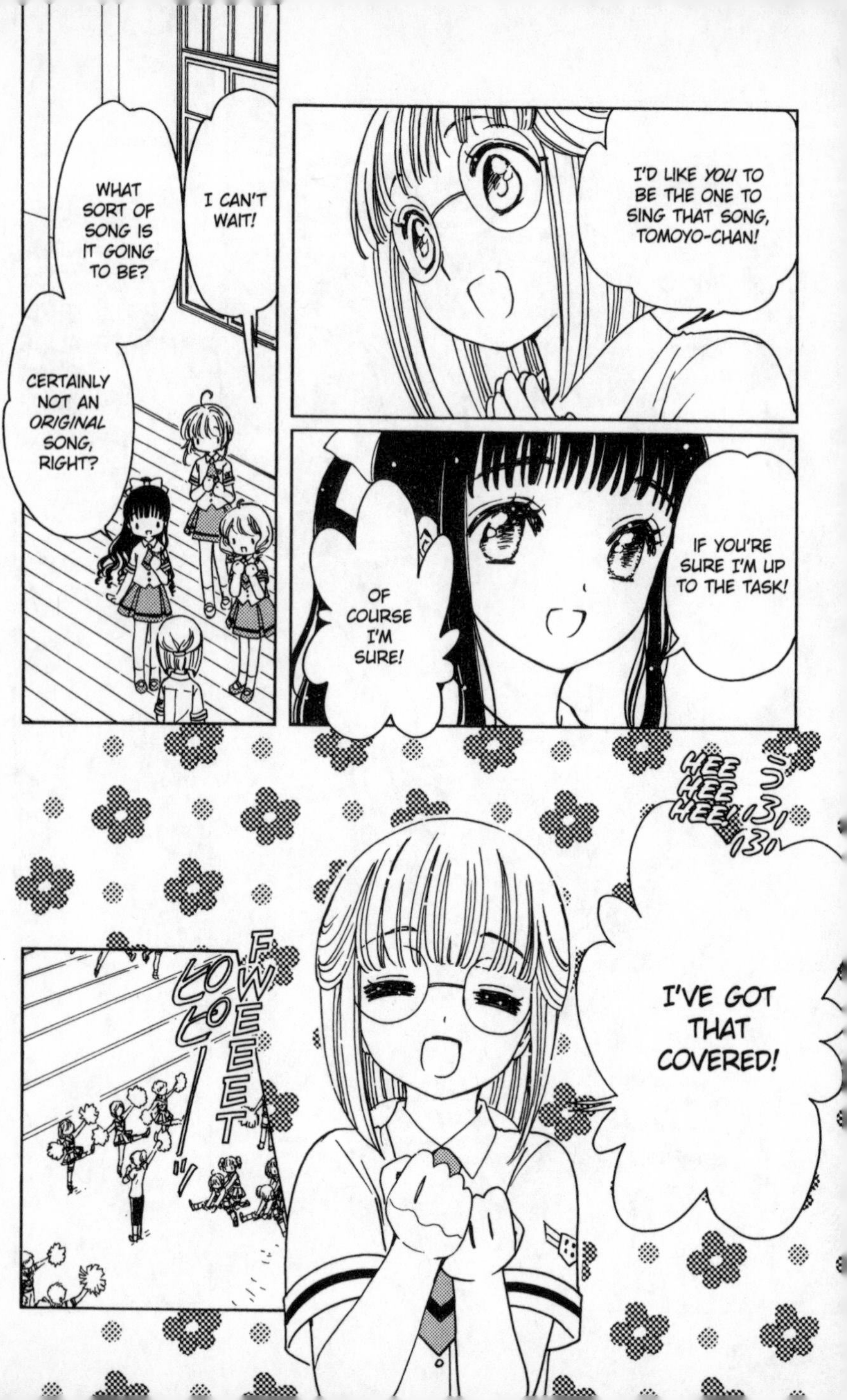
I'D LIKE YOU TO BE THE ONE TO SING THAT SONG, TOMOYO-CHAN!
IF YOU'RE SURE I'M UP TO THE TASK!
OF COURSE I'M SURE!
I CAN'T WAIT!
WHAT SORT OF SONG IS IT GOING TO BE?
CERTAINLY NOT AN ORIGINAL SONG, RIGHT?
HEE HEE HEE!
I'VE GOT THAT COVERED!
FWEEEET

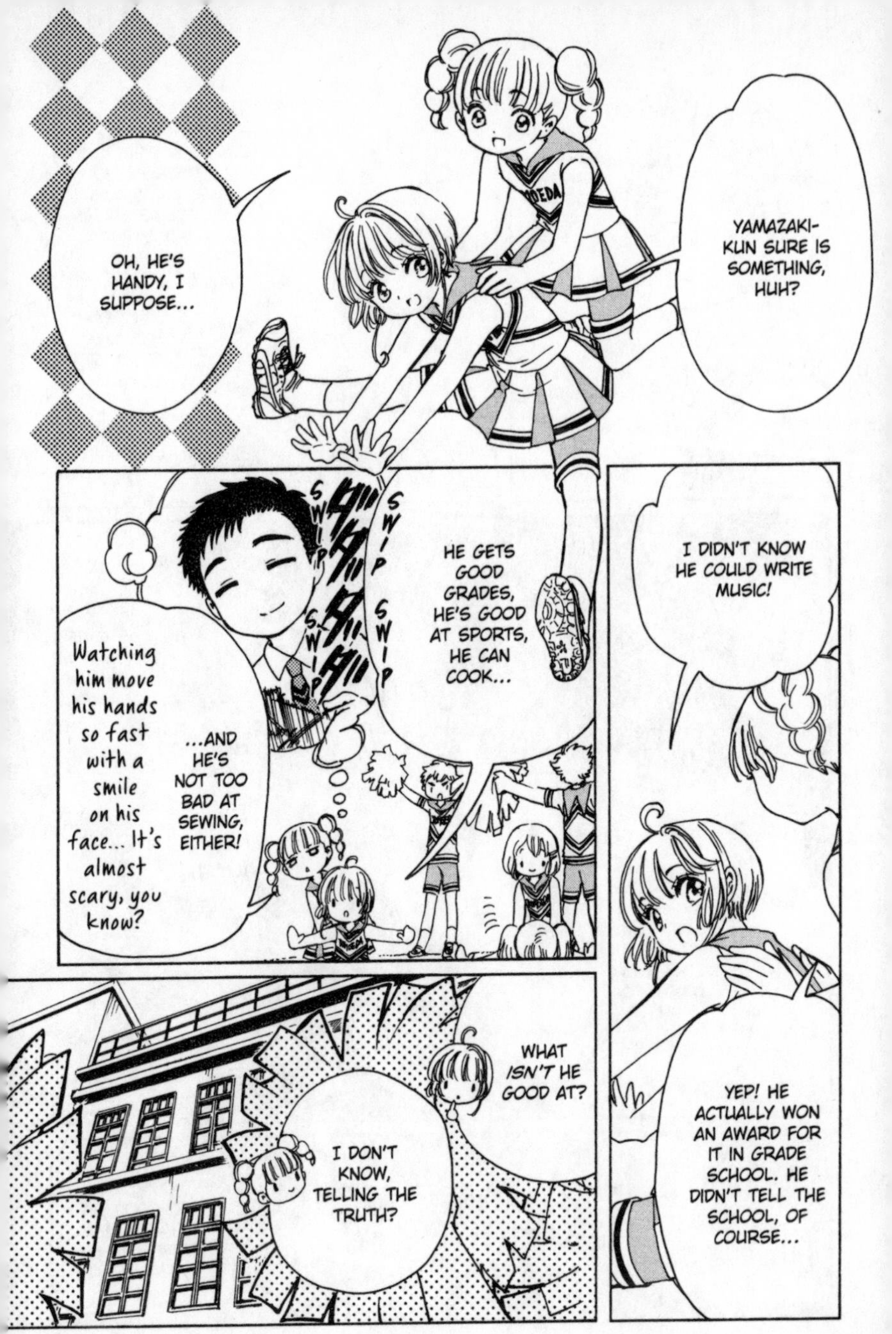
YAMAZAKI-KUN SURE IS SOMETHING, HUH?
OH, HE'S HANDY, I SUPPOSE...
I DIDN'T KNOW HE COULD WRITE MUSIC!
YEP! HE ACTUALLY WON AN AWARD FOR IT IN GRADE SCHOOL. HE DIDN'T TELL THE SCHOOL, OF COURSE...
SWIP
SWIP
HE GETS GOOD GRADES, HE'S GOOD AT SPORTS, HE CAN COOK...
SWIP
SWIP
...AND HE'S NOT TOO BAD AT SEWING, EITHER!
Watching him move his hands so fast with a smile on his face... It's almost scary, you know?
WHAT *ISN'T* HE GOOD AT?
I DON'T KNOW, TELLING THE TRUTH?

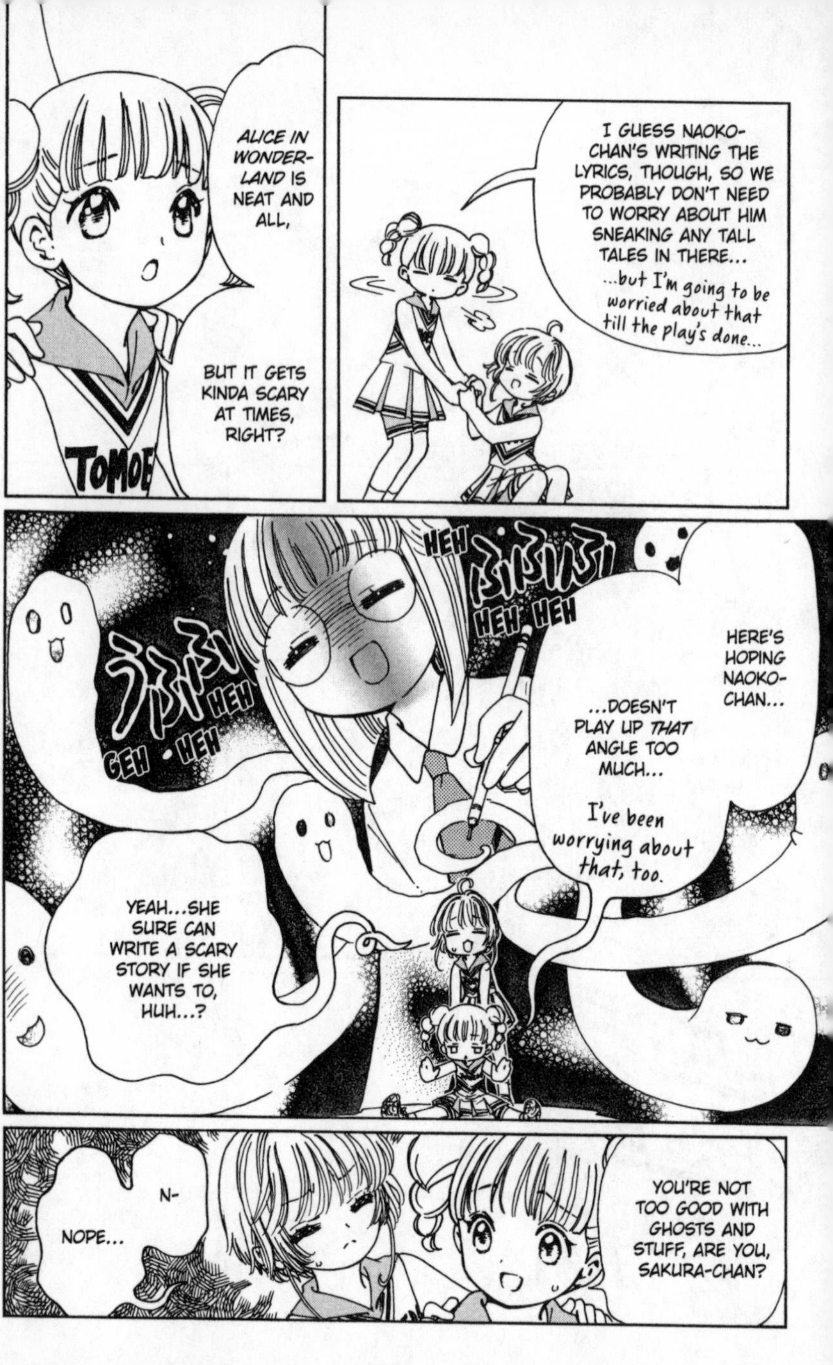
I GUESS NAOKO-CHAN'S WRITING THE LYRICS, THOUGH, SO WE PROBABLY DON'T NEED TO WORRY ABOUT HIM SNEAKING ANY TALL TALES IN THERE...
...but I'm going to be worried about that till the play's done...
ALICE IN WONDERLAND IS NEAT AND ALL,
BUT IT GETS KINDA SCARY AT TIMES, RIGHT?
TOMOE
HERE'S HOPING NAOKO-CHAN...
...DOESN'T PLAY UP *THAT* ANGLE TOO MUCH...
I've been worrying about that, too.
HEH HEH HEH
ふふふ
うふふ
HEH GEH HEH
YEAH...SHE SURE CAN WRITE A SCARY STORY IF SHE WANTS TO, HUH...?
YOU'RE NOT TOO GOOD WITH GHOSTS AND STUFF, ARE YOU, SAKURA-CHAN?
N-
NOPE...

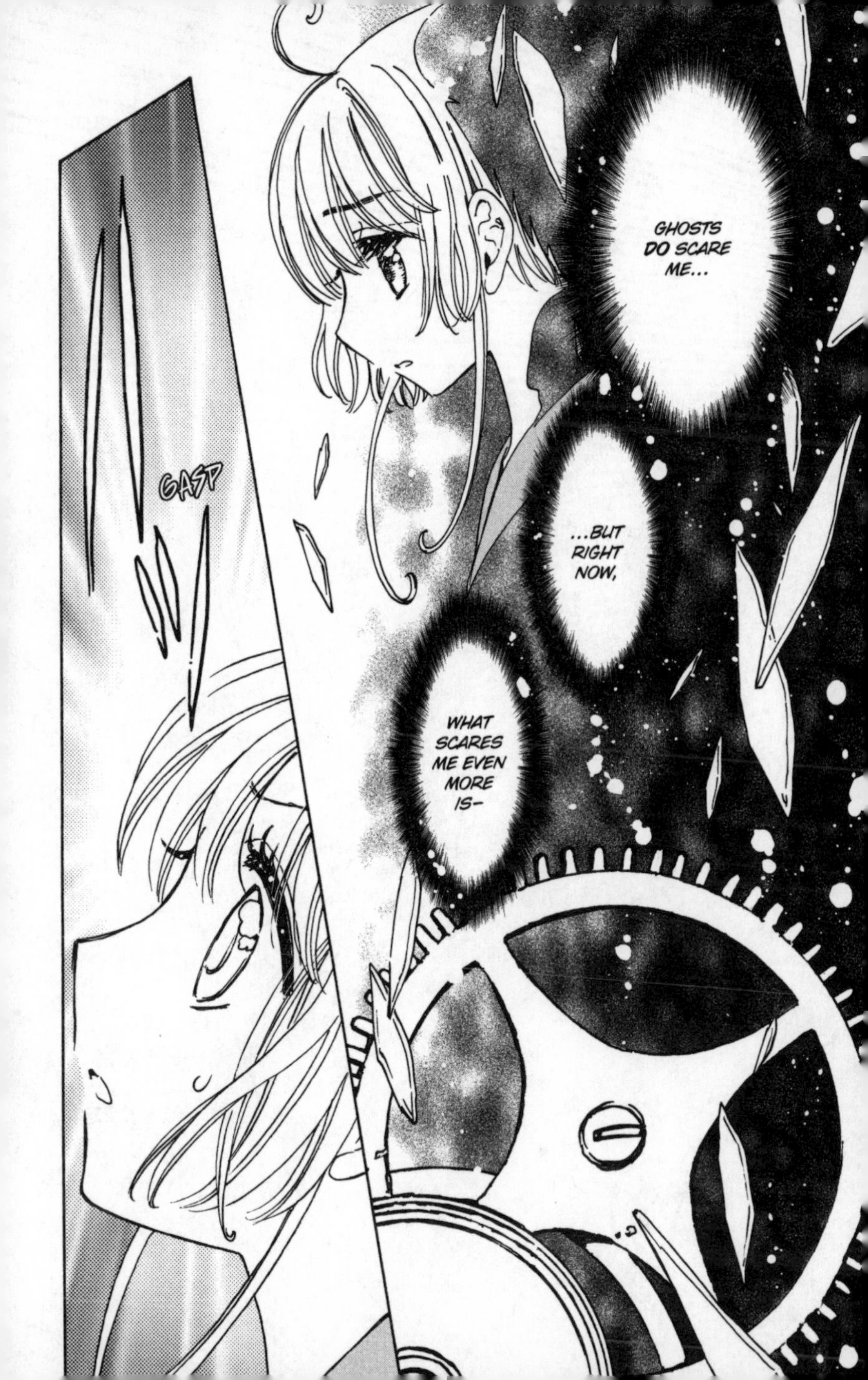
GHOSTS DO SCARE ME...
...BUT RIGHT NOW,
WHAT SCARES ME EVEN MORE IS-
GASP

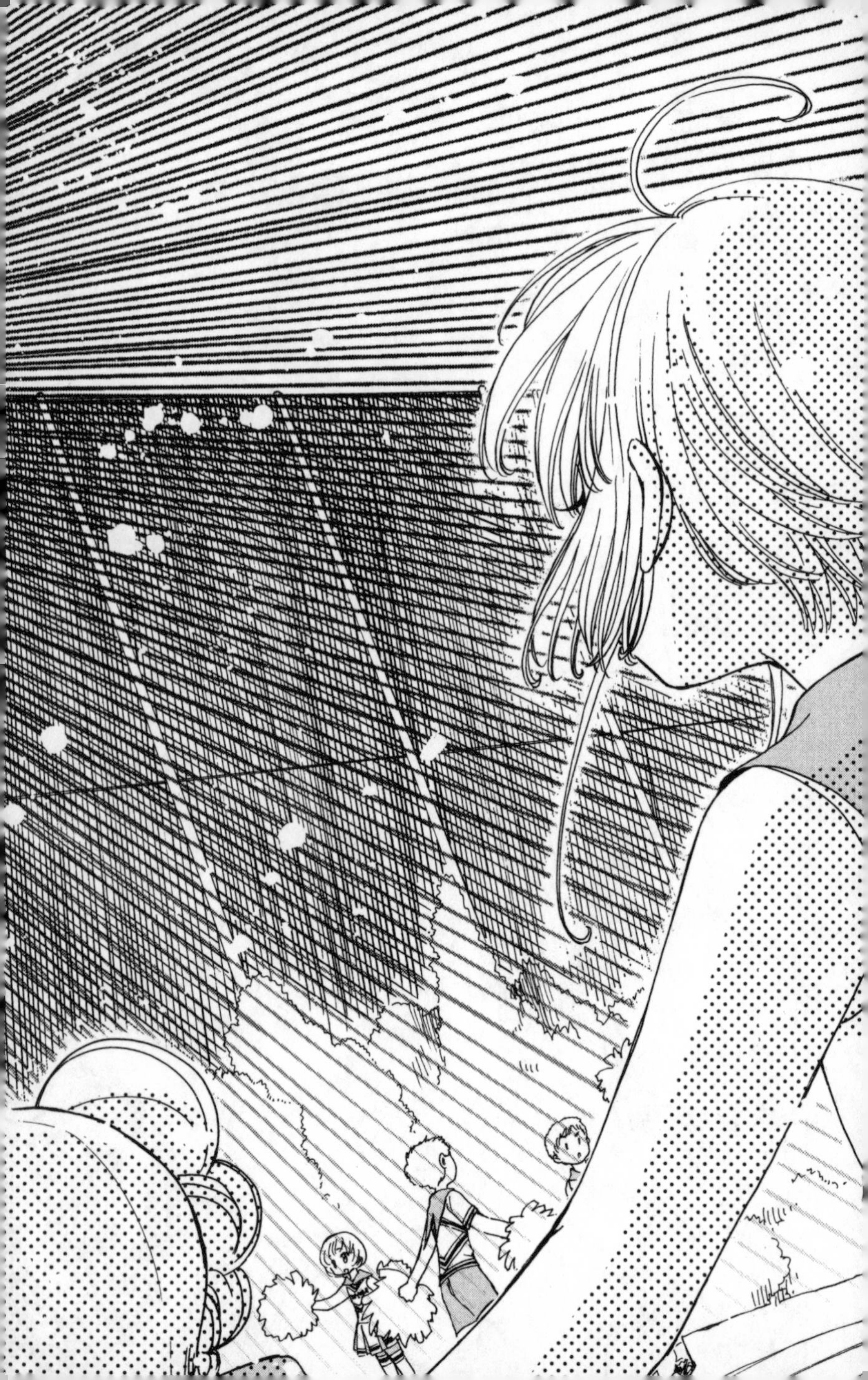

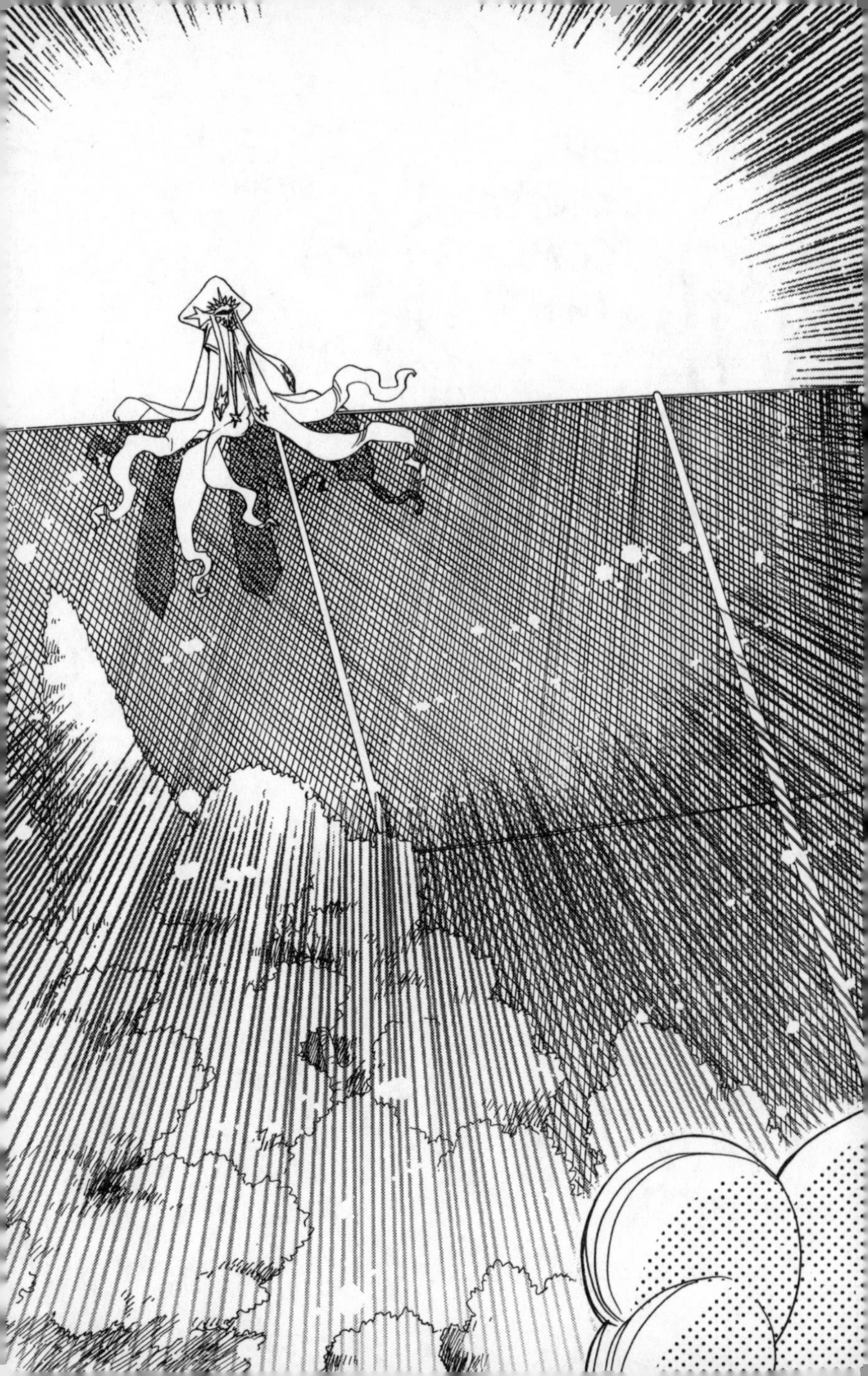

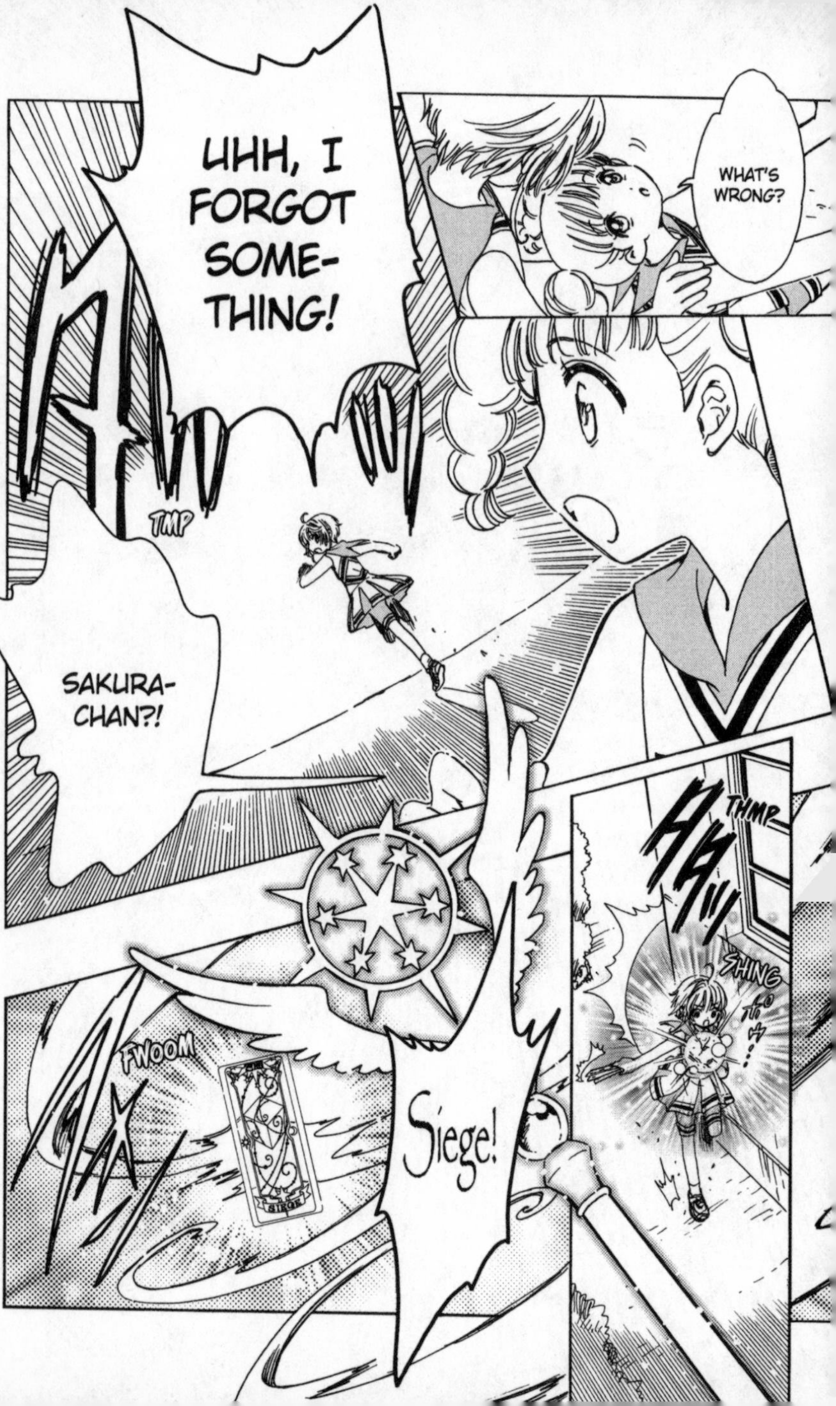
WHAT'S WRONG?
UHH, I FORGOT SOME-THING!
TMP
SAKURA-CHAN?!
THMP
SHING
Siege!
FWOOM

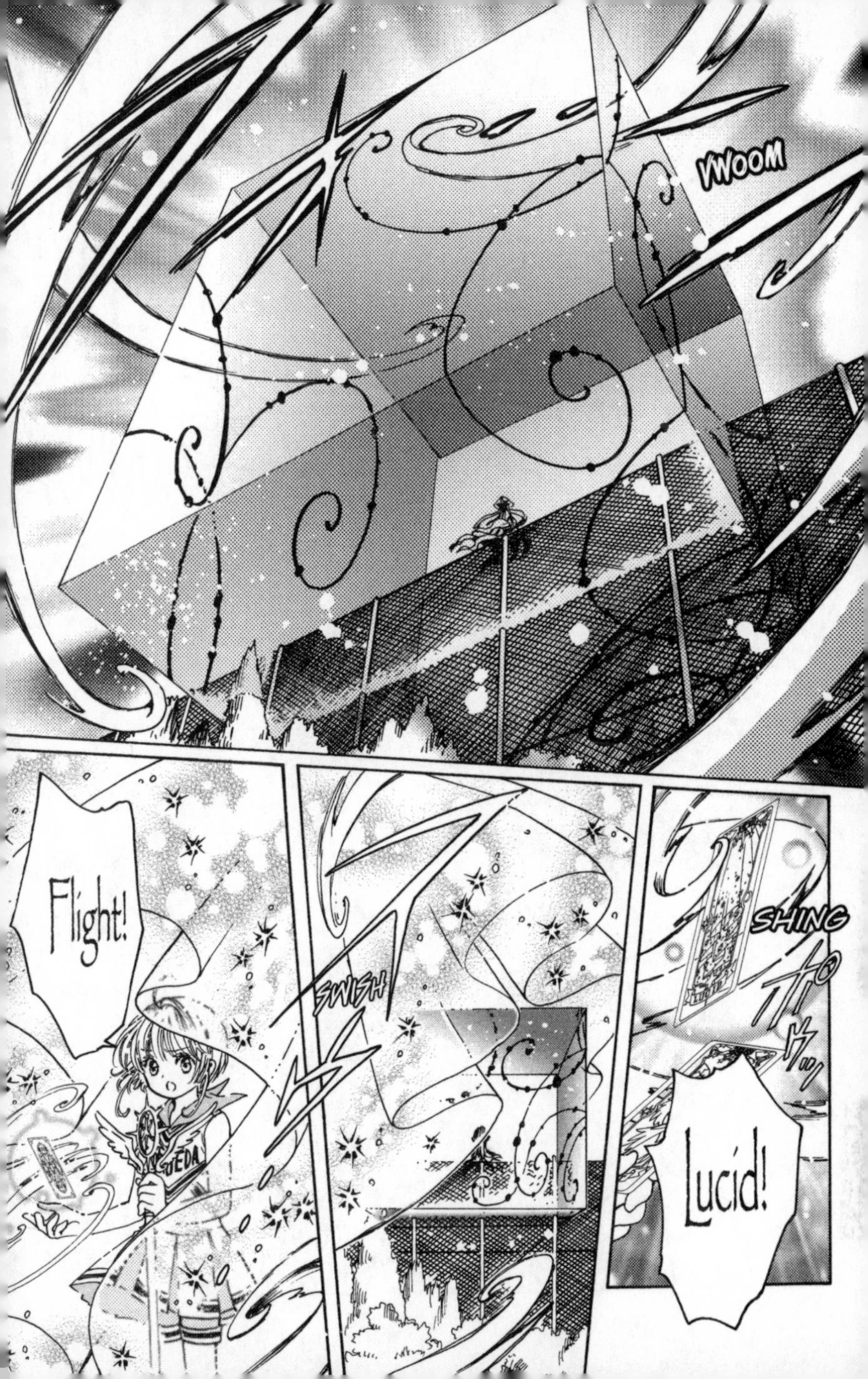
VWOOM
SHING
Lucid!
SWISH
Flight!

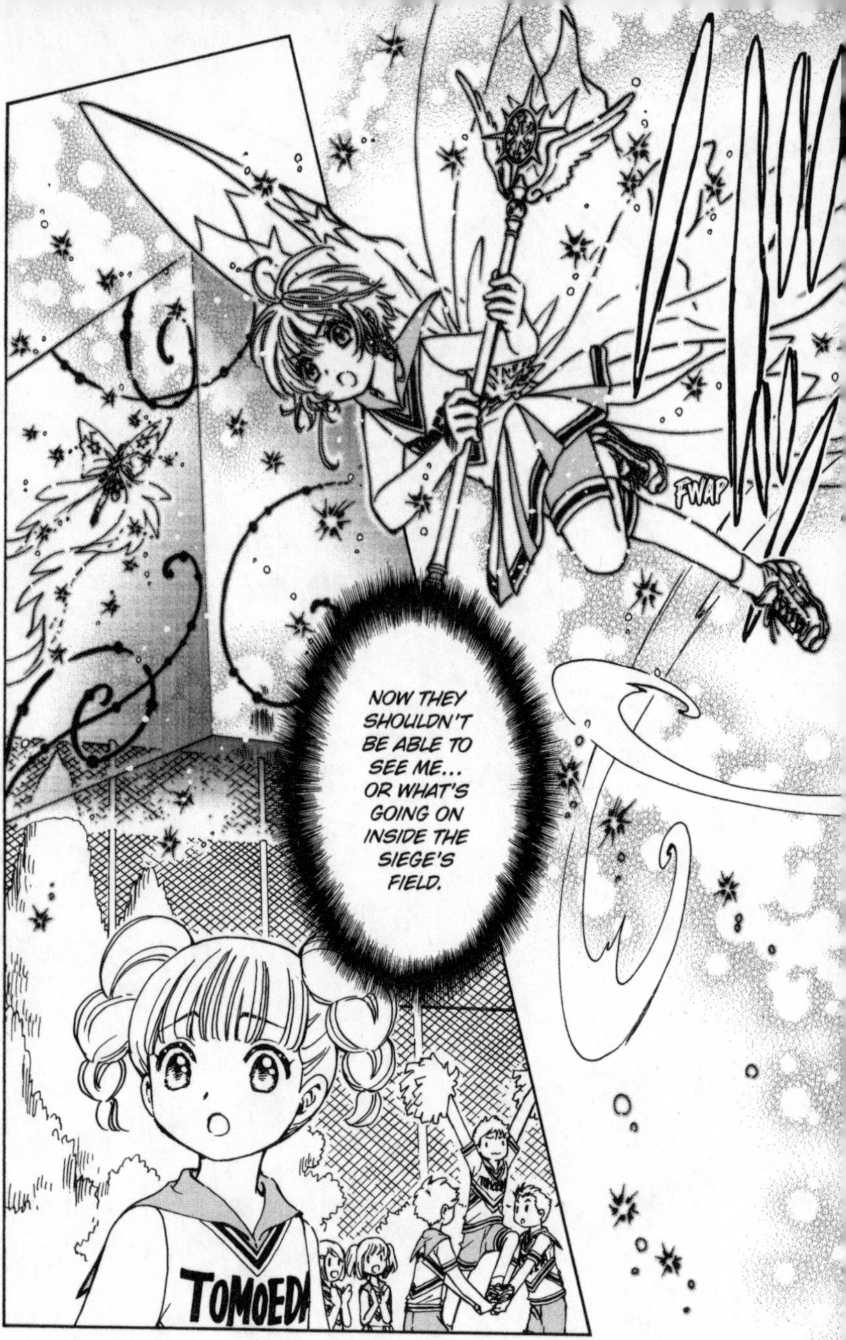
FWAP
NOW THEY SHOULDN'T BE ABLE TO SEE ME... OR WHAT'S GOING ON INSIDE THE SIEGE'S FIELD.
TOMOEDA

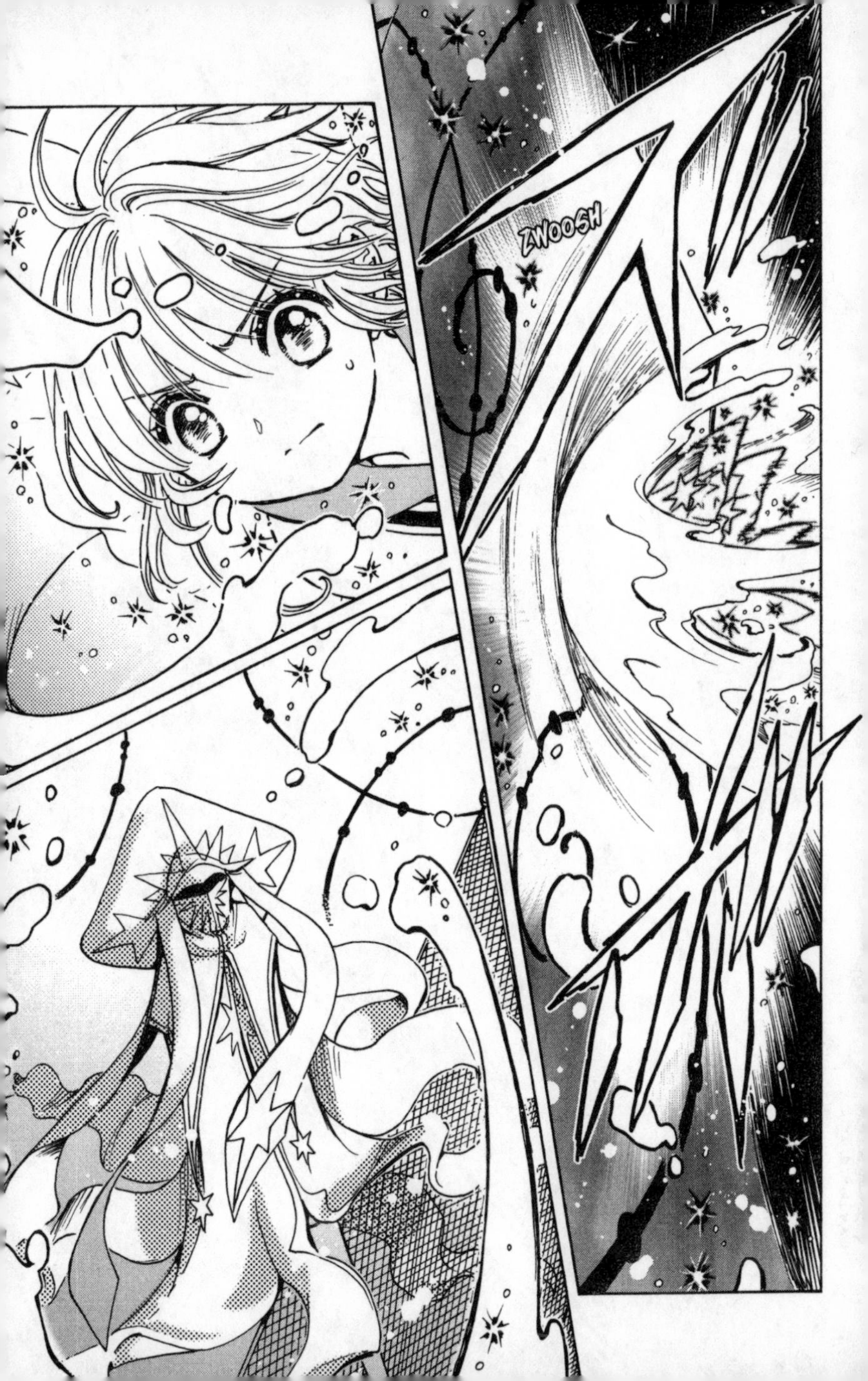
ZWOOSH

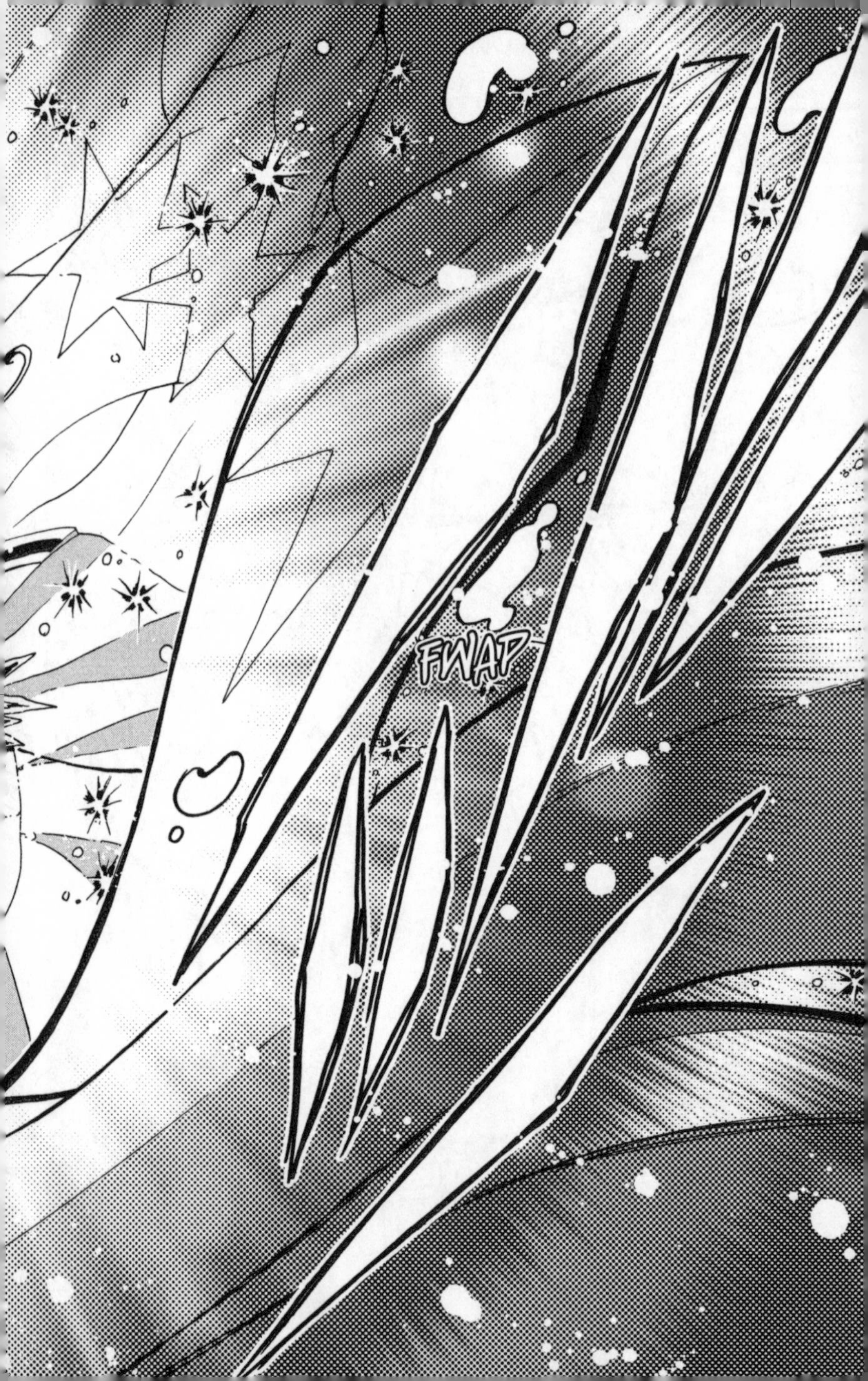
FWAP

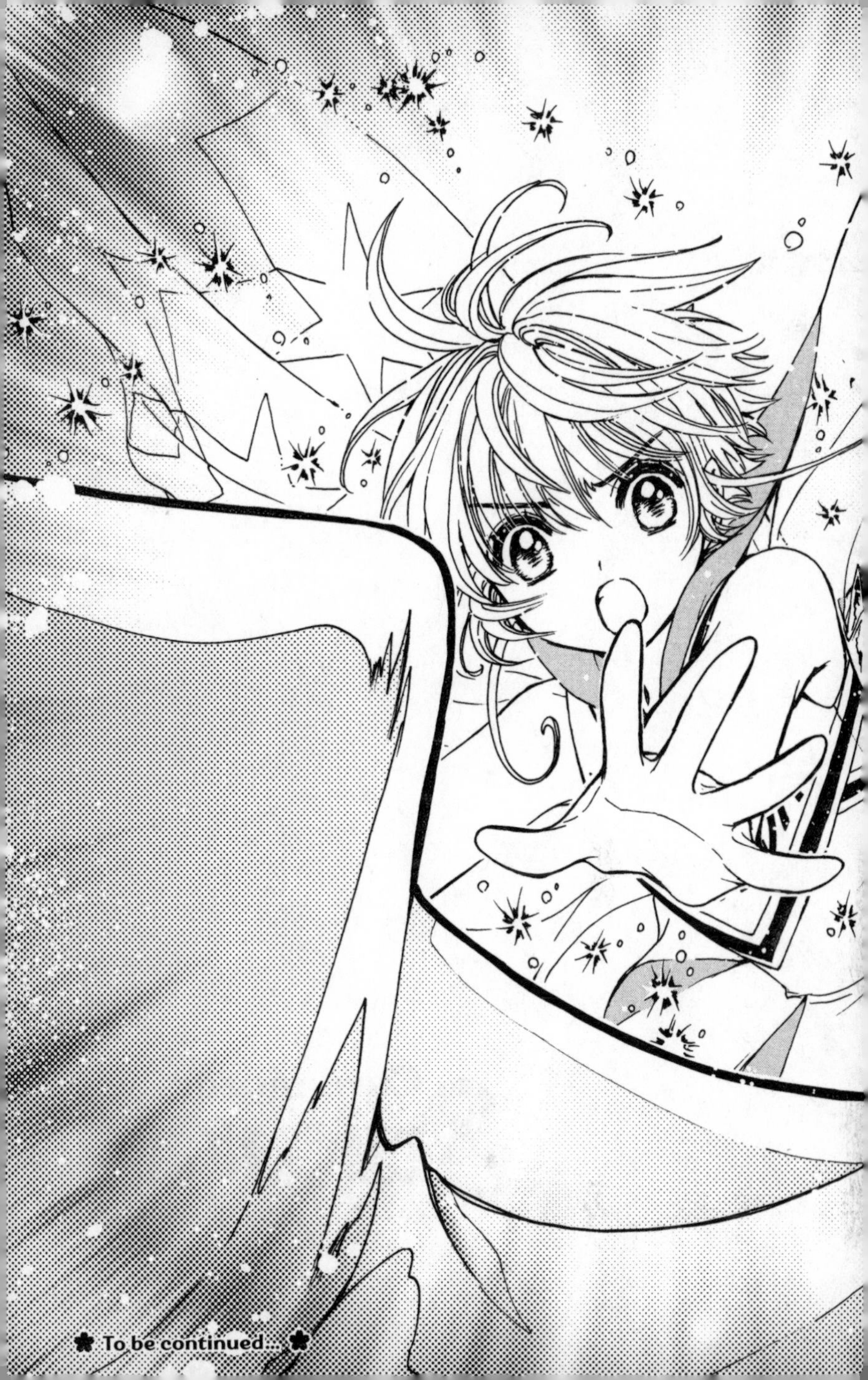
To be continued...

Cardcaptor
Sakura
CLEAR CARD

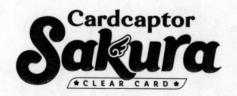

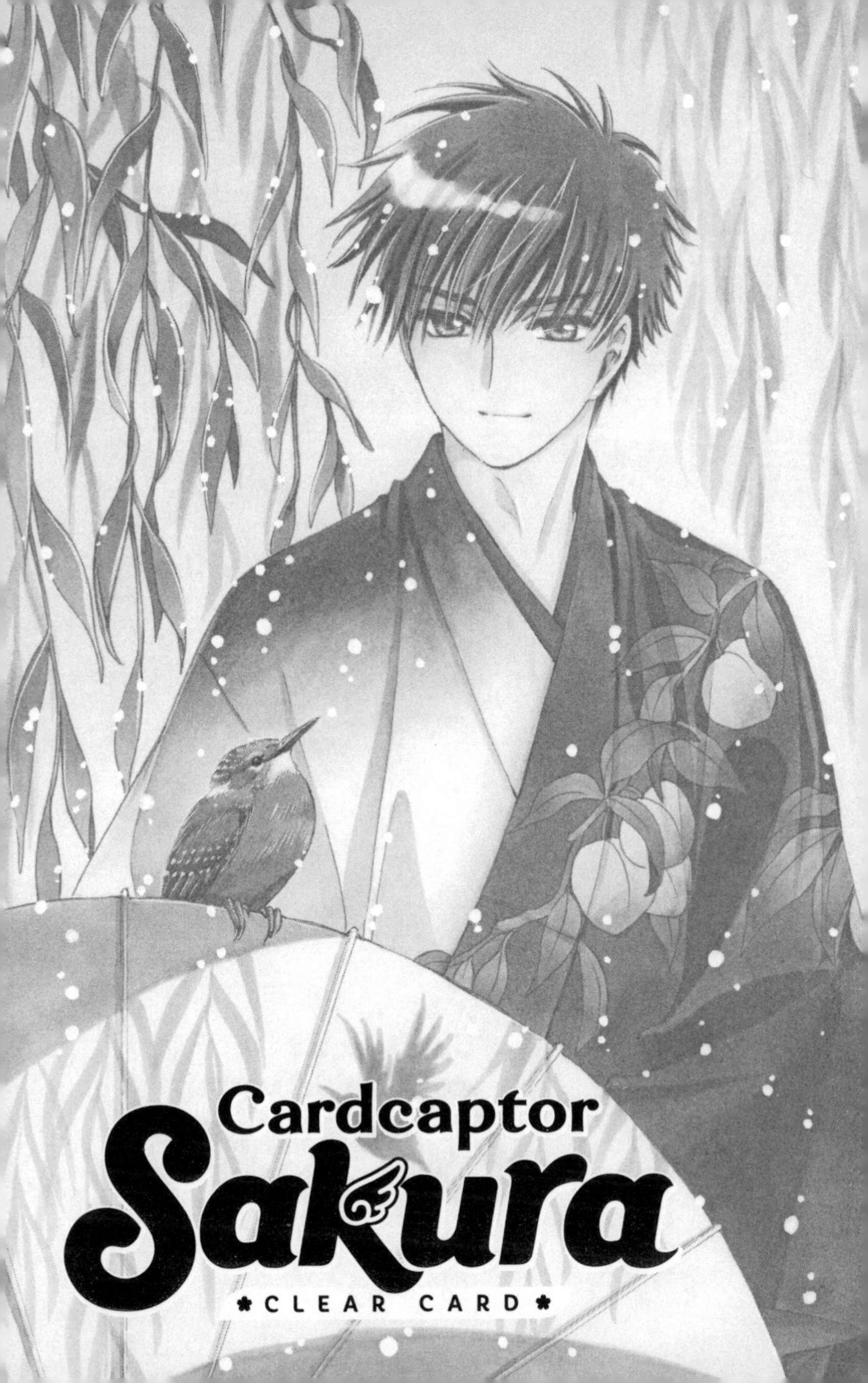
Cardcaptor
Sakura
CLEAR CARD

Cardcaptor Sakura

CLEAR CARD

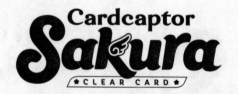

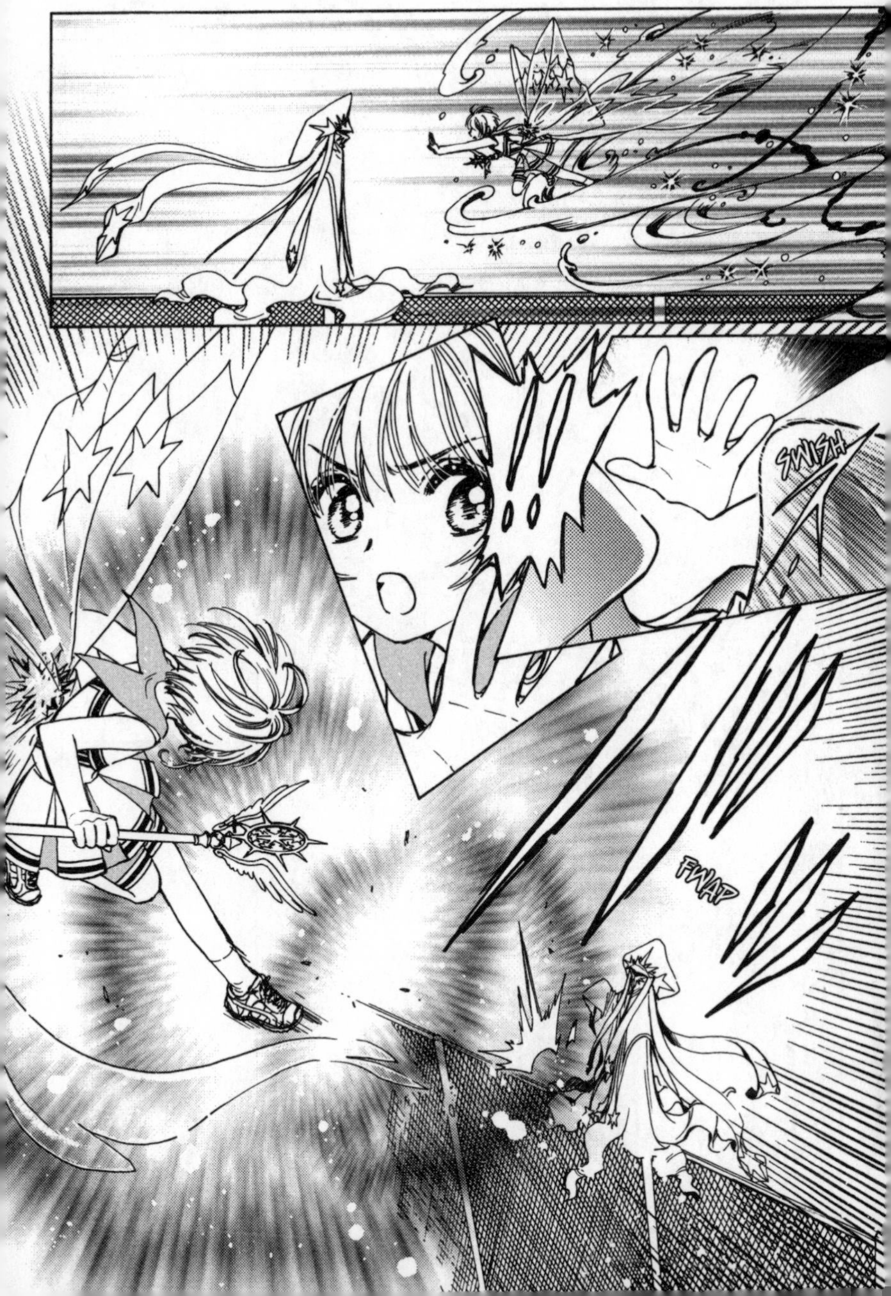
SWISH
FWAP

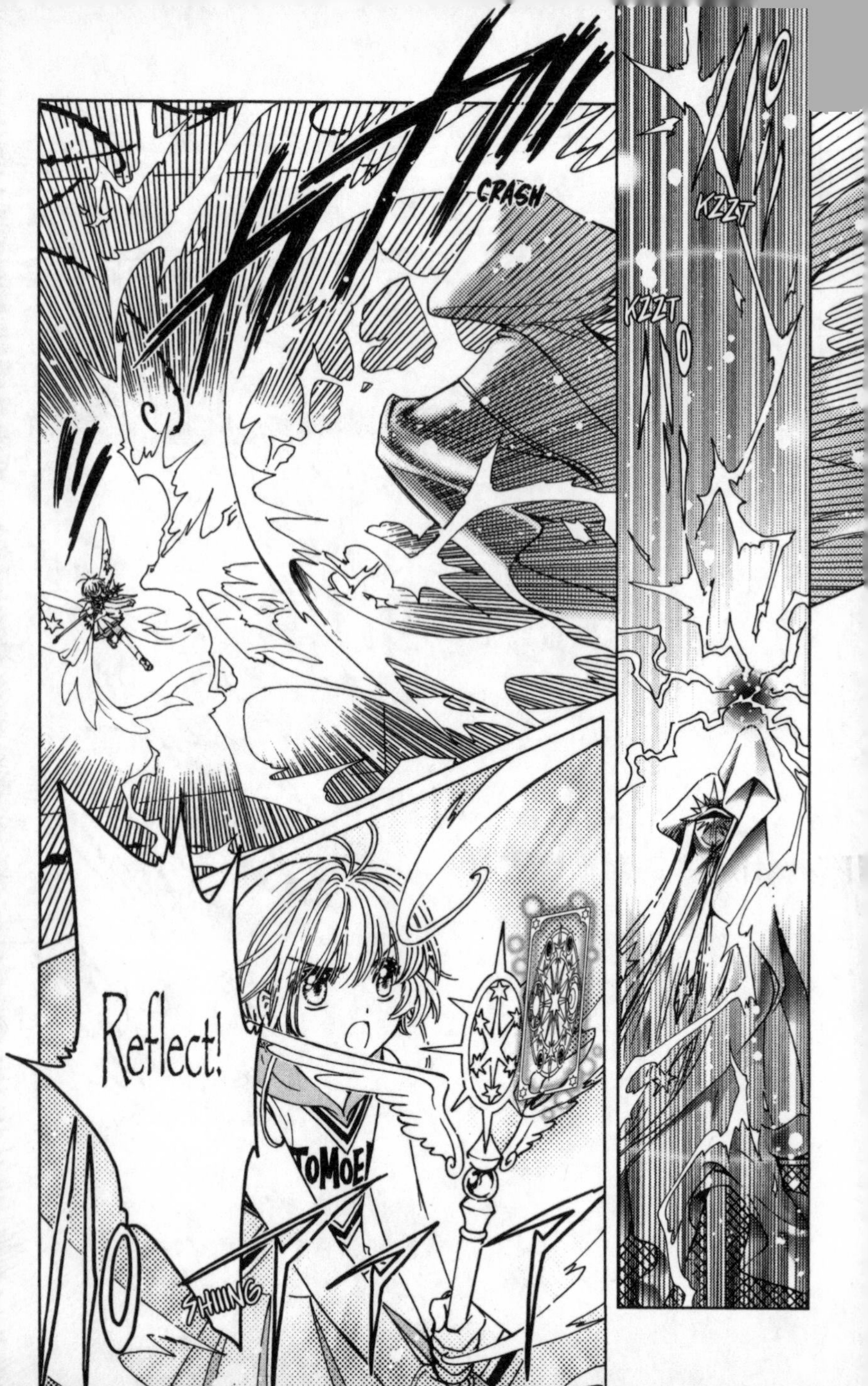
KZZT
KZZT
CRASH
Reflect!
TOMOE
SHIIING

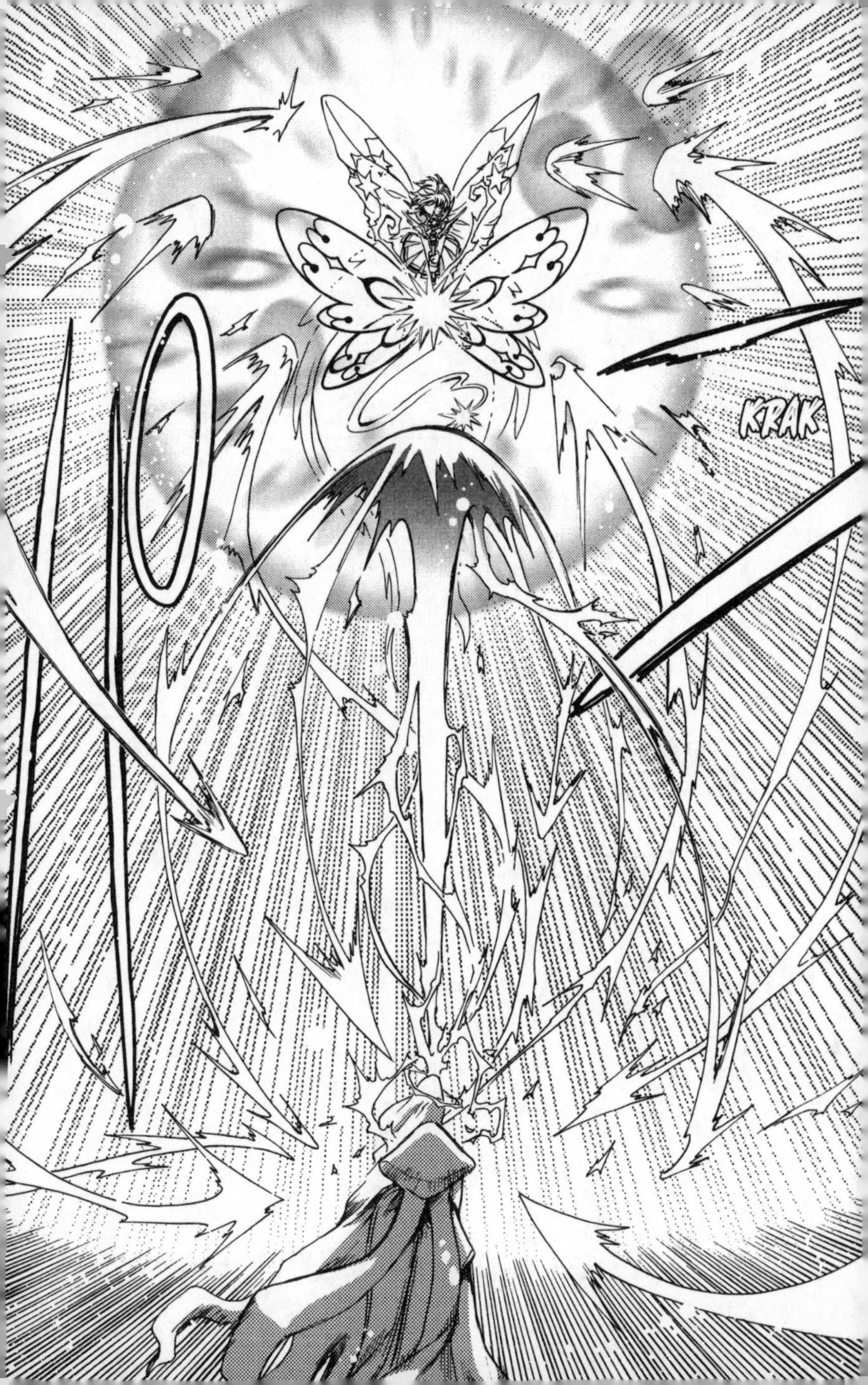
KRAK

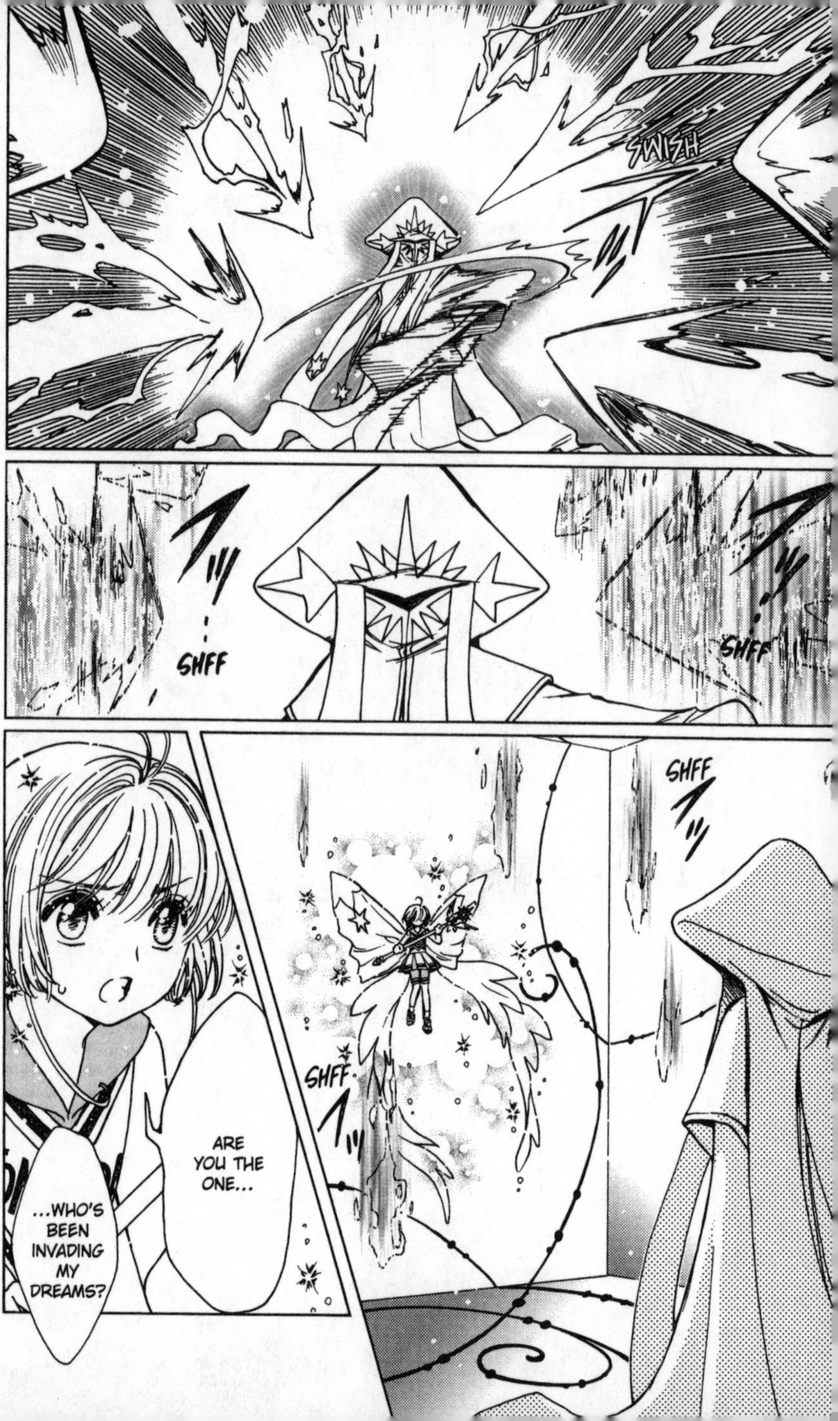
SWISH
SHFF
SHFF
SHFF
SHFF
ARE YOU THE ONE...
...WHO'S BEEN INVADING MY DREAMS?

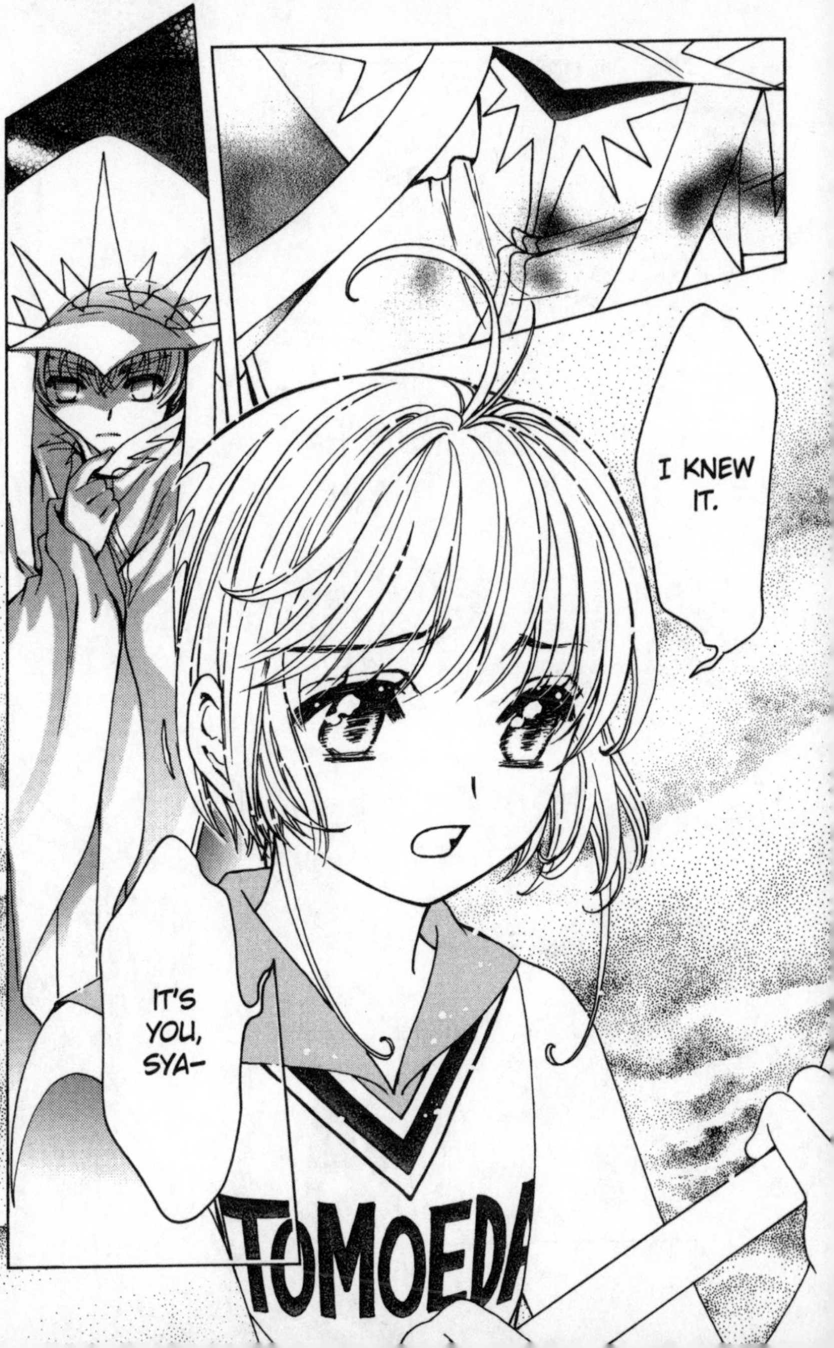
I KNEW IT.
IT'S YOU, SYA-
TOMOEDA

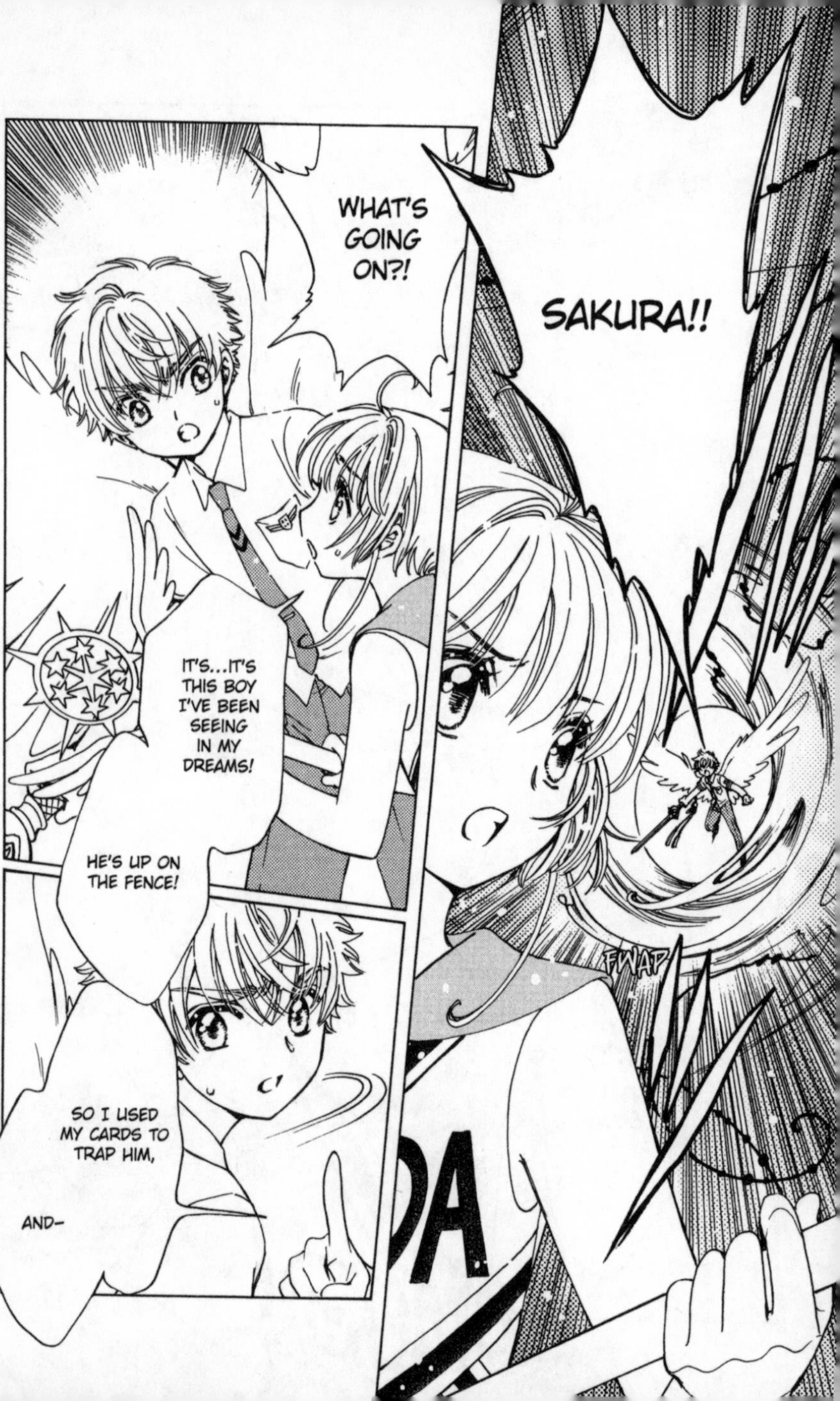
SAKURA!!
FWAP
DA
WHAT'S GOING ON?!
IT'S...IT'S THIS BOY I'VE BEEN SEEING IN MY DREAMS!
HE'S UP ON THE FENCE!
SO I USED MY CARDS TO TRAP HIM,
AND–

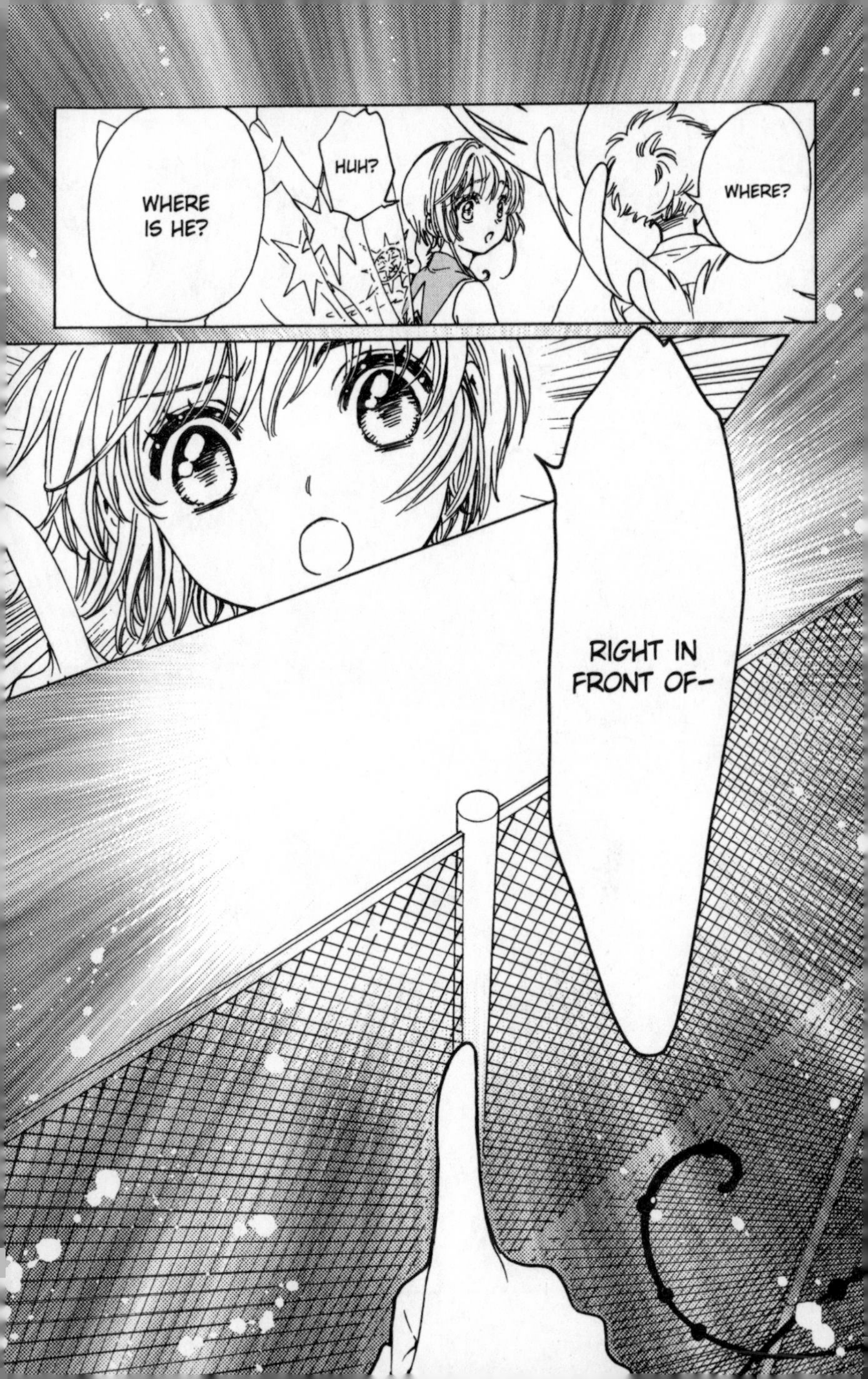
WHERE?
HUH?
WHERE IS HE?
RIGHT IN FRONT OF–

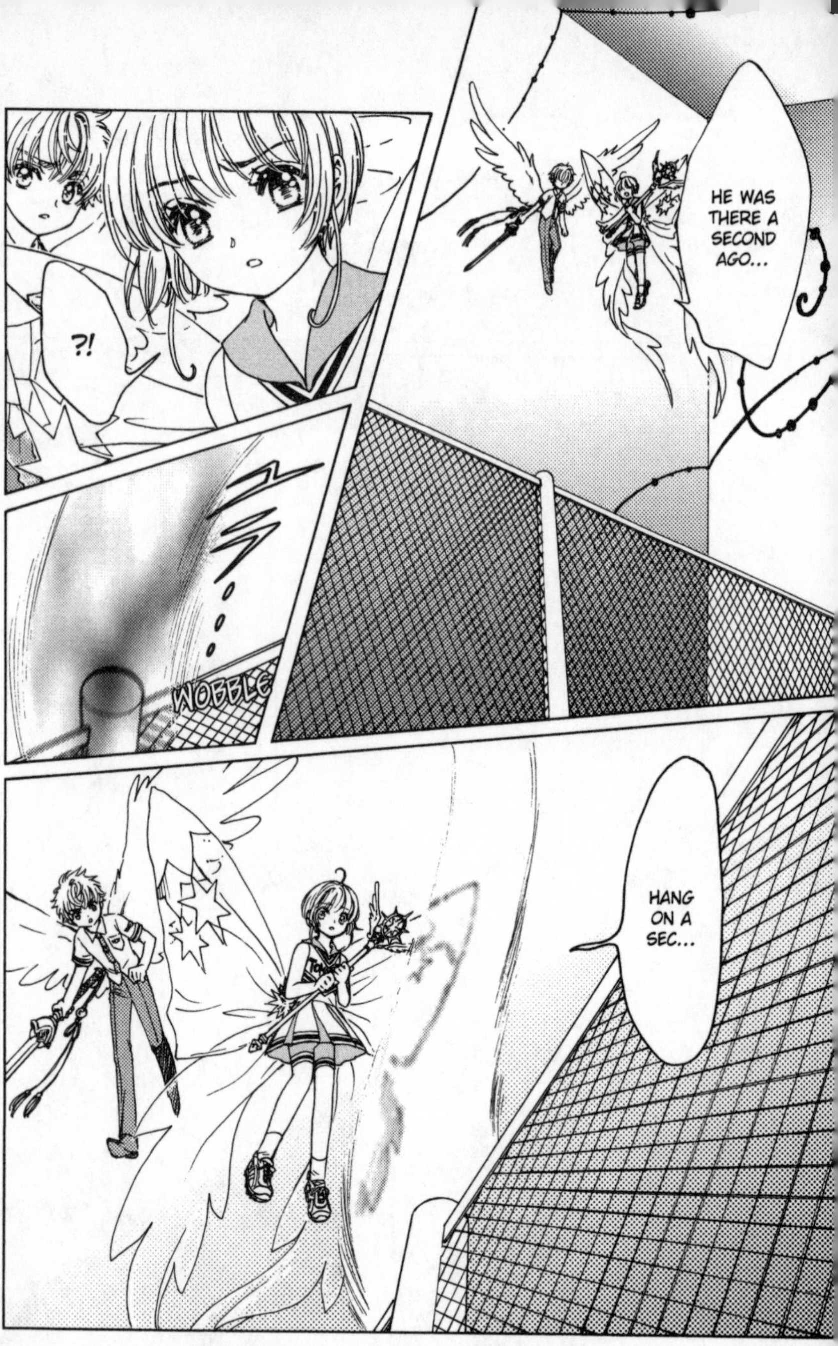
HE WAS THERE A SECOND AGO...
?!
WOBBLE
HANG ON A SEC...

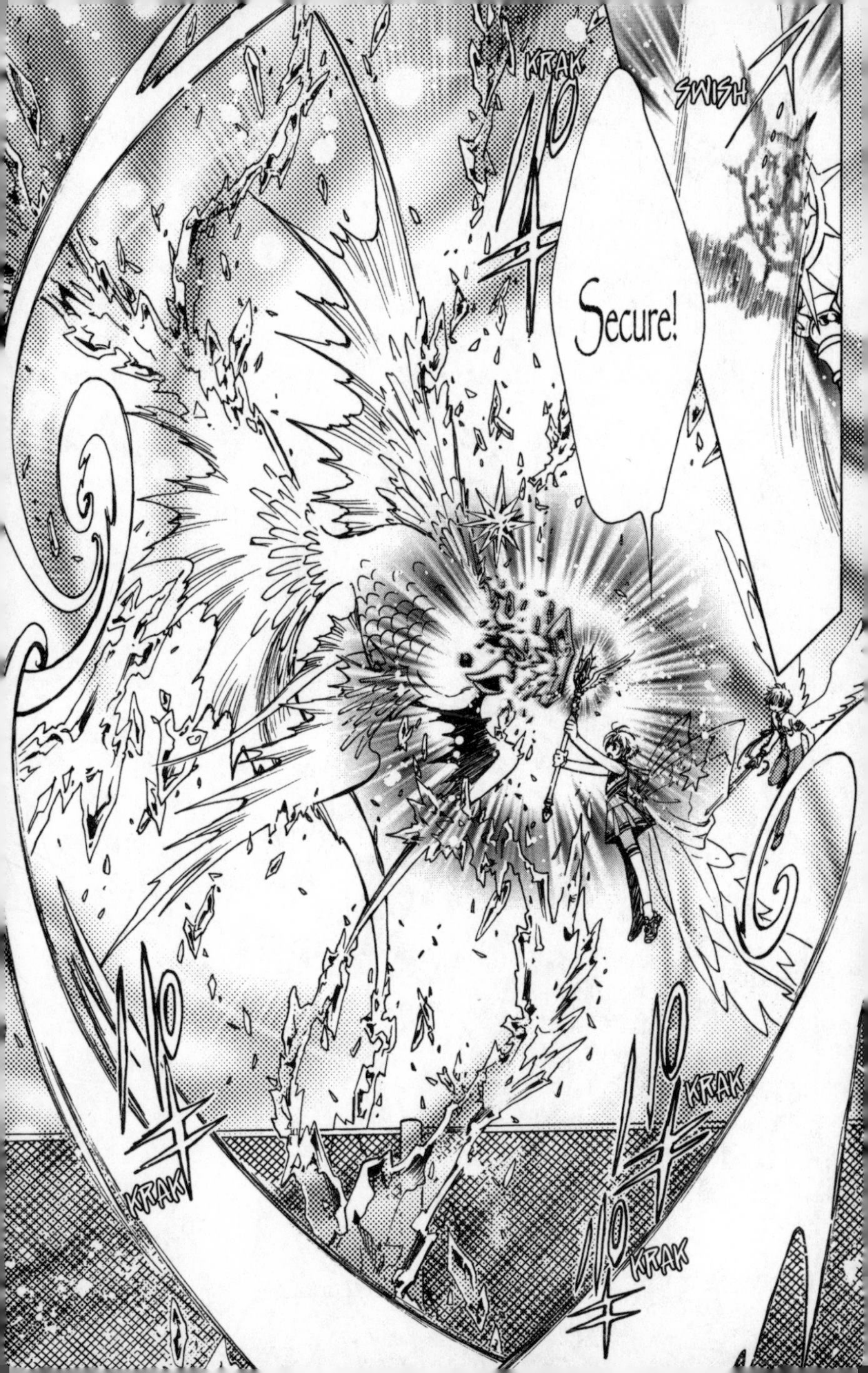
SWISH
KRAK
Secure!
KRAK
KRAK
KRAK

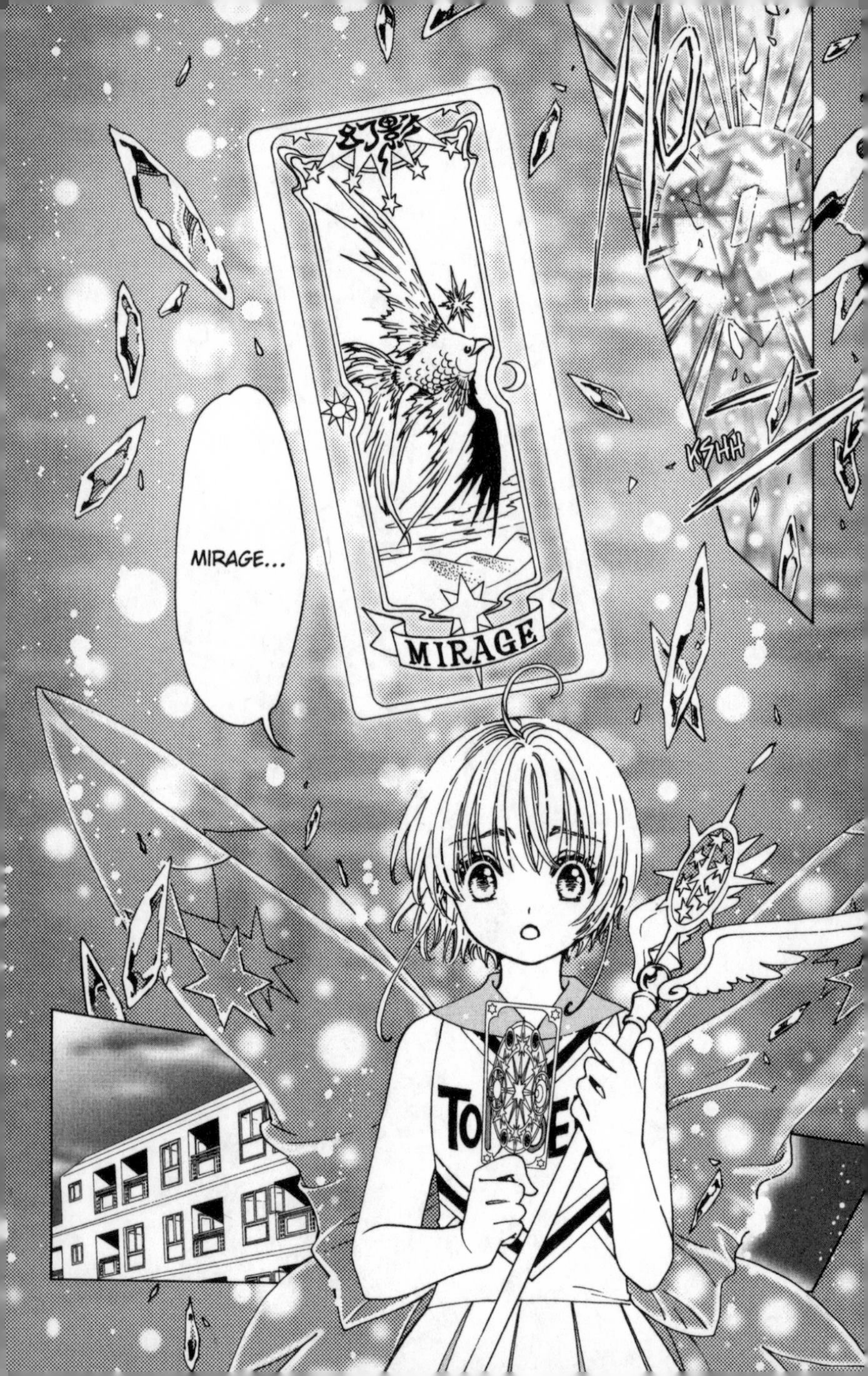
KSHH
MIRAGE
MIRAGE...

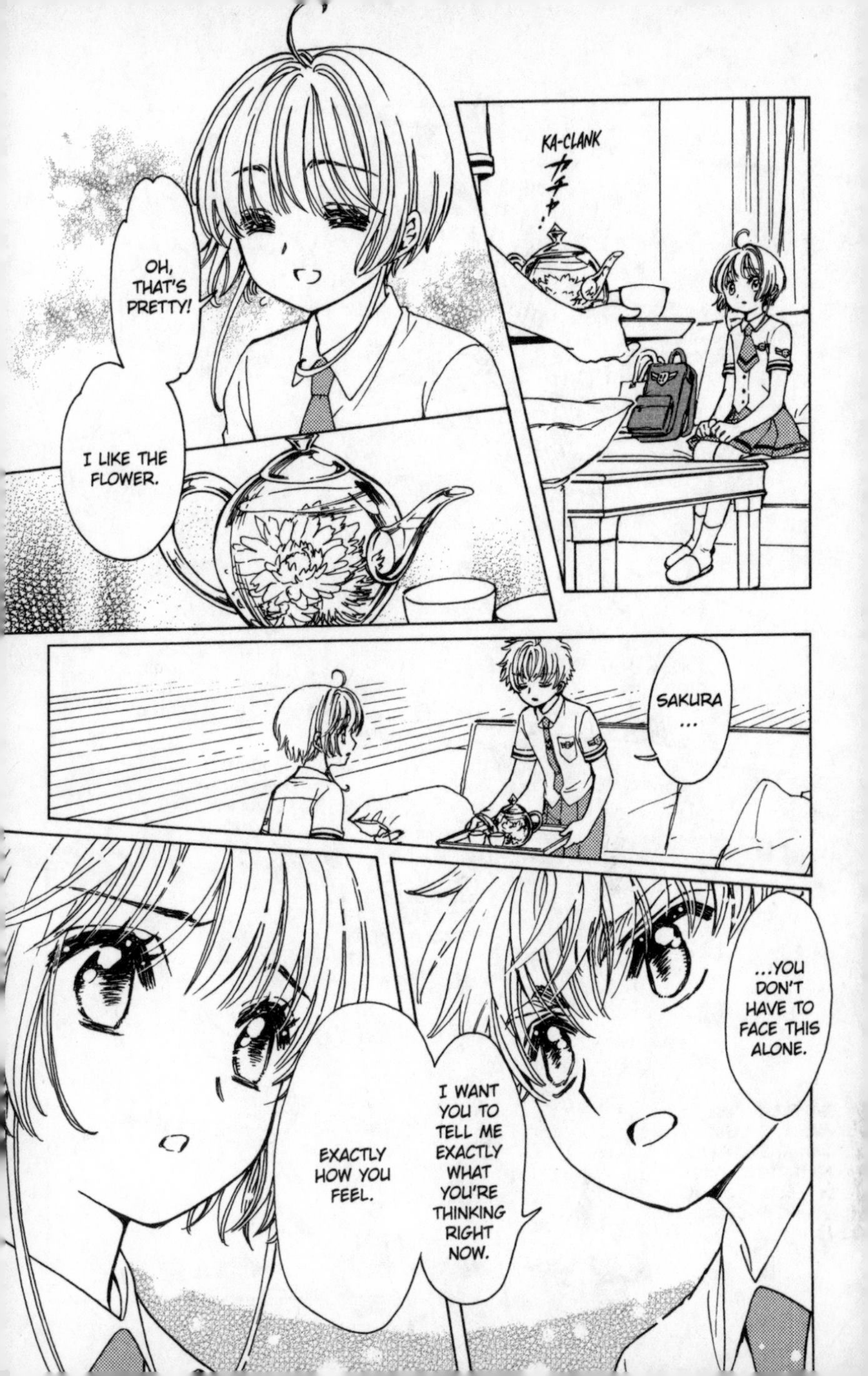
KA-CLANK
カチャ!
OH, THAT'S PRETTY!
I LIKE THE FLOWER.
SAKURA...
...YOU DON'T HAVE TO FACE THIS ALONE.
I WANT YOU TO TELL ME EXACTLY WHAT YOU'RE THINKING RIGHT NOW.
EXACTLY HOW YOU FEEL.

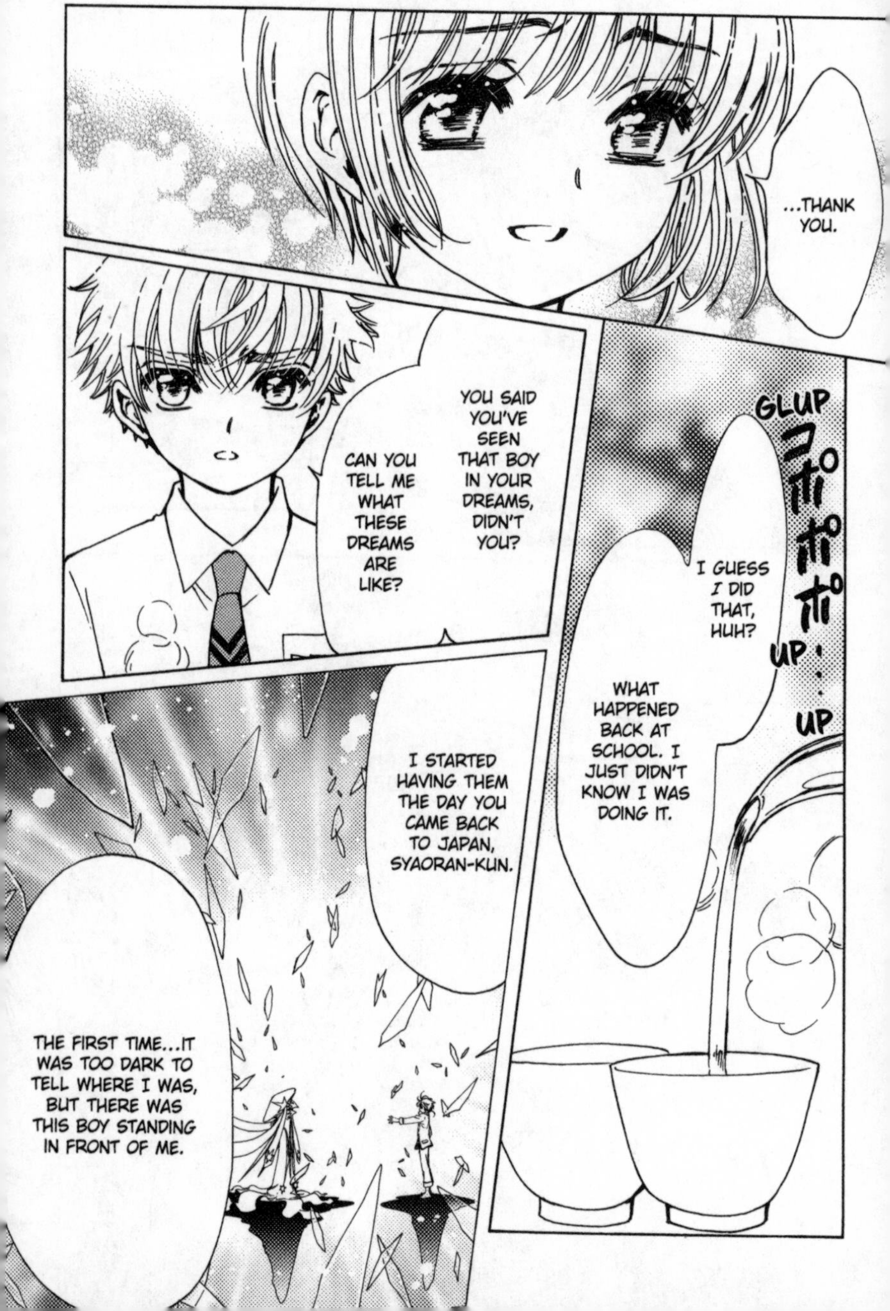
...THANK YOU.
I GUESS *I* DID THAT, HUH?
WHAT HAPPENED BACK AT SCHOOL. I JUST DIDN'T KNOW I WAS DOING IT.
GLUP
コポポポポ
UP... UP
YOU SAID YOU'VE SEEN THAT BOY IN YOUR DREAMS, DIDN'T YOU?
CAN YOU TELL ME WHAT THESE DREAMS ARE LIKE?
I STARTED HAVING THEM THE DAY YOU CAME BACK TO JAPAN, SYAORAN-KUN.
THE FIRST TIME...IT WAS TOO DARK TO TELL WHERE I WAS, BUT THERE WAS THIS BOY STANDING IN FRONT OF ME.

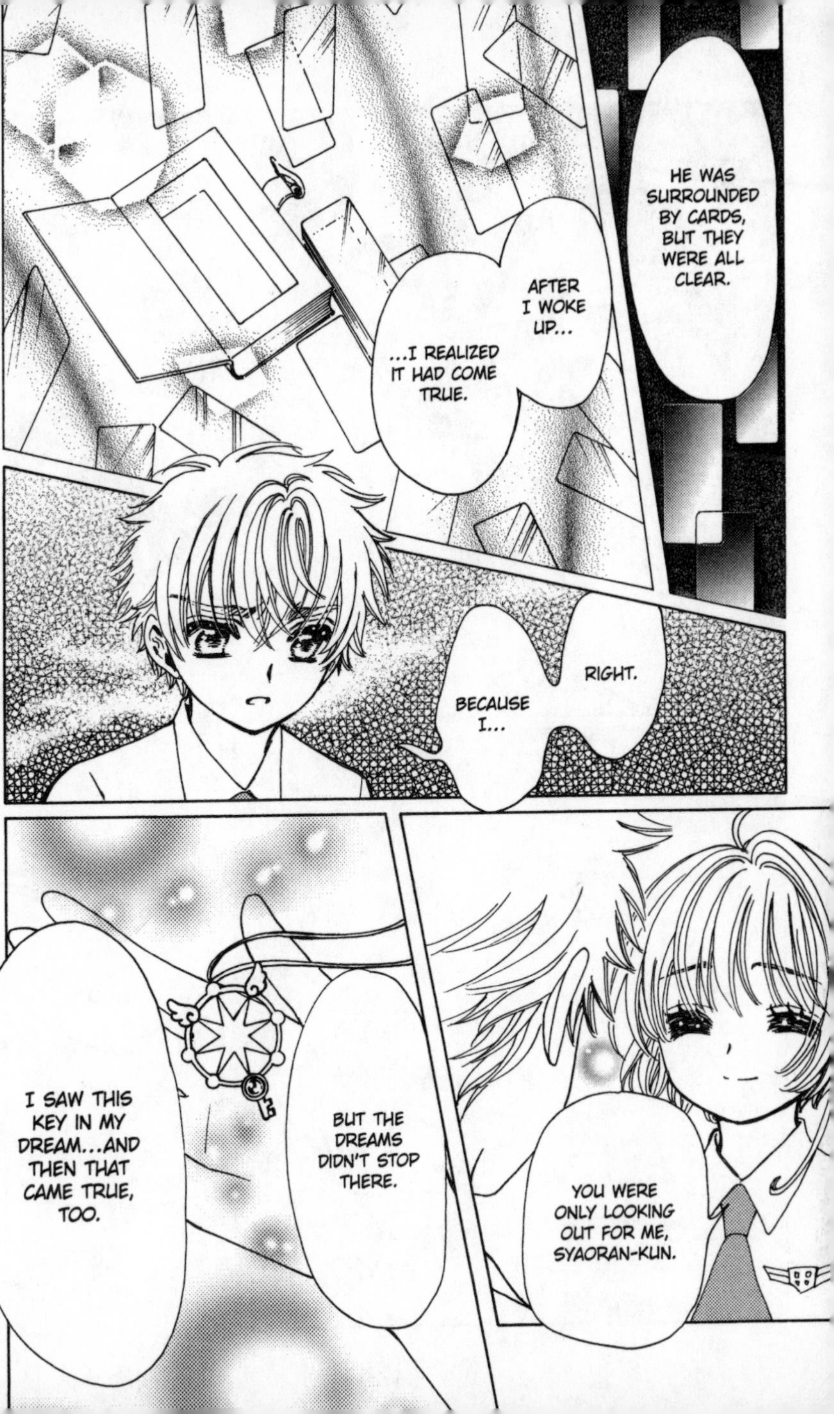
HE WAS SURROUNDED BY CARDS, BUT THEY WERE ALL CLEAR.
AFTER I WOKE UP...
...I REALIZED IT HAD COME TRUE.
RIGHT.
BECAUSE I...
YOU WERE ONLY LOOKING OUT FOR ME, SYAORAN-KUN.
I SAW THIS KEY IN MY DREAM...AND THEN THAT CAME TRUE, TOO.
BUT THE DREAMS DIDN'T STOP THERE.

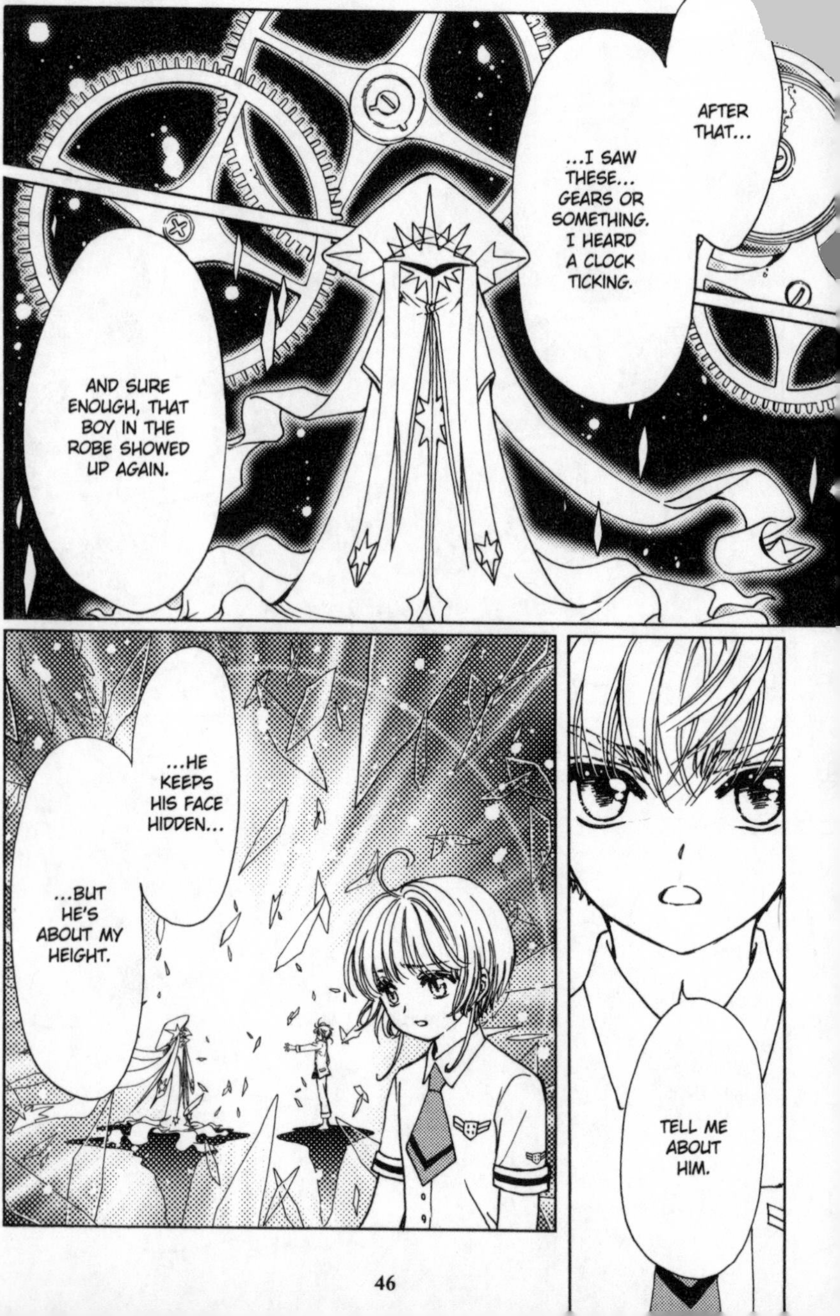
AFTER THAT...
...I SAW THESE... GEARS OR SOMETHING. I HEARD A CLOCK TICKING.
AND SURE ENOUGH, THAT BOY IN THE ROBE SHOWED UP AGAIN.
TELL ME ABOUT HIM.
...HE KEEPS HIS FACE HIDDEN...
...BUT HE'S ABOUT MY HEIGHT.

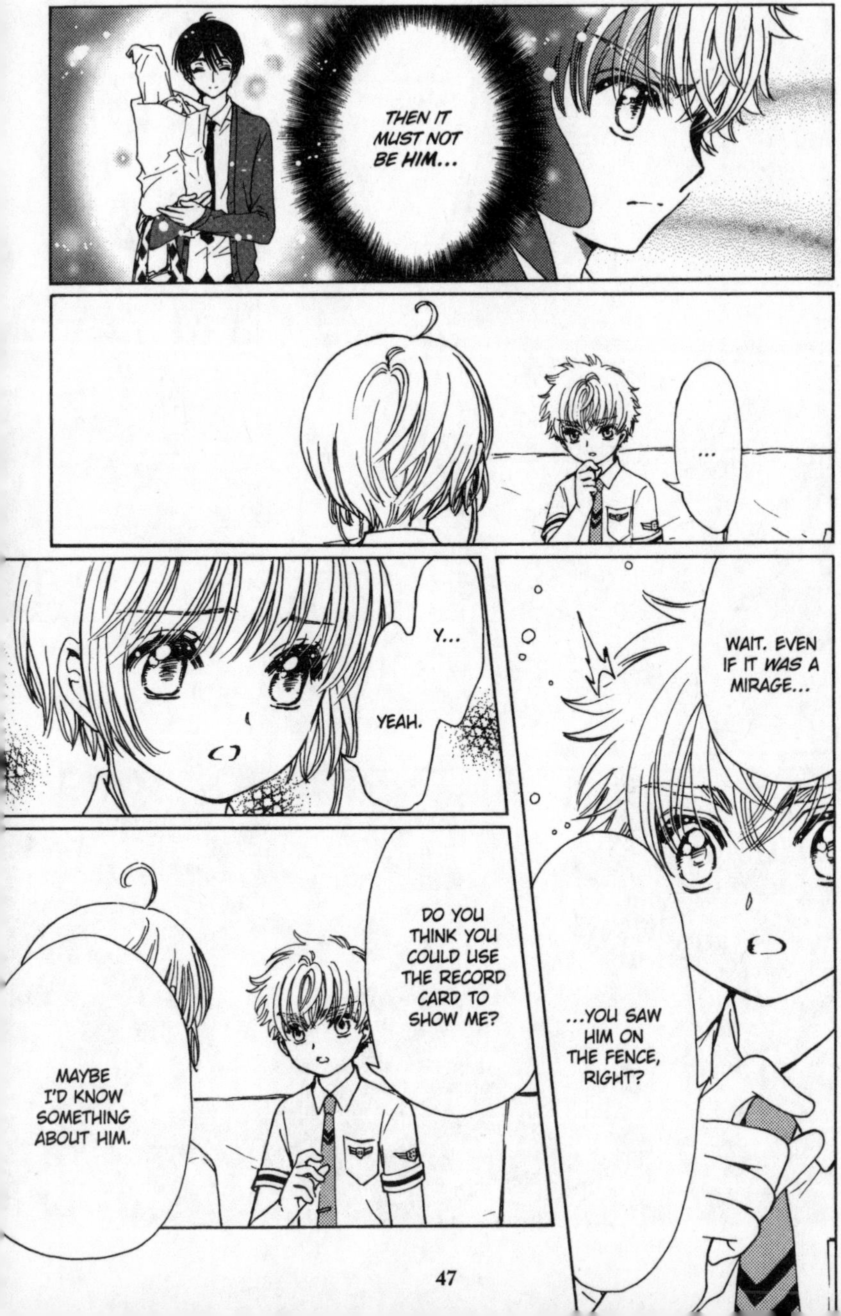
THEN IT MUST NOT BE HIM...
...
WAIT. EVEN IF IT WAS A MIRAGE...
...YOU SAW HIM ON THE FENCE, RIGHT?
Y...
YEAH.
DO YOU THINK YOU COULD USE THE RECORD CARD TO SHOW ME?
MAYBE I'D KNOW SOMETHING ABOUT HIM.

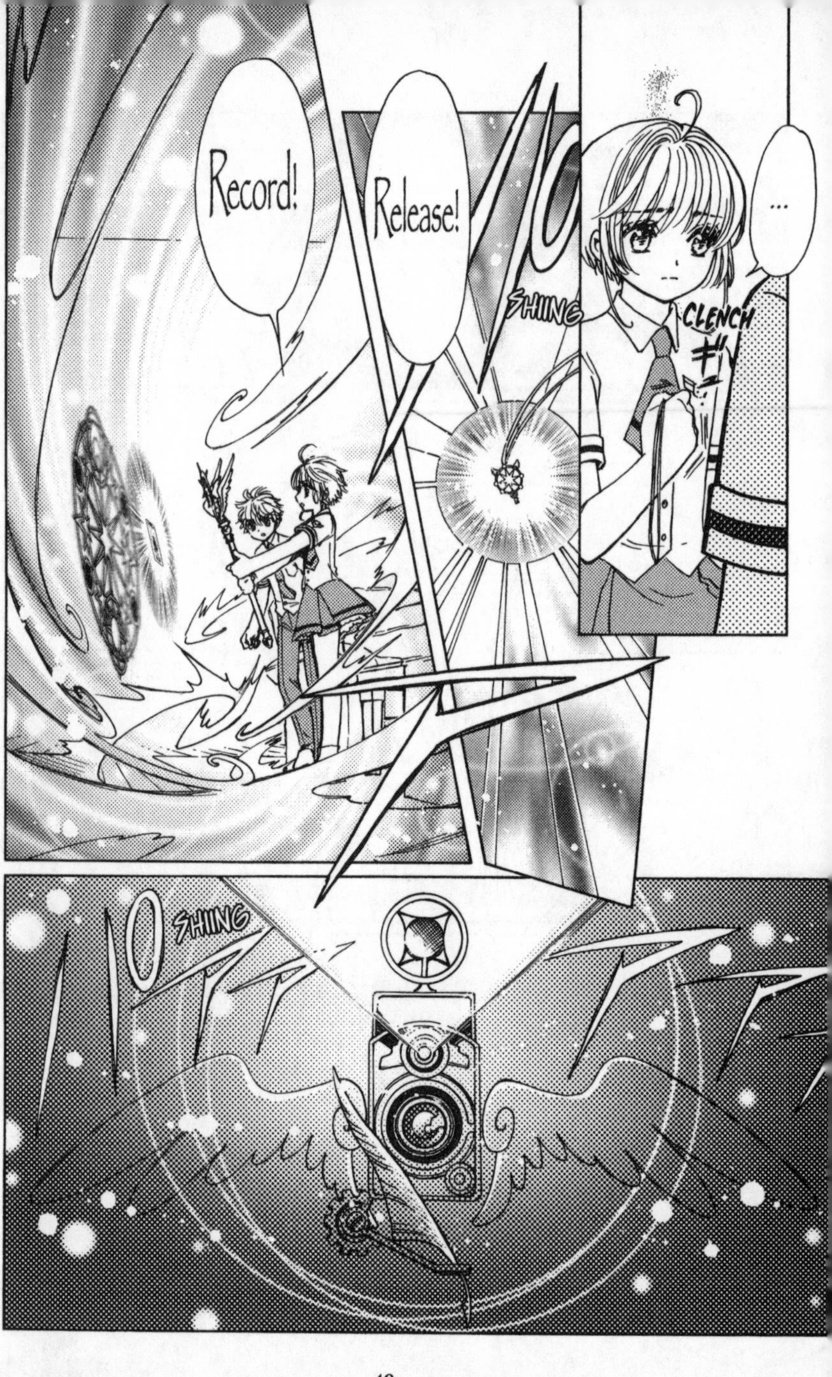
...
CLENCH
ギュ
Release!
SHIING
Record!
SHIING

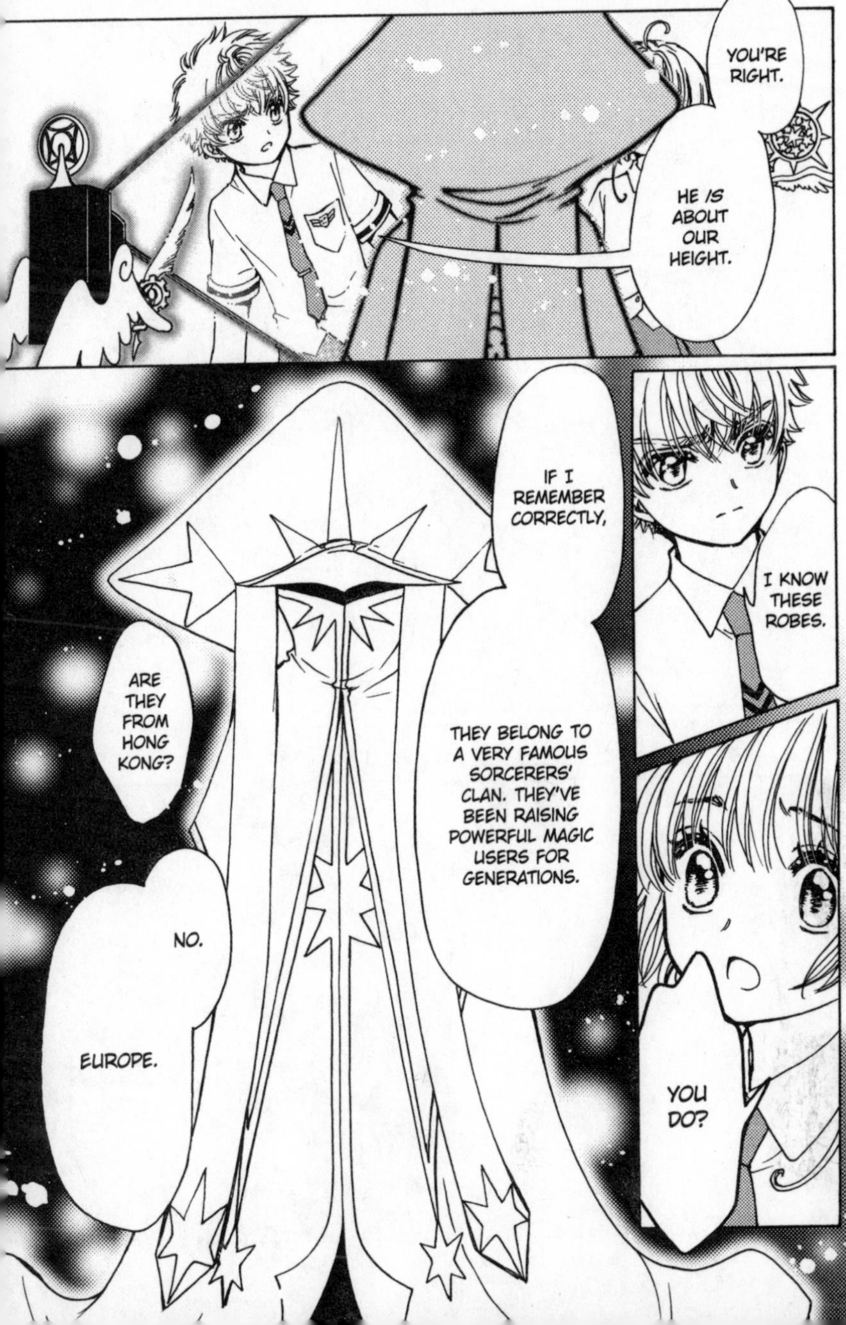
YOU'RE RIGHT.
HE IS ABOUT OUR HEIGHT.
I KNOW THESE ROBES.
YOU DO?
IF I REMEMBER CORRECTLY,
THEY BELONG TO A VERY FAMOUS SORCERERS' CLAN. THEY'VE BEEN RAISING POWERFUL MAGIC USERS FOR GENERATIONS.
ARE THEY FROM HONG KONG?
NO.
EUROPE.

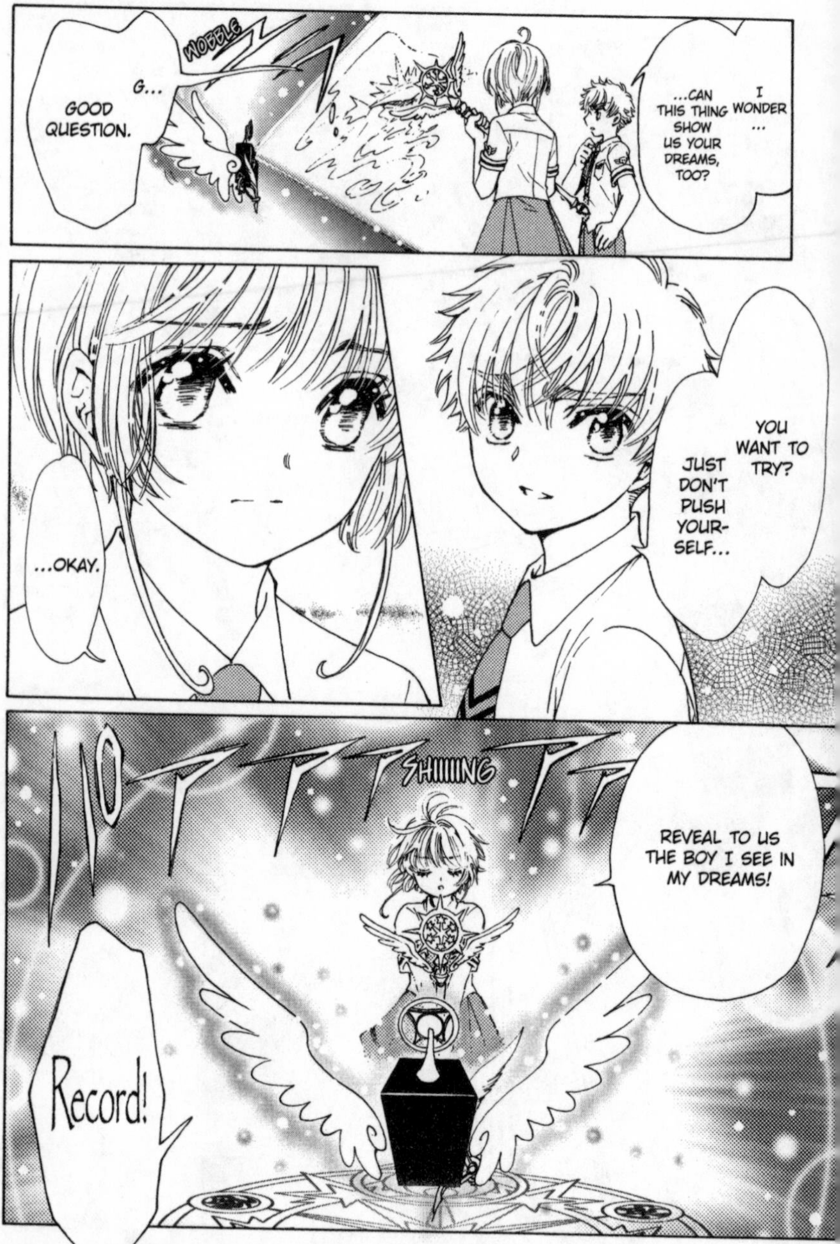

I WONDER ...
...CAN THIS THING SHOW US YOUR DREAMS, TOO?
WOBBLE
G... GOOD QUESTION.
YOU WANT TO TRY?
JUST DON'T PUSH YOUR-SELF...
...OKAY.
REVEAL TO US THE BOY I SEE IN MY DREAMS!
SHIIIIING
Record!

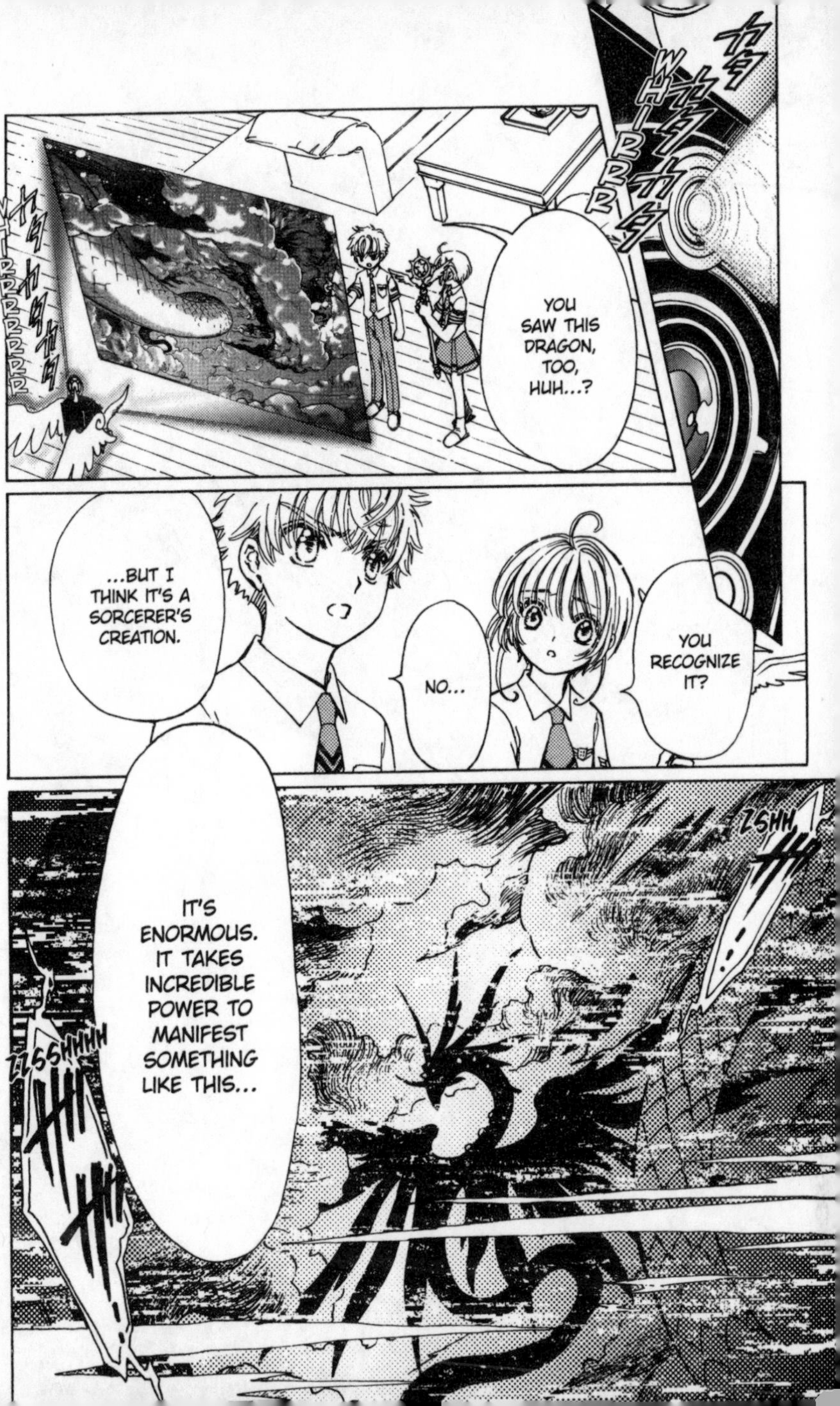
WHIRRRR
YOU SAW THIS DRAGON, TOO, HUH...?
WHIRRRRRRR
YOU RECOGNIZE IT?
NO...
...BUT I THINK IT'S A SORCERER'S CREATION.
ZSHH
IT'S ENORMOUS. IT TAKES INCREDIBLE POWER TO MANIFEST SOMETHING LIKE THIS...
ZZSSHHHH

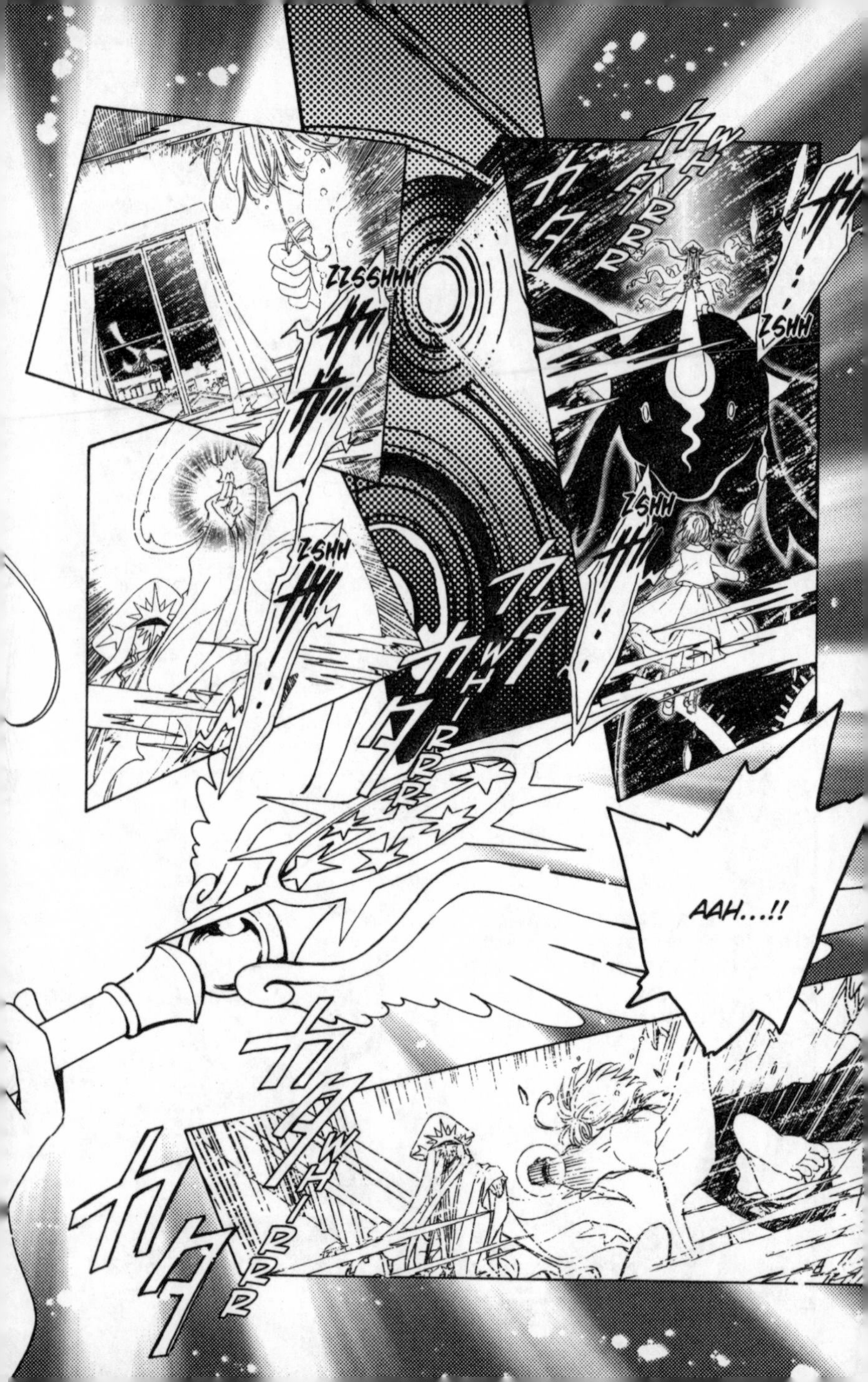
WHIRRRR
ZSHH
ZSHH
WHIRRRR
ZZSSHHH
ZSHH
AAH...!!
WHIRRRR

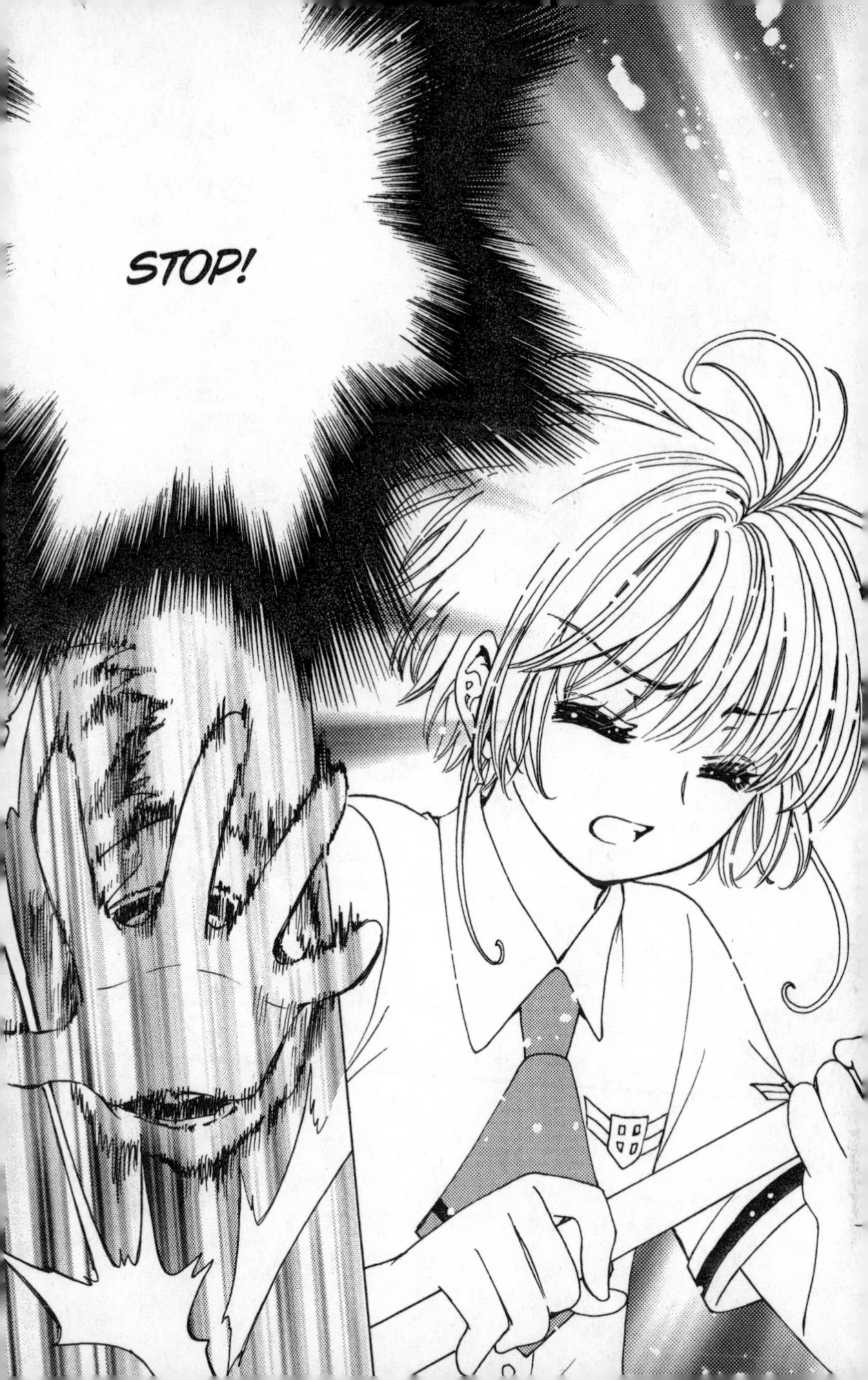
STOP!

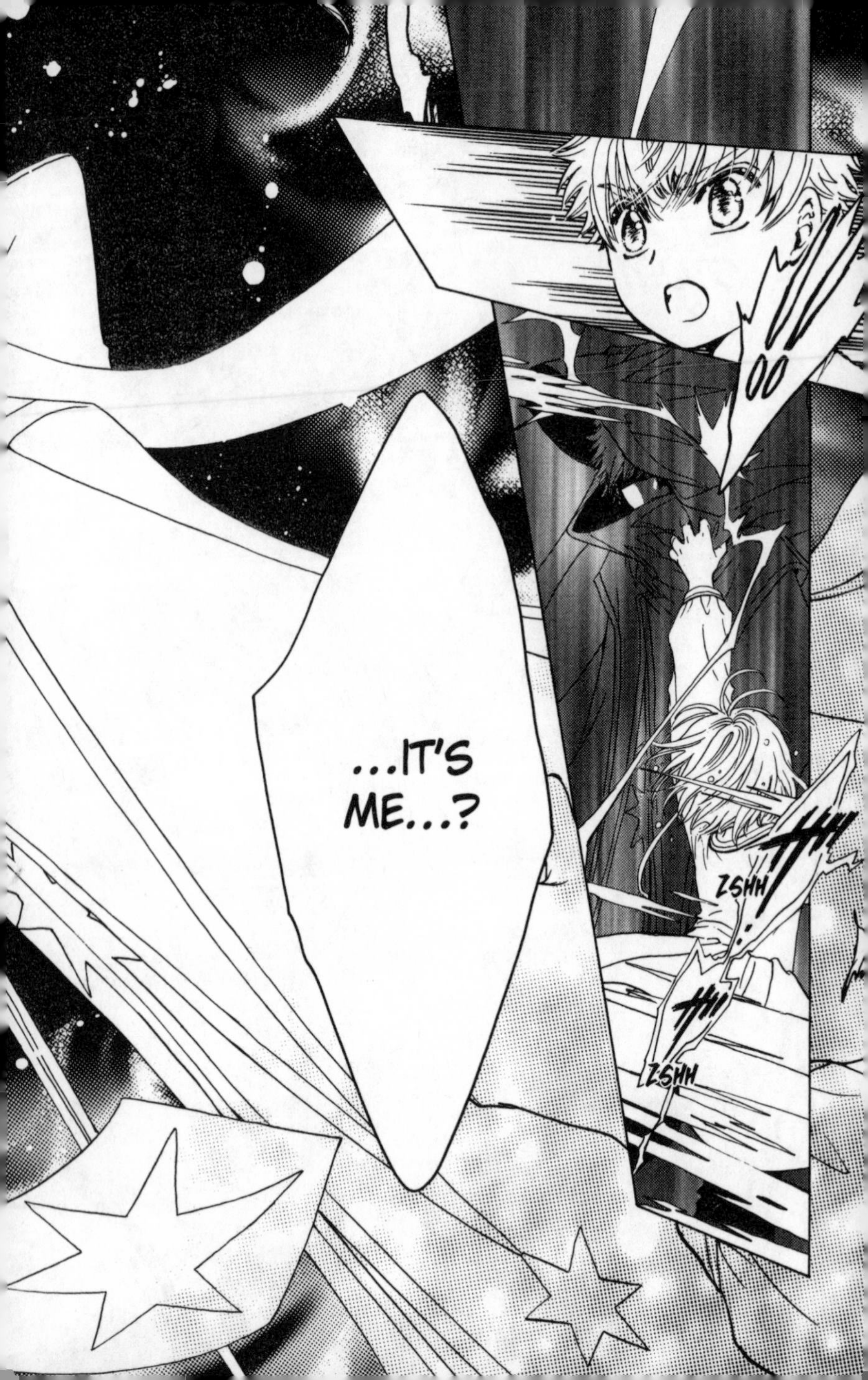
ZSHH
ZSHH
...IT'S ME...?

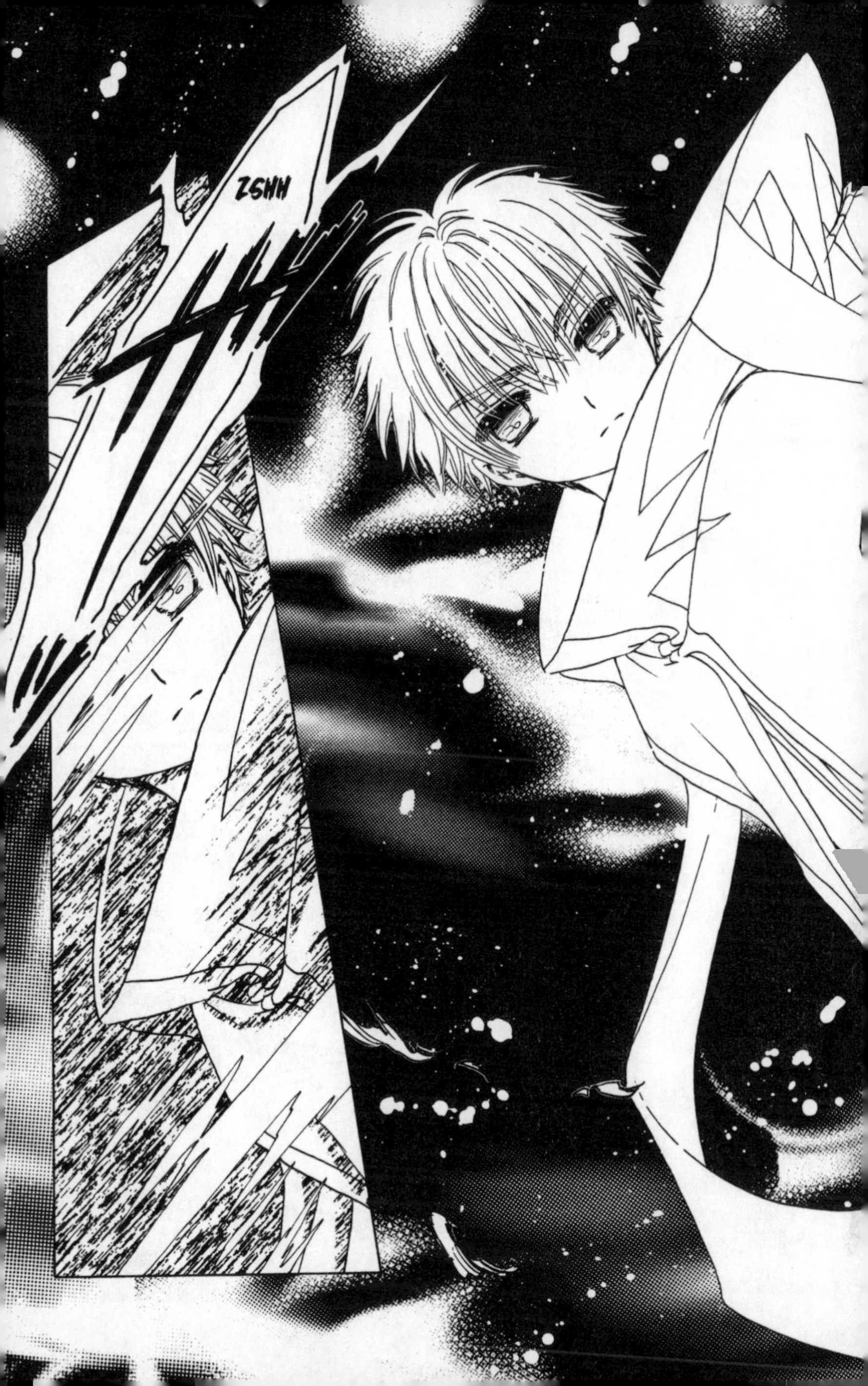
ZSHH

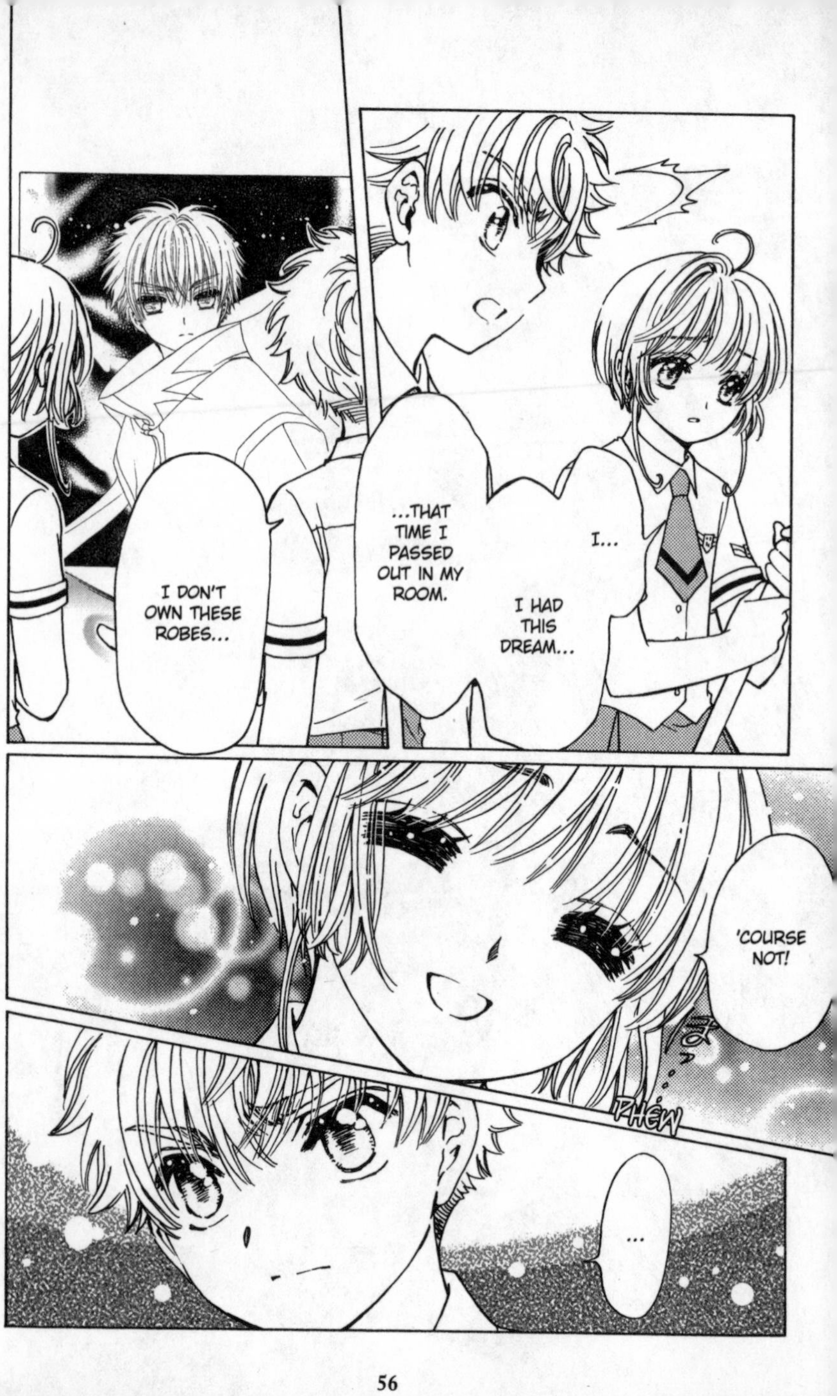
I...
I HAD THIS DREAM...
...THAT TIME I PASSED OUT IN MY ROOM.
I DON'T OWN THESE ROBES...
'COURSE NOT!
PHEW
...

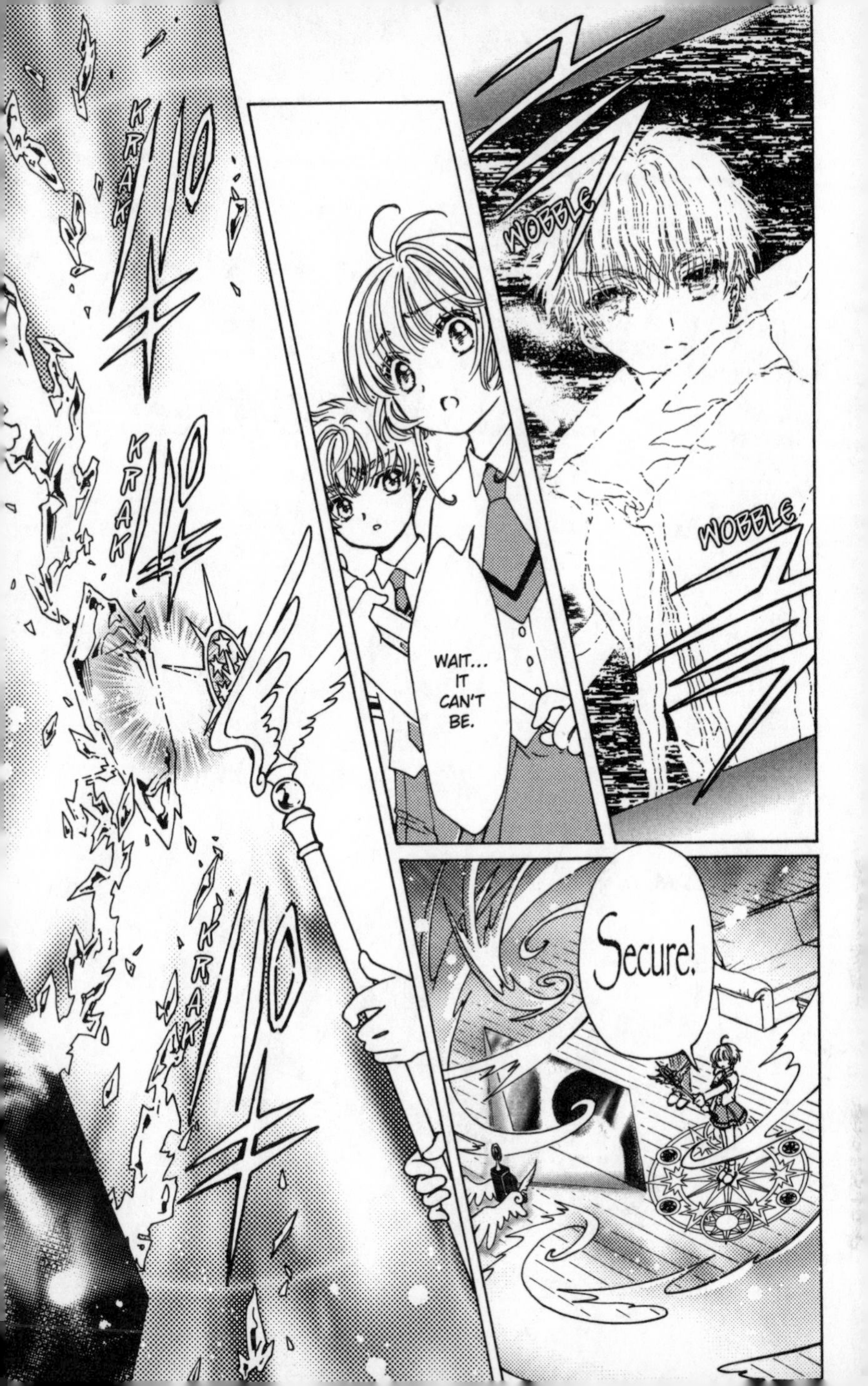
WOBBLE
WOBBLE
WAIT... IT CAN'T BE.
KRAK
KRAK
KRAK
Secure!

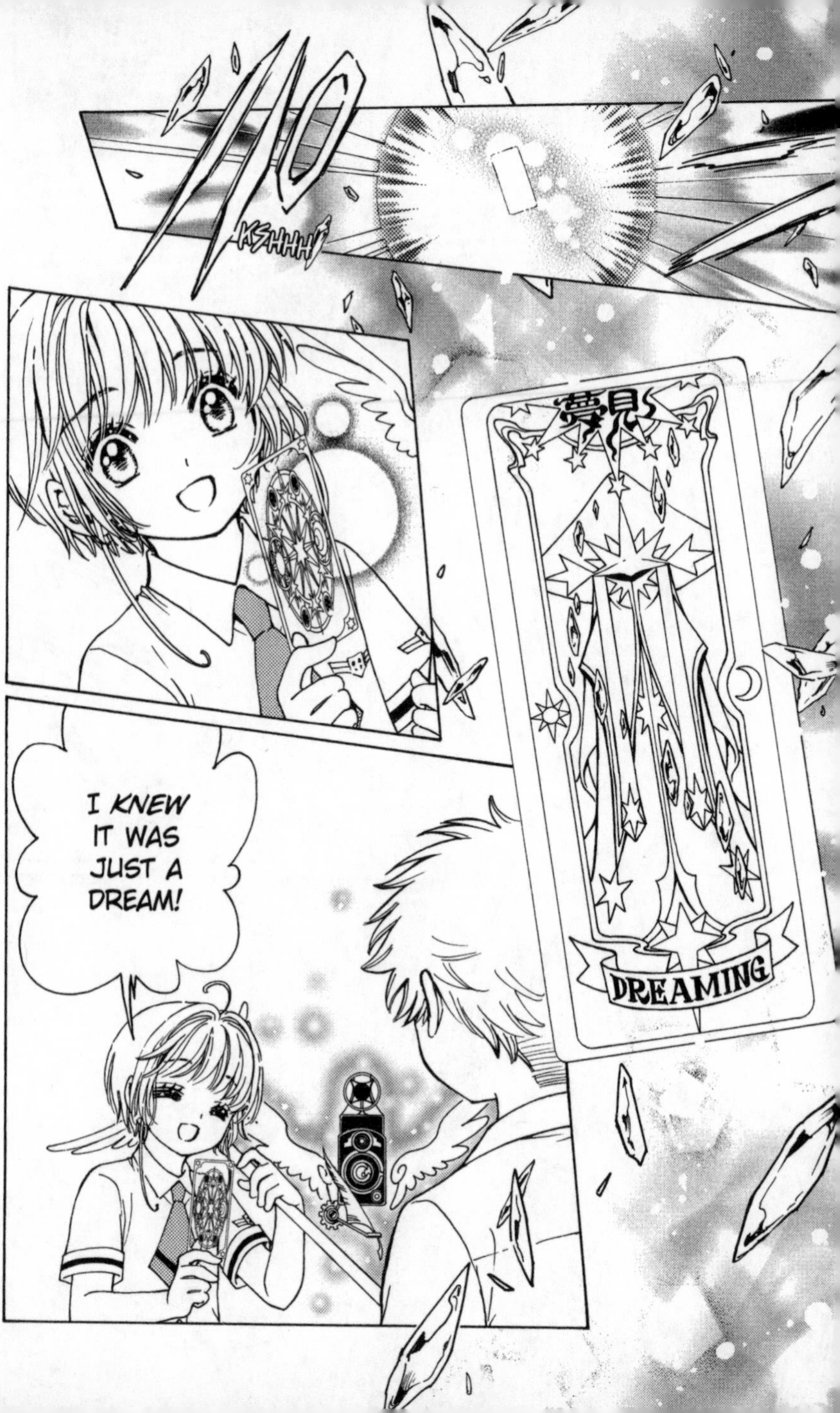
KSHHH
夢見
DREAMING
I KNEW IT WAS JUST A DREAM!

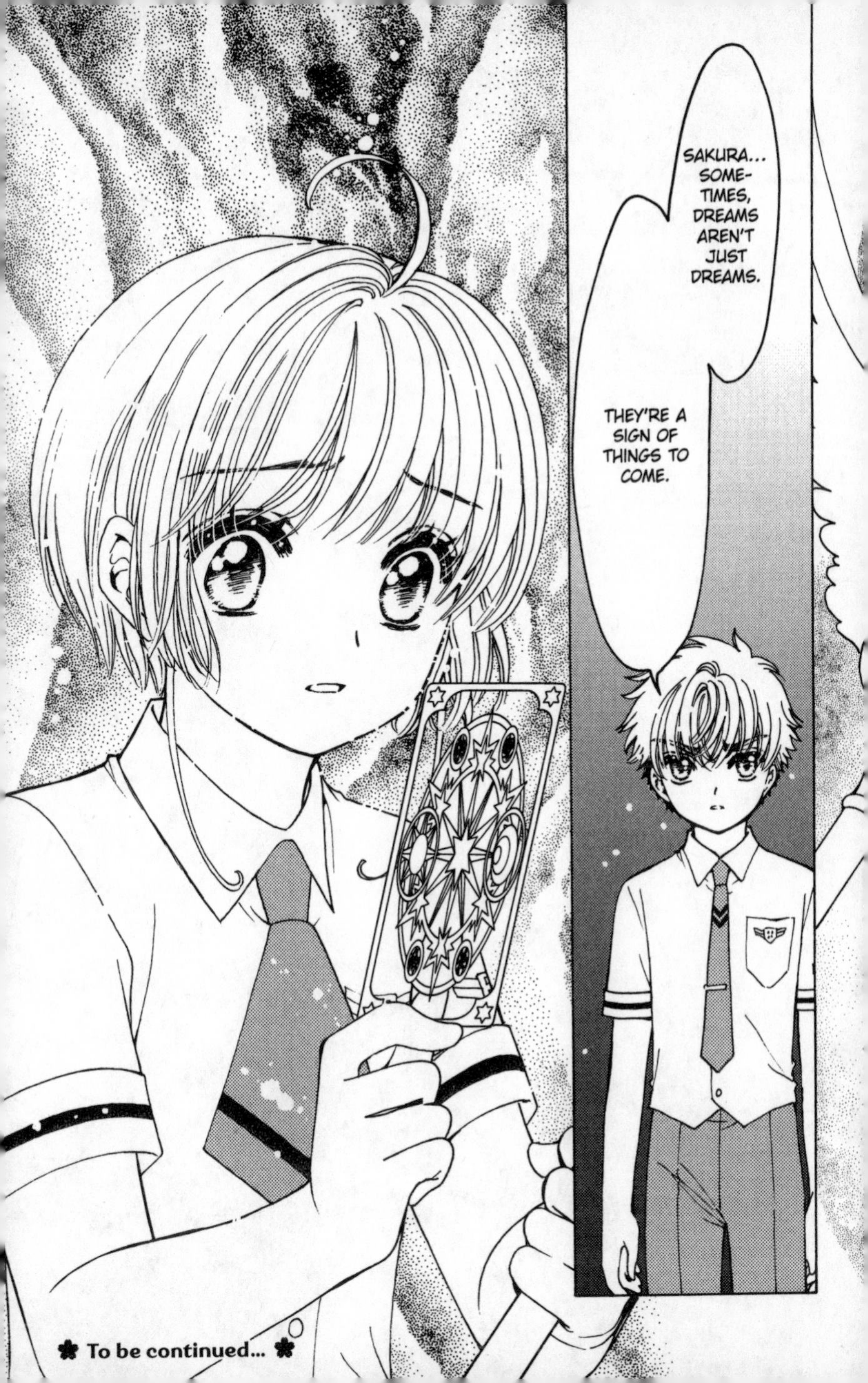
SAKURA... SOME-TIMES, DREAMS AREN'T JUST DREAMS.
THEY'RE A SIGN OF THINGS TO COME.
To be continued...

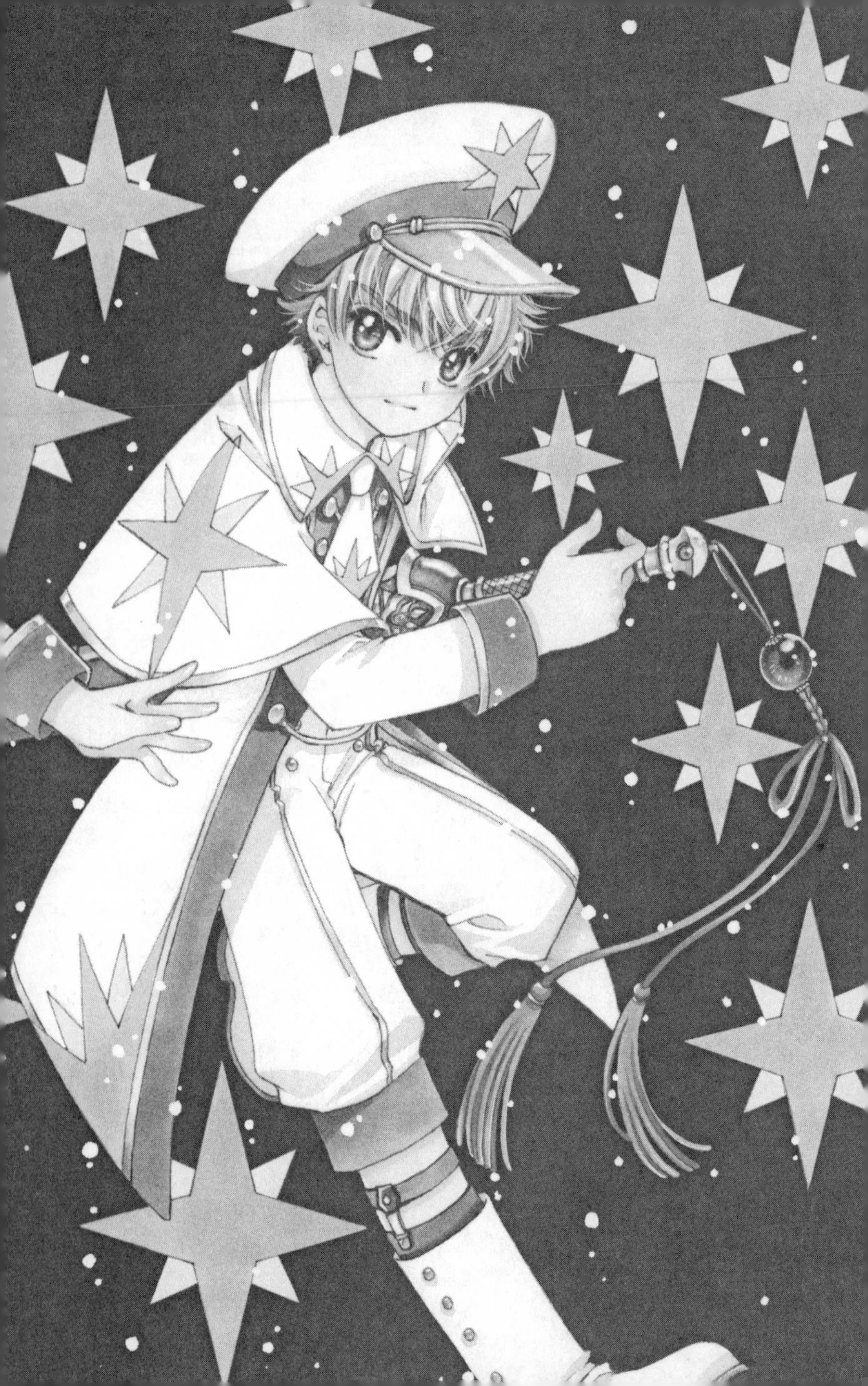

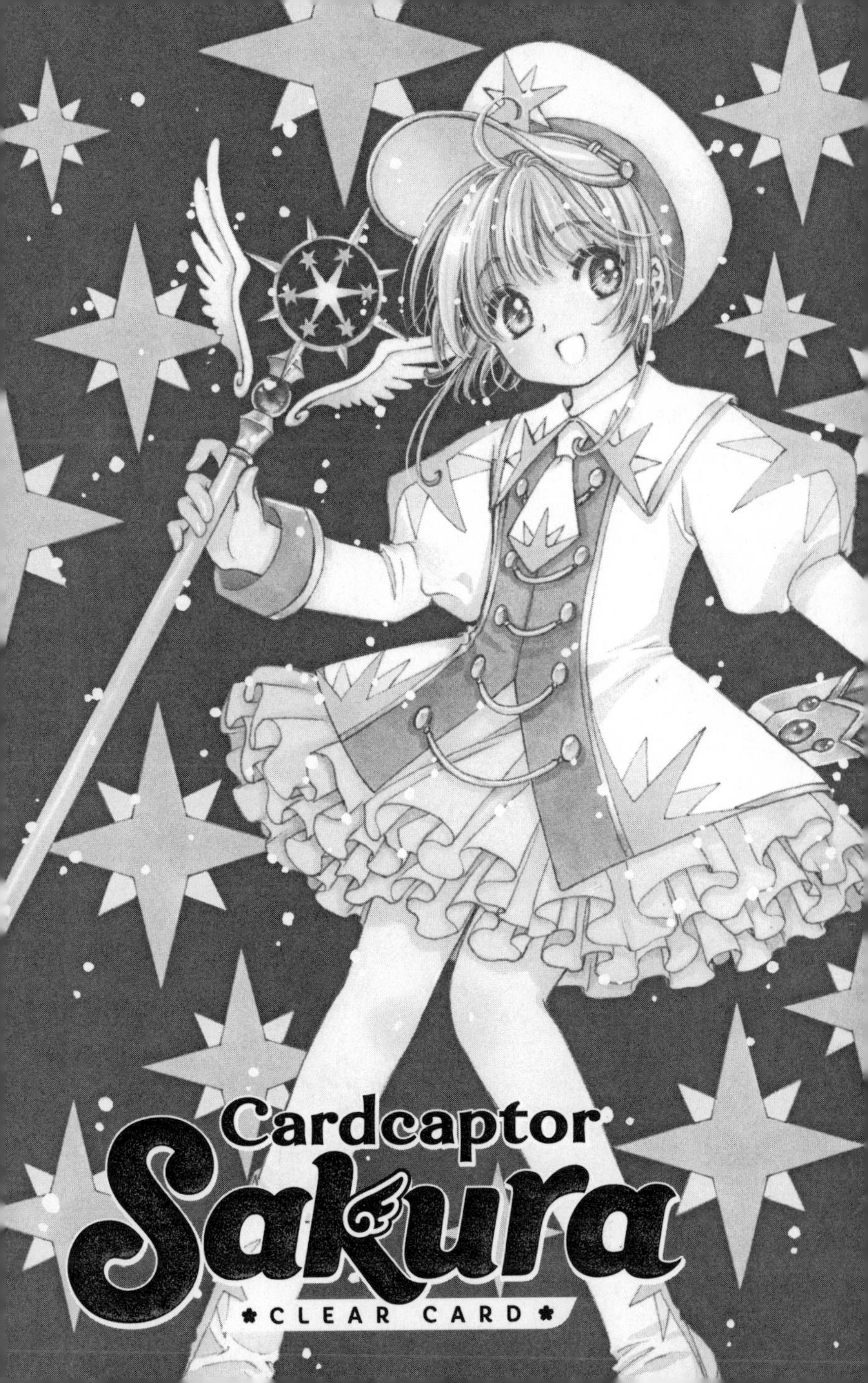
Cardcaptor
Sakura
CLEAR CARD

Cardcaptor Sakura

CLEAR CARD

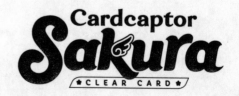

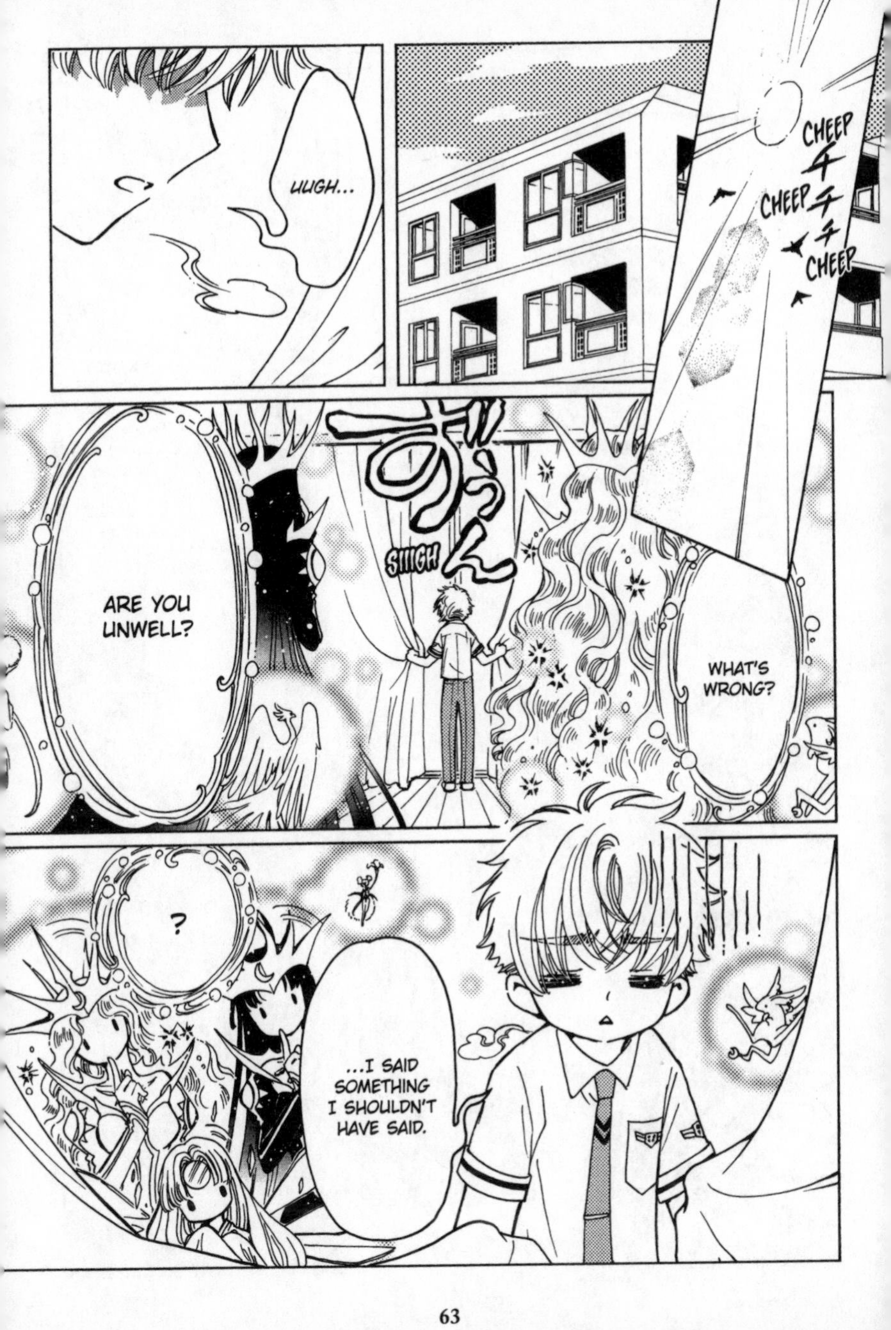
CHEEP
CHEEP
CHEEP
UUGH...
WHAT'S WRONG?
SIIIGH
ARE YOU UNWELL?
...I SAID SOMETHING I SHOULDN'T HAVE SAID.
?

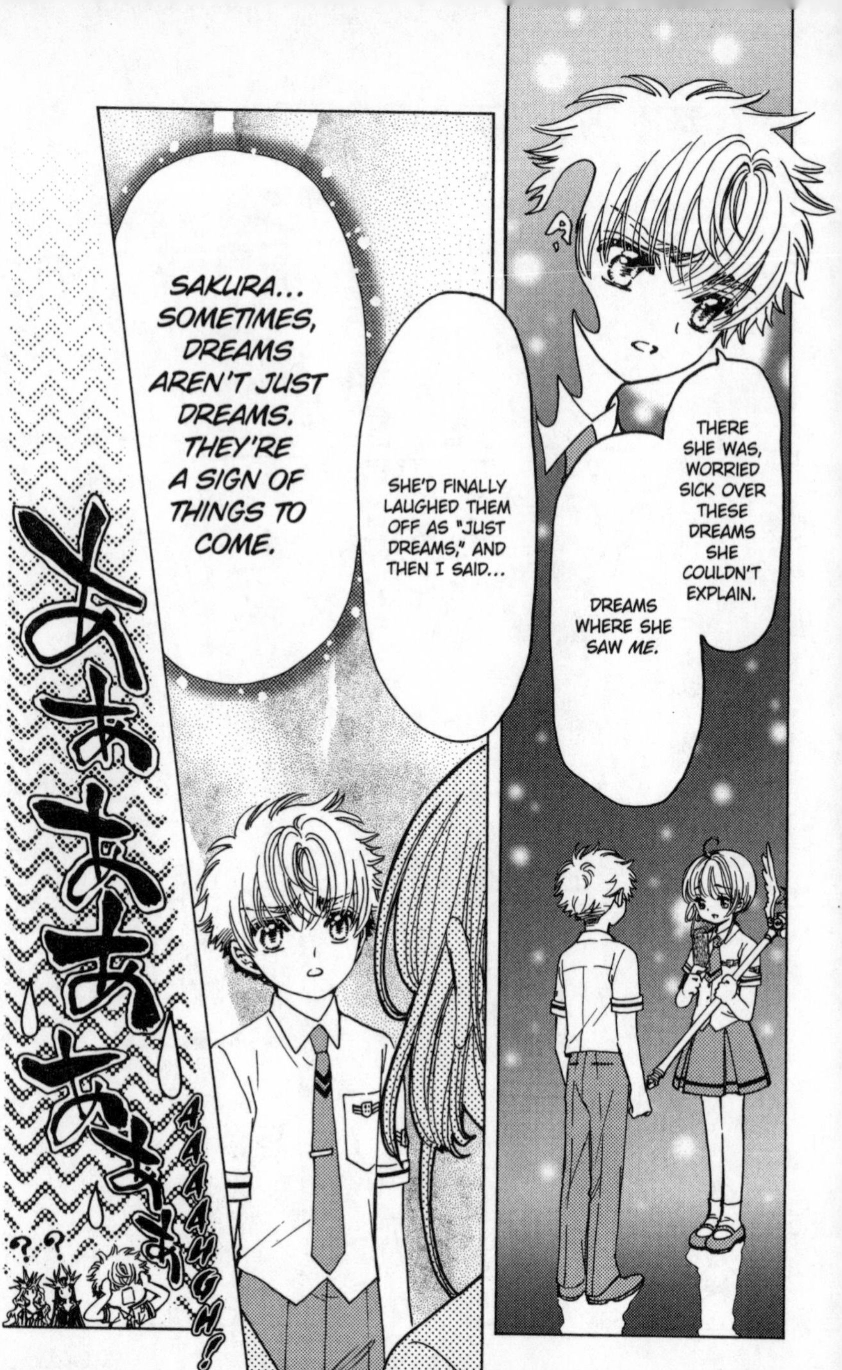
THERE SHE WAS, WORRIED SICK OVER THESE DREAMS SHE COULDN'T EXPLAIN.
DREAMS WHERE SHE SAW ME.
SHE'D FINALLY LAUGHED THEM OFF AS "JUST DREAMS," AND THEN I SAID...
SAKURA... SOMETIMES, DREAMS AREN'T JUST DREAMS. THEY'RE A SIGN OF THINGS TO COME.
ああああ
AAAAAUGH!
? ?

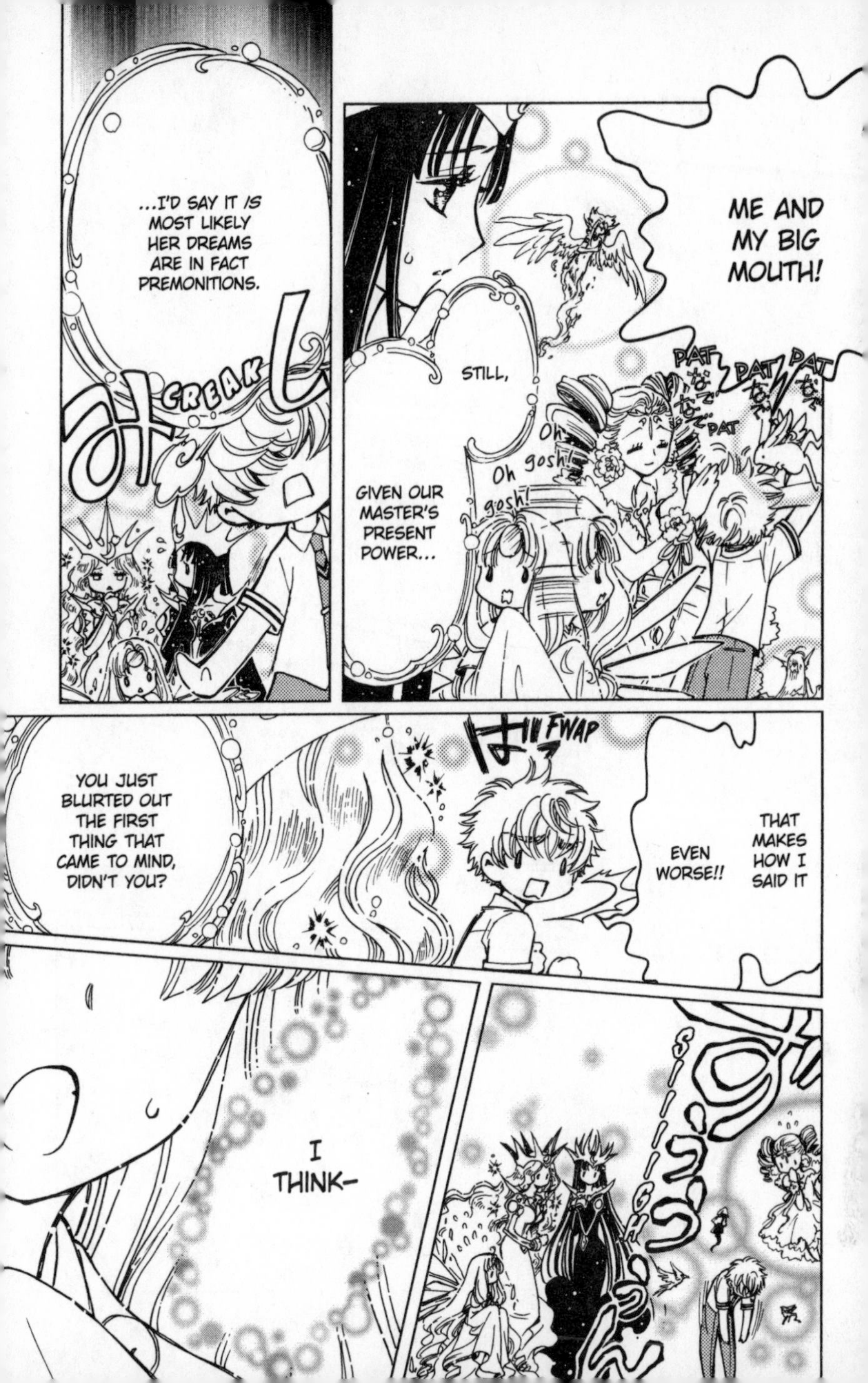
ME AND MY BIG MOUTH!
PAT PAT PAT PAT
Oh gosh! Oh gosh!
STILL,
GIVEN OUR MASTER'S PRESENT POWER...
...I'D SAY IT IS MOST LIKELY HER DREAMS ARE IN FACT PREMONITIONS.
CREAK
THAT MAKES HOW I SAID IT
EVEN WORSE!!
FWAP
YOU JUST BLURTED OUT THE FIRST THING THAT CAME TO MIND, DIDN'T YOU?
SIIIIGH
I THINK-

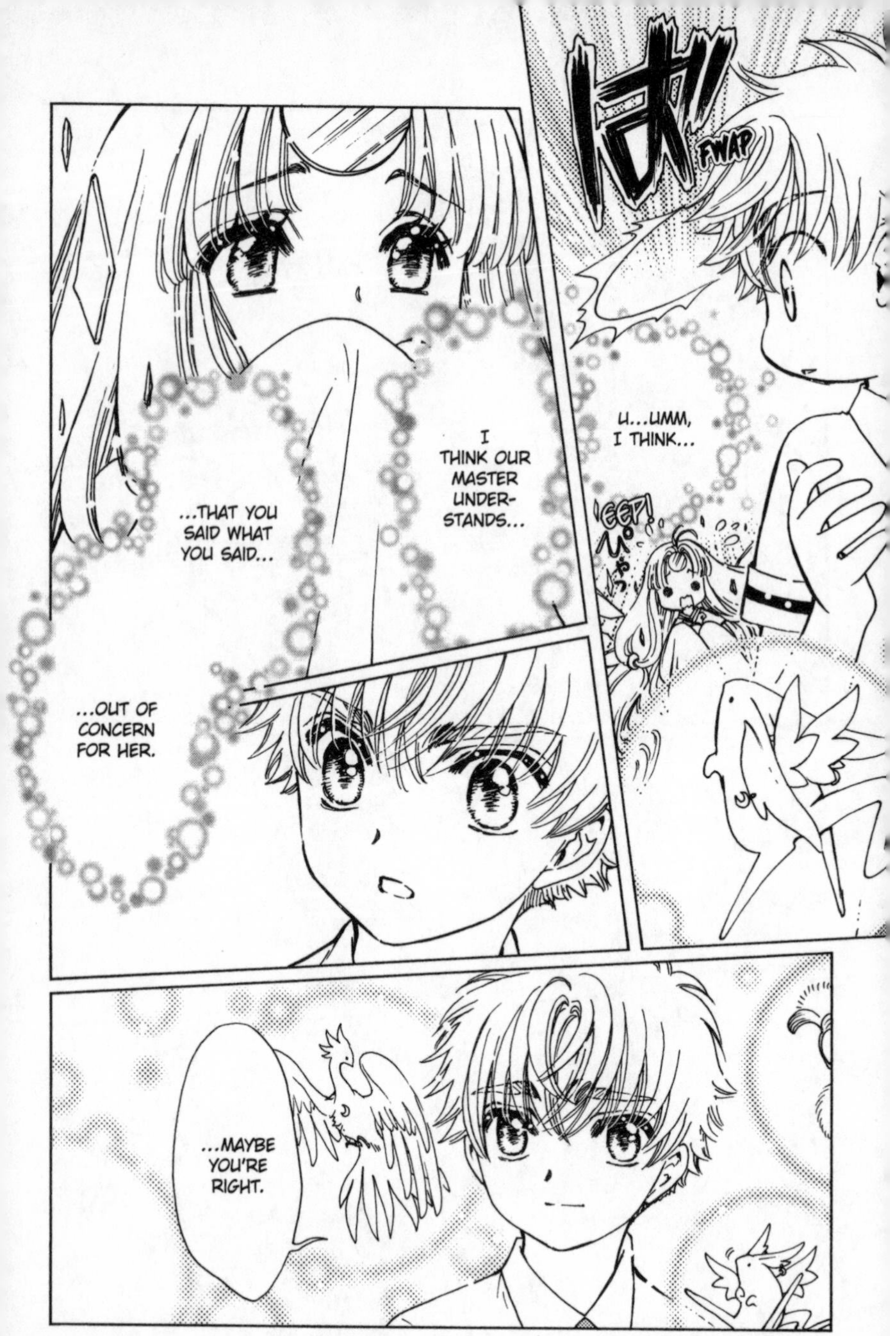
FWAP
U...UMM, I THINK...
EEP!
I THINK OUR MASTER UNDERSTANDS...
...THAT YOU SAID WHAT YOU SAID...
...OUT OF CONCERN FOR HER.
...MAYBE YOU'RE RIGHT.

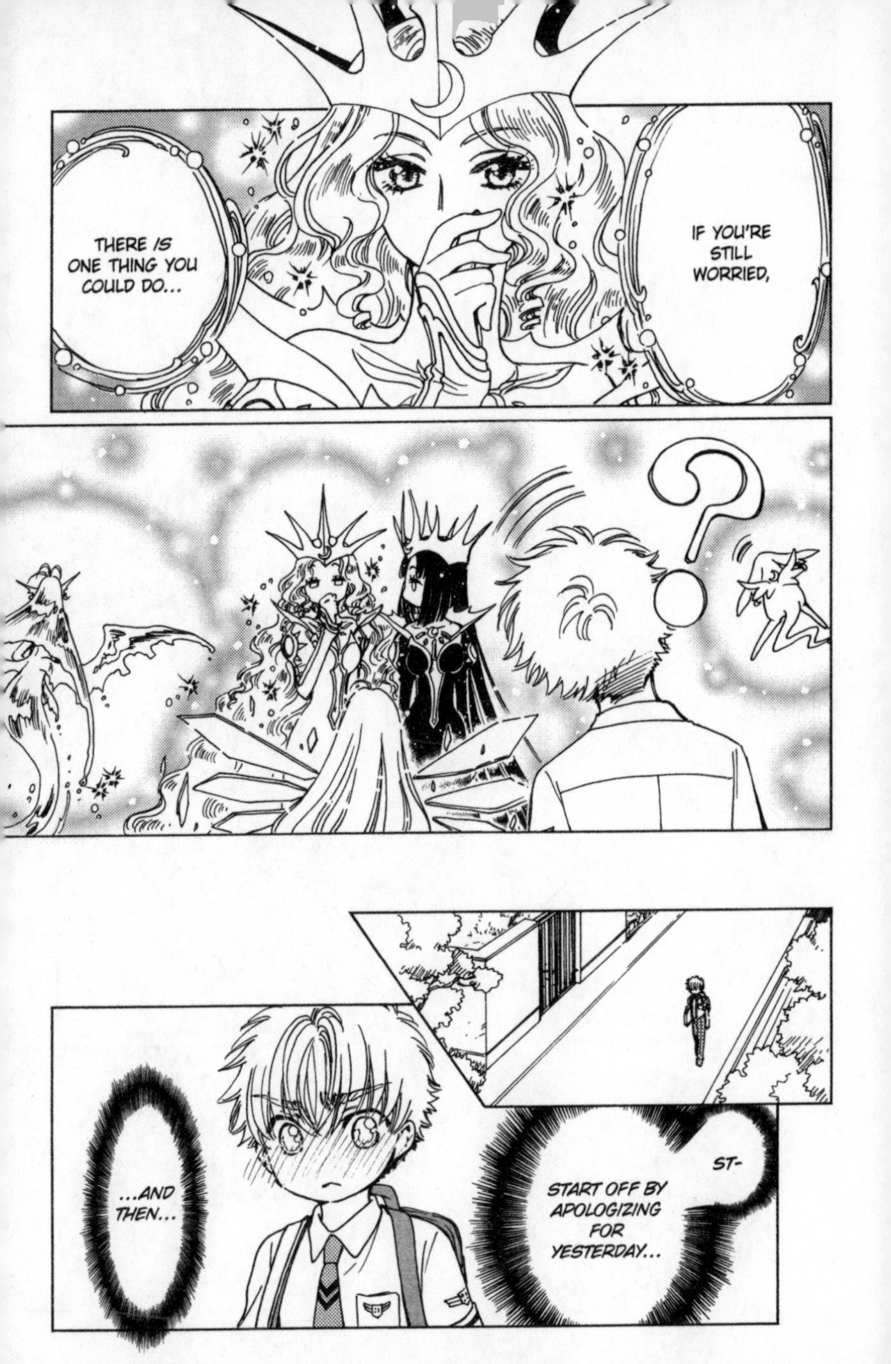
IF YOU'RE STILL WORRIED,
THERE IS ONE THING YOU COULD DO...
ST-
START OFF BY APOLOGIZING FOR YESTERDAY...
...AND THEN...

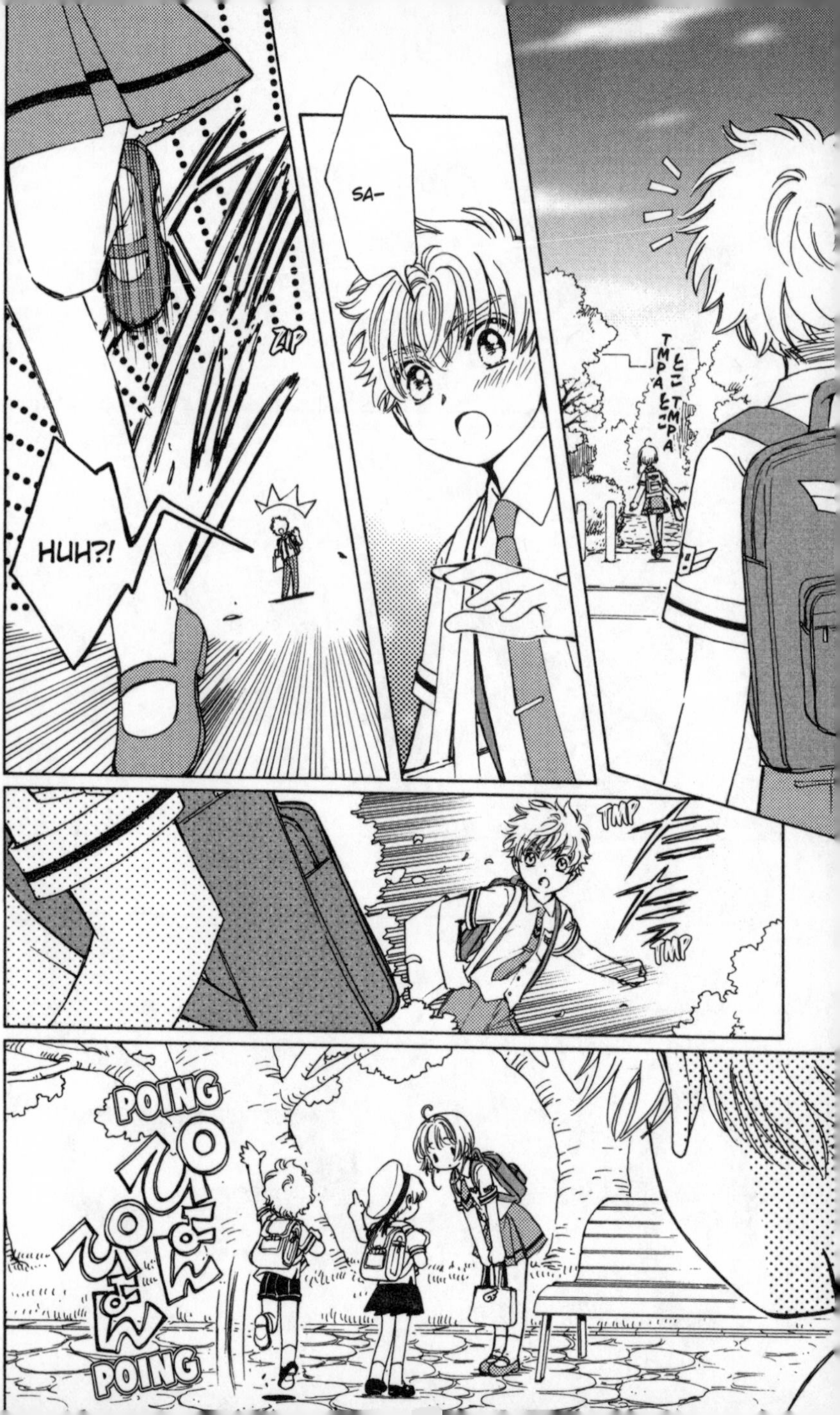

TMPA
TMPA
SA-
ZIP
HUH?!
TMP
TMP
POING
POING

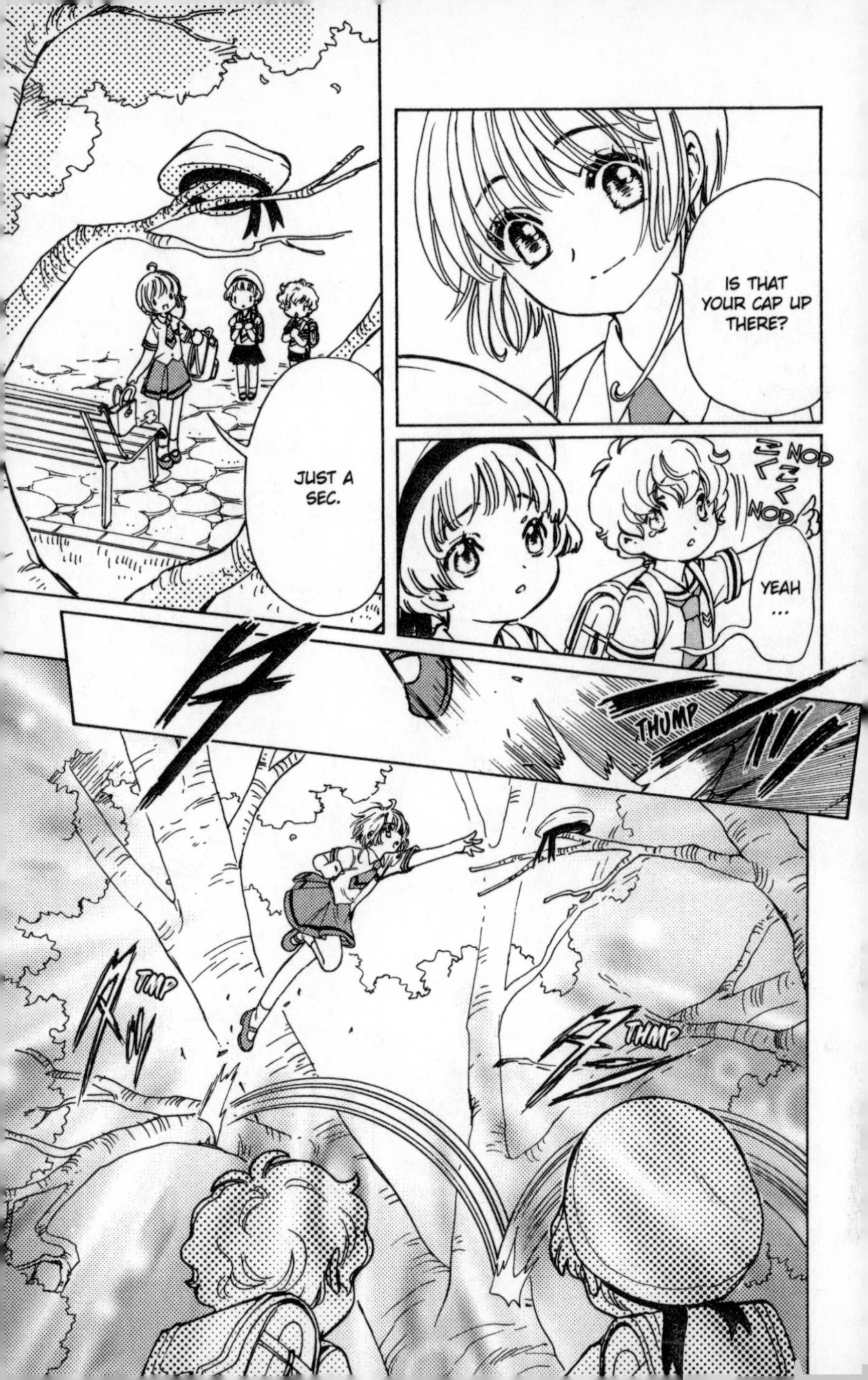
IS THAT YOUR CAP UP THERE?
こく NOD
こく NOD
YEAH ...
JUST A SEC.
THUMP
TMP
THMP

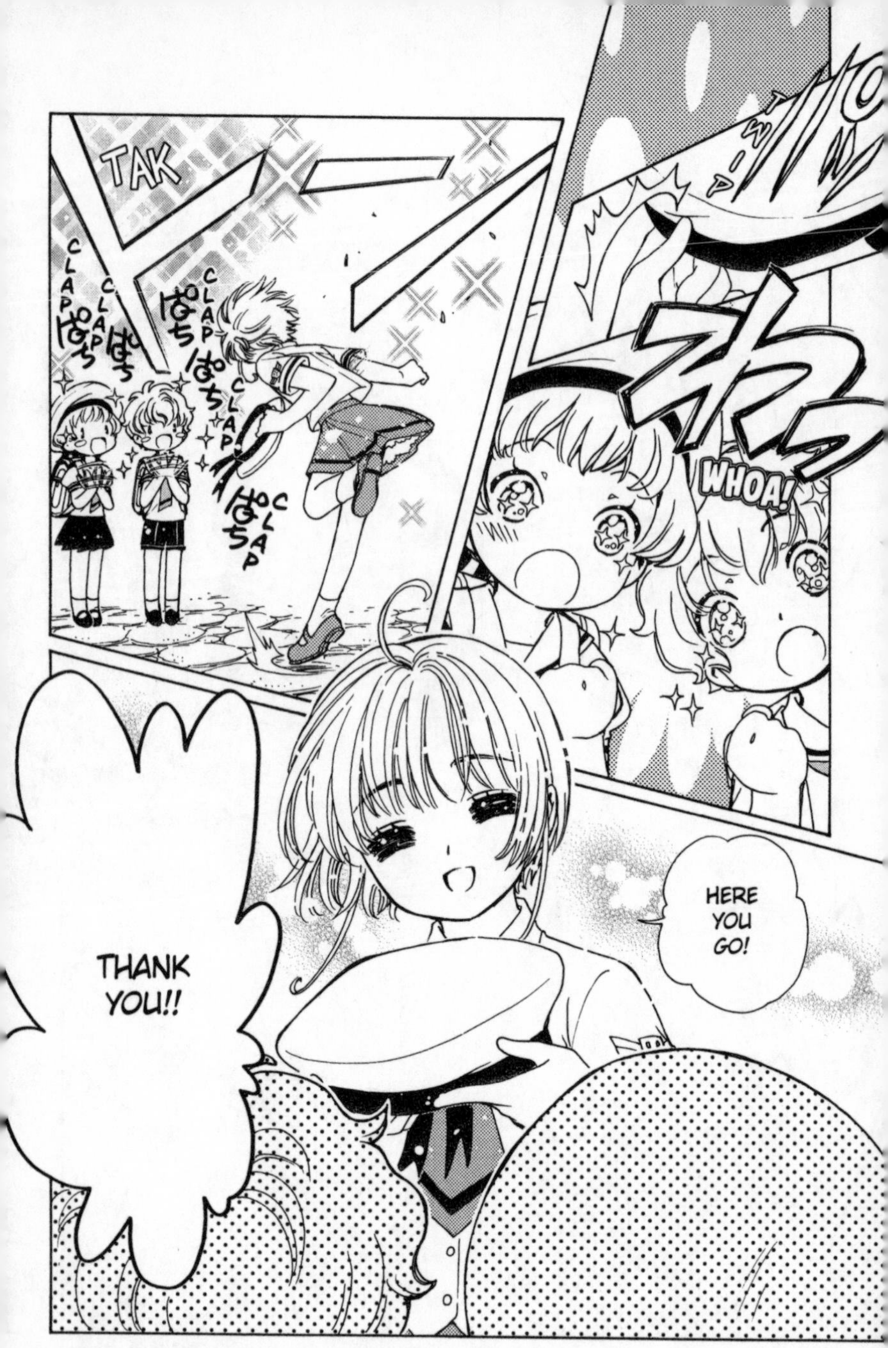
WHIP
WHOA!
TAK
ぱち CLAP
ぱち CLAP
ぱち CLAP
ぱち CLAP
ぱち CLAP
HERE YOU GO!
THANK YOU!!

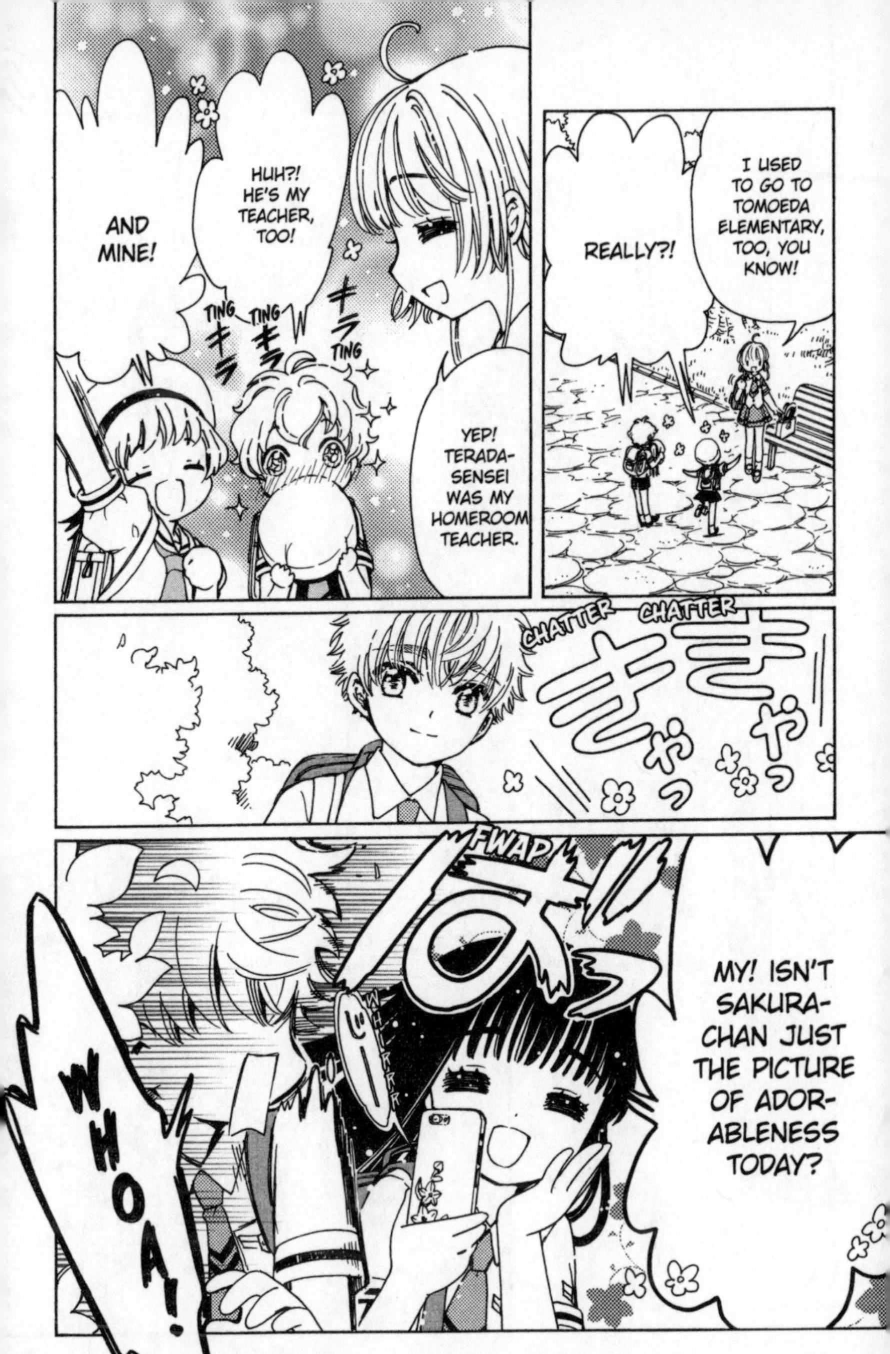
I USED TO GO TO TOMOEDA ELEMENTARY, TOO, YOU KNOW!
REALLY?!
YEP! TERADA-SENSEI WAS MY HOMEROOM TEACHER.
HUH?! HE'S MY TEACHER, TOO!
AND MINE!
TING
TING
TING
CHATTER
CHATTER
MY! ISN'T SAKURA-CHAN JUST THE PICTURE OF ADOR-ABLENESS TODAY?
FWAP
WHIRRR
WHOA!

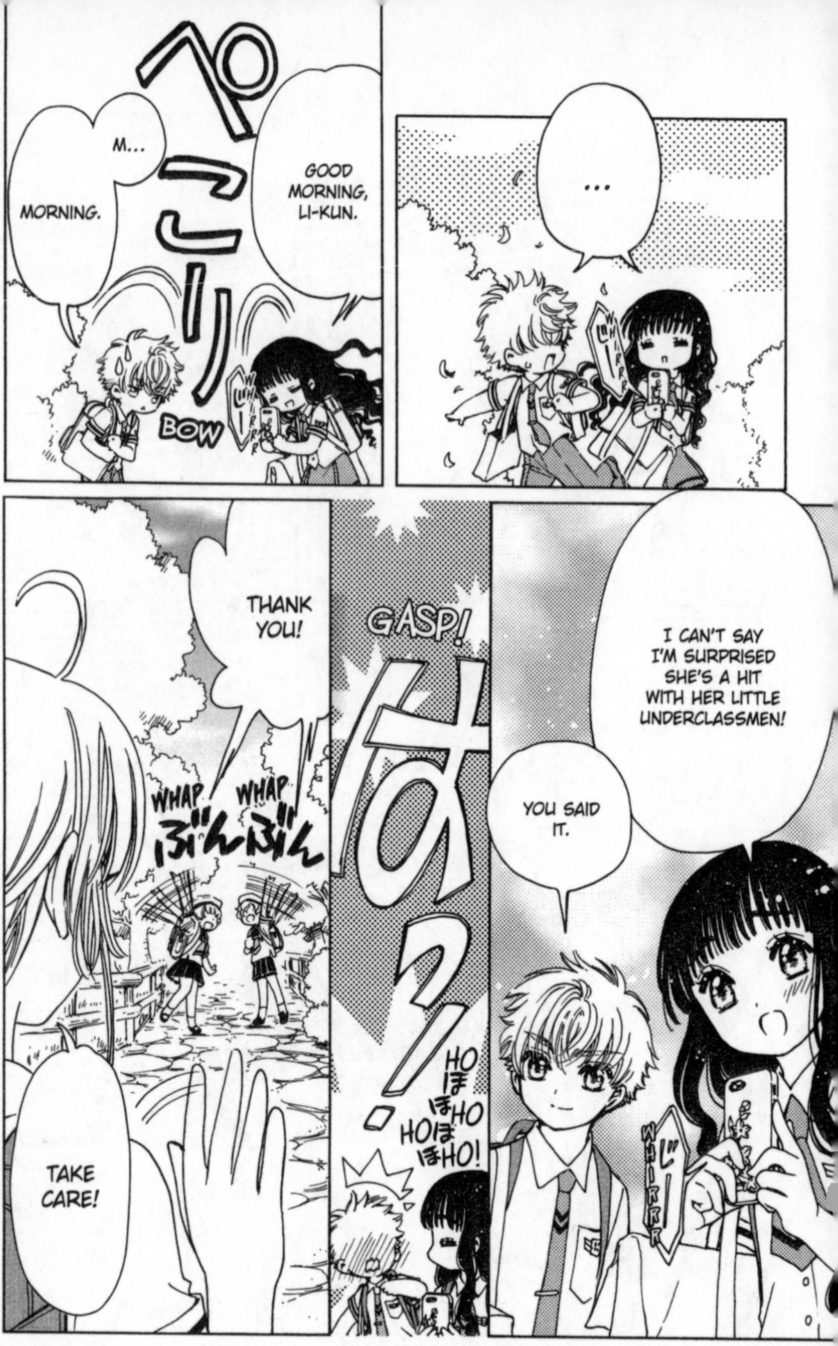
...
WHIRRR
GOOD MORNING, LI-KUN.
M... MORNING.
BOW
WHIRRR
I CAN'T SAY I'M SURPRISED SHE'S A HIT WITH HER LITTLE UNDERCLASSMEN!
YOU SAID IT.
WHIRRR
GASP!
HO HO HO HO!
THANK YOU!
WHAP WHAP
TAKE CARE!

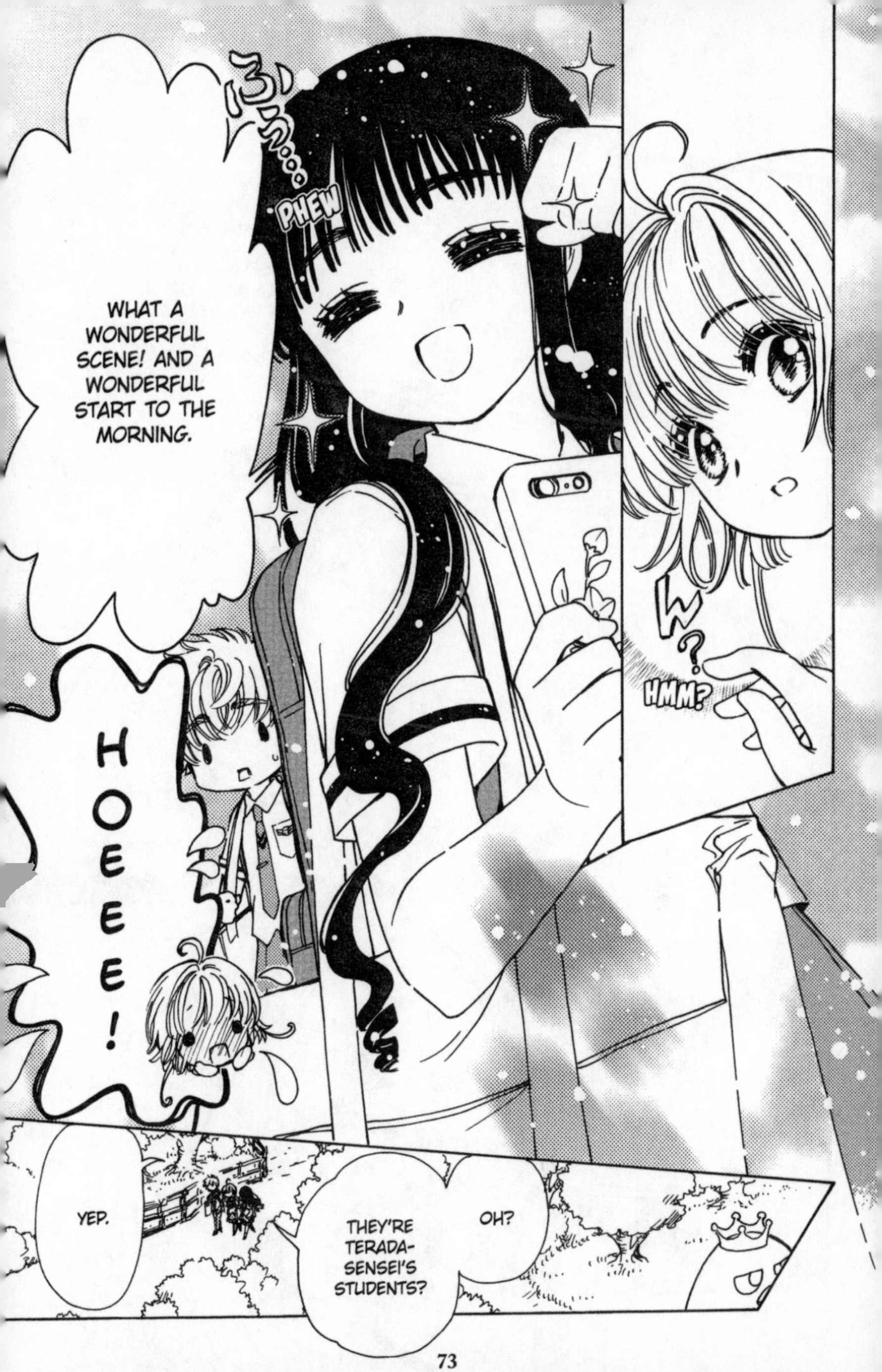
HMM?
PHEW
WHAT A WONDERFUL SCENE! AND A WONDERFUL START TO THE MORNING.
HOEEE!
OH?
THEY'RE TERADA-SENSEI'S STUDENTS?
YEP.

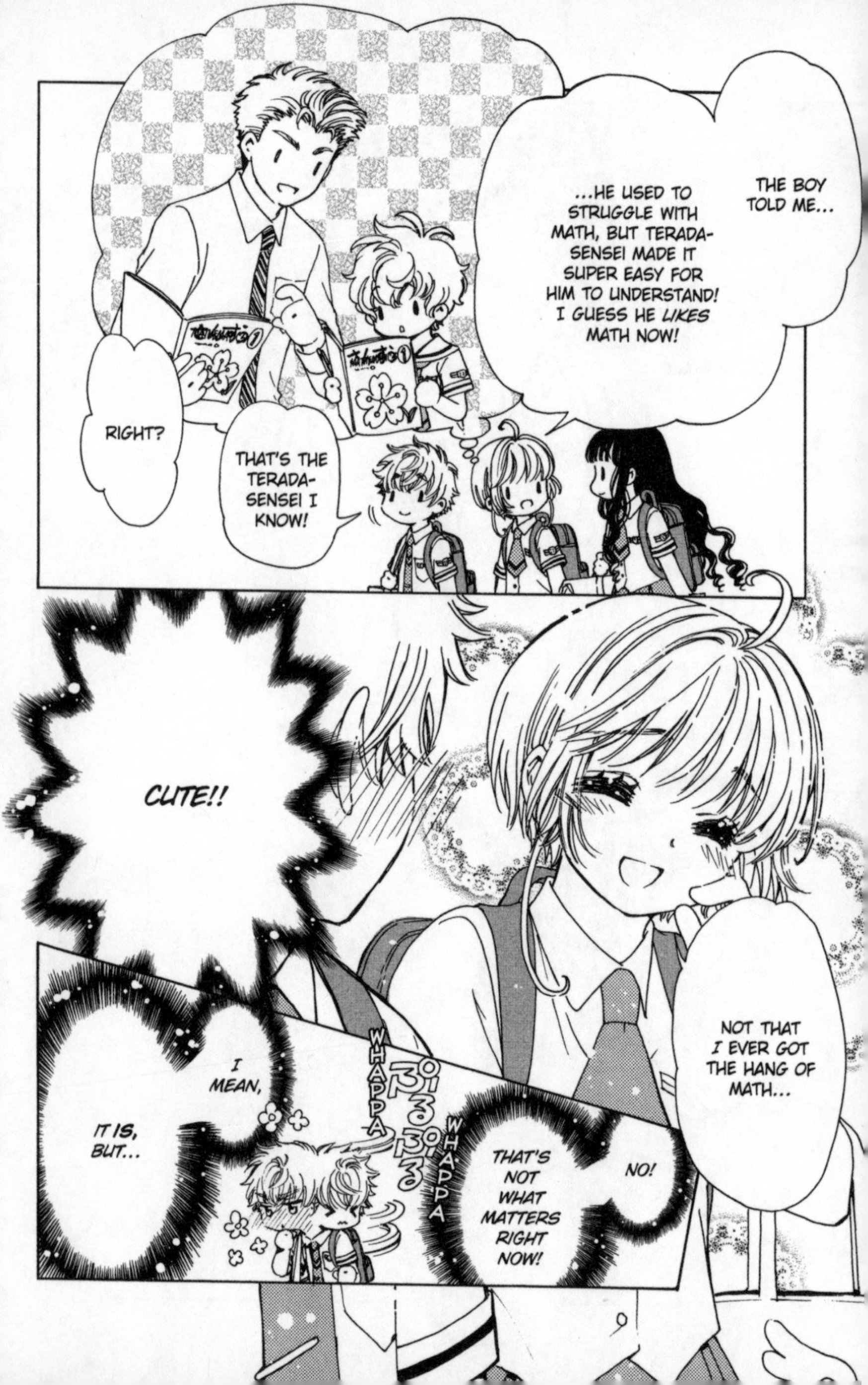
THE BOY TOLD ME...
...HE USED TO STRUGGLE WITH MATH, BUT TERADA-SENSEI MADE IT SUPER EASY FOR HIM TO UNDERSTAND! I GUESS HE *LIKES* MATH NOW!
THAT'S THE TERADA-SENSEI I KNOW!
RIGHT?
NOT THAT I EVER GOT THE HANG OF MATH...
CUTE!!
NO!
THAT'S NOT WHAT MATTERS RIGHT NOW!
WHAPPA WHAPPA
I MEAN,
IT IS, BUT...

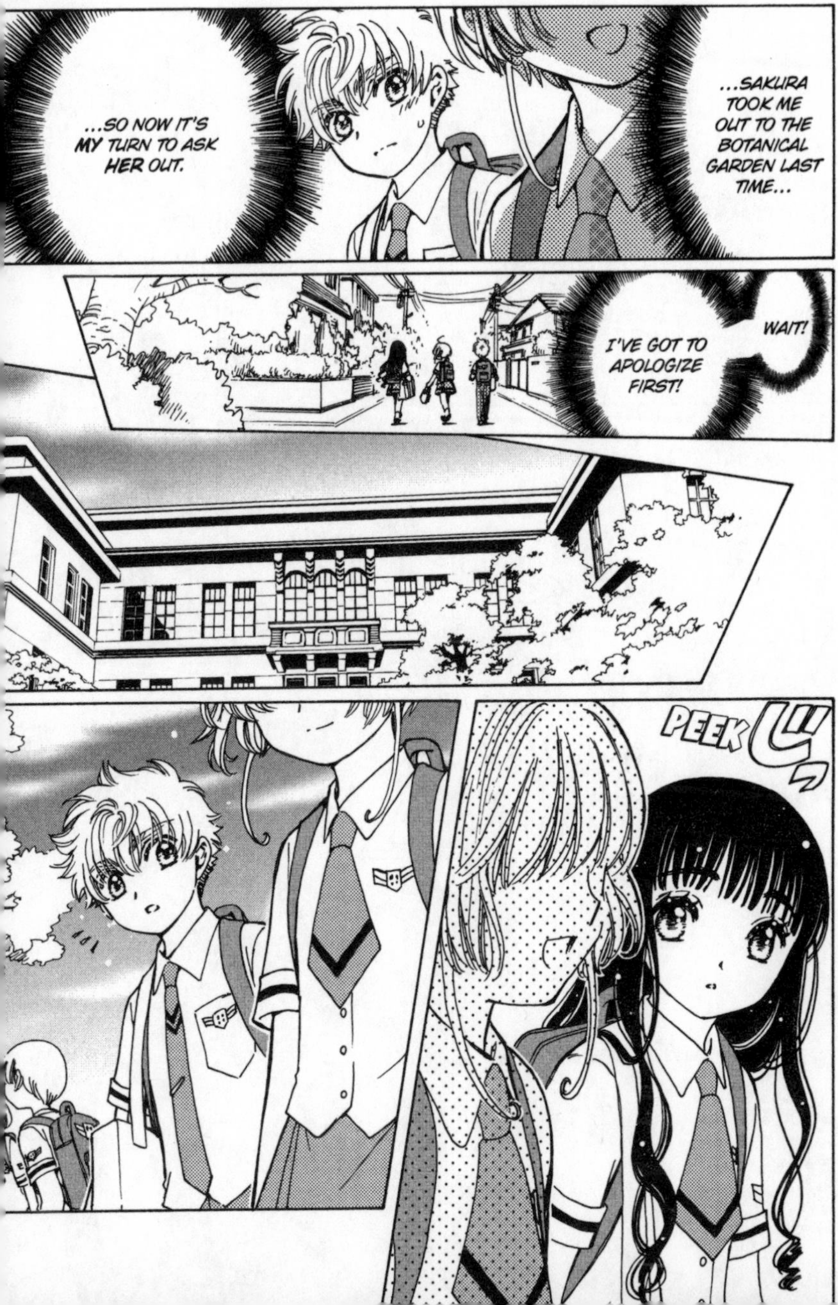
...SAKURA TOOK ME OUT TO THE BOTANICAL GARDEN LAST TIME...
...SO NOW IT'S MY TURN TO ASK HER OUT.
WAIT!
I'VE GOT TO APOLOGIZE FIRST!
PEEK

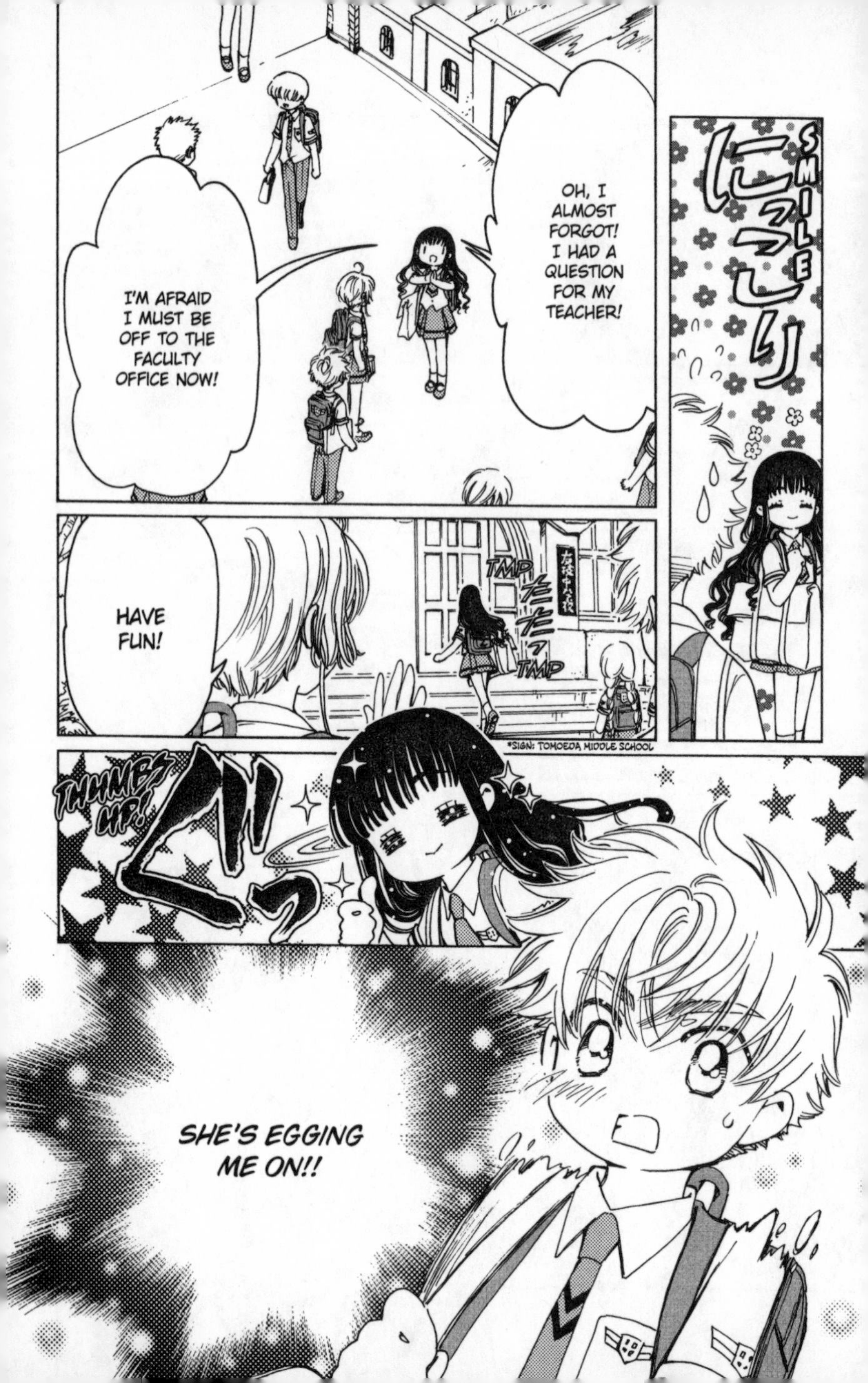
SMILE
OH, I ALMOST FORGOT! I HAD A QUESTION FOR MY TEACHER!
I'M AFRAID I MUST BE OFF TO THE FACULTY OFFICE NOW!
TMP
TMP
HAVE FUN!
*SIGN: TOMOEDA MIDDLE SCHOOL
THUMBS UP!
SHE'S EGGING ME ON!!

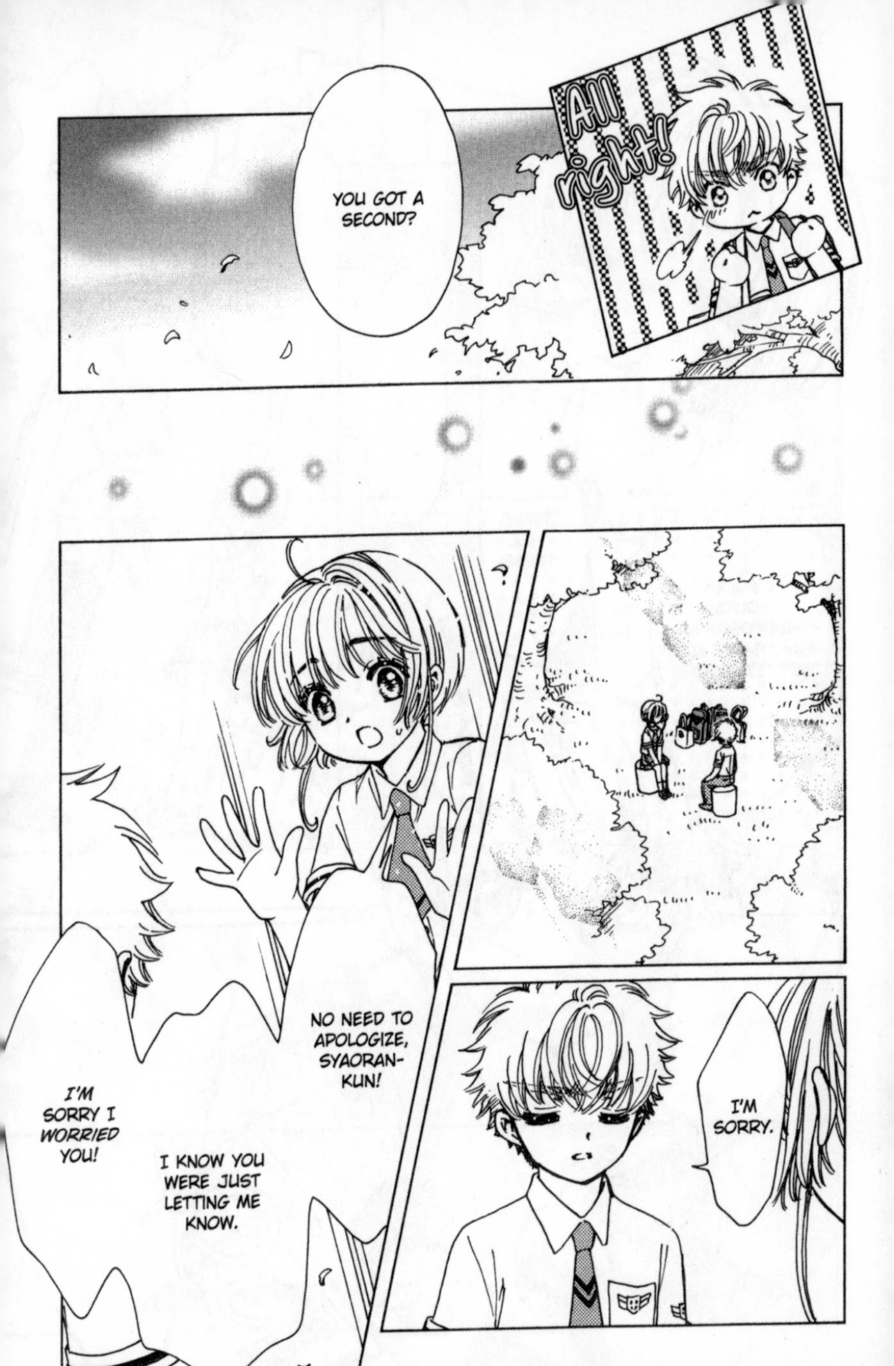
All right!
YOU GOT A SECOND?
I'M SORRY.
NO NEED TO APOLOGIZE, SYAORAN-KUN!
I KNOW YOU WERE JUST LETTING ME KNOW.
I'M SORRY I WORRIED YOU!

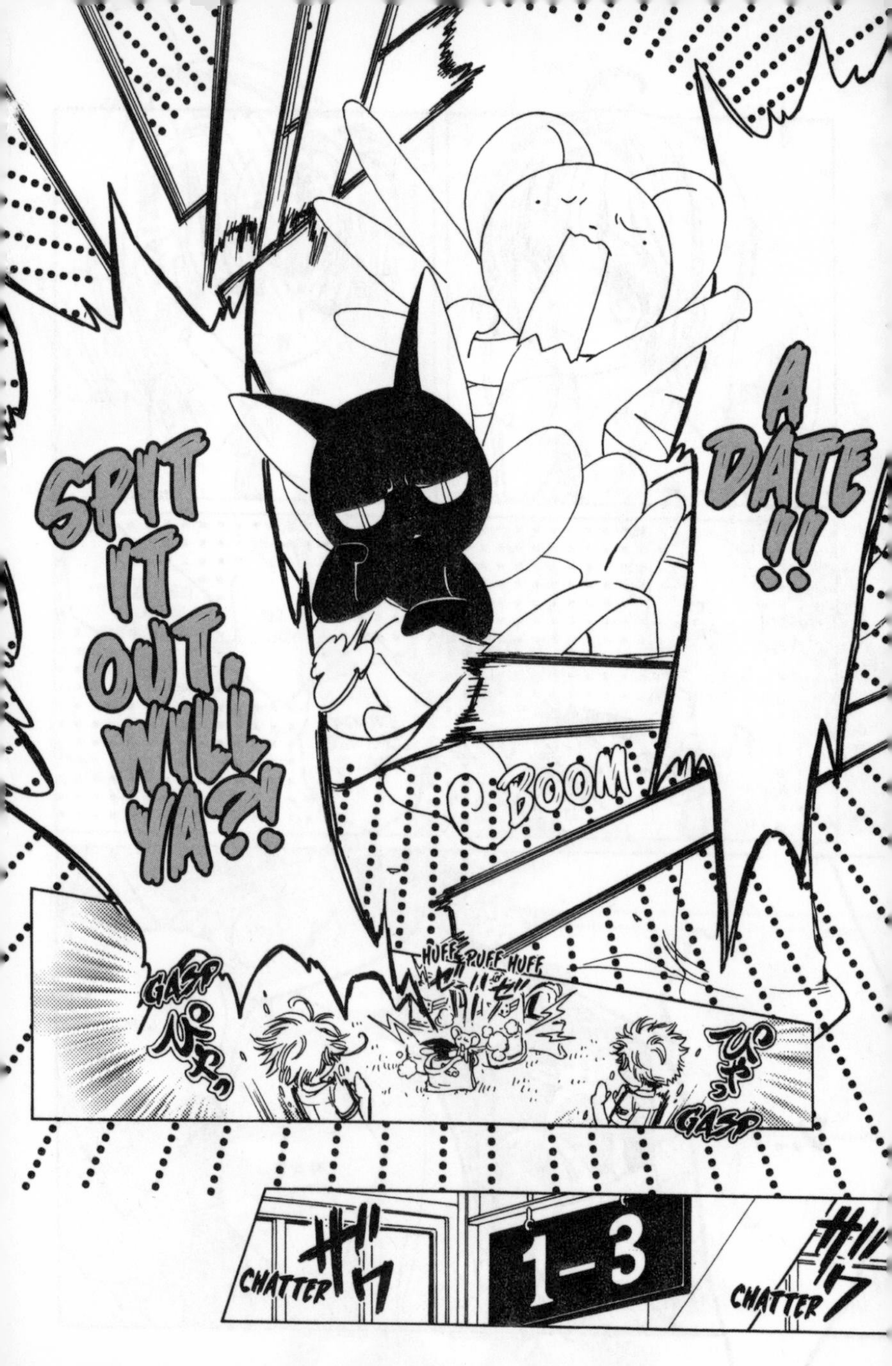
A DATE!!
SPIT IT OUT, WILL YA?!
BOOM
GASP
HUFF PUFF HUFF
GASP
CHATTER
1-3
CHATTER

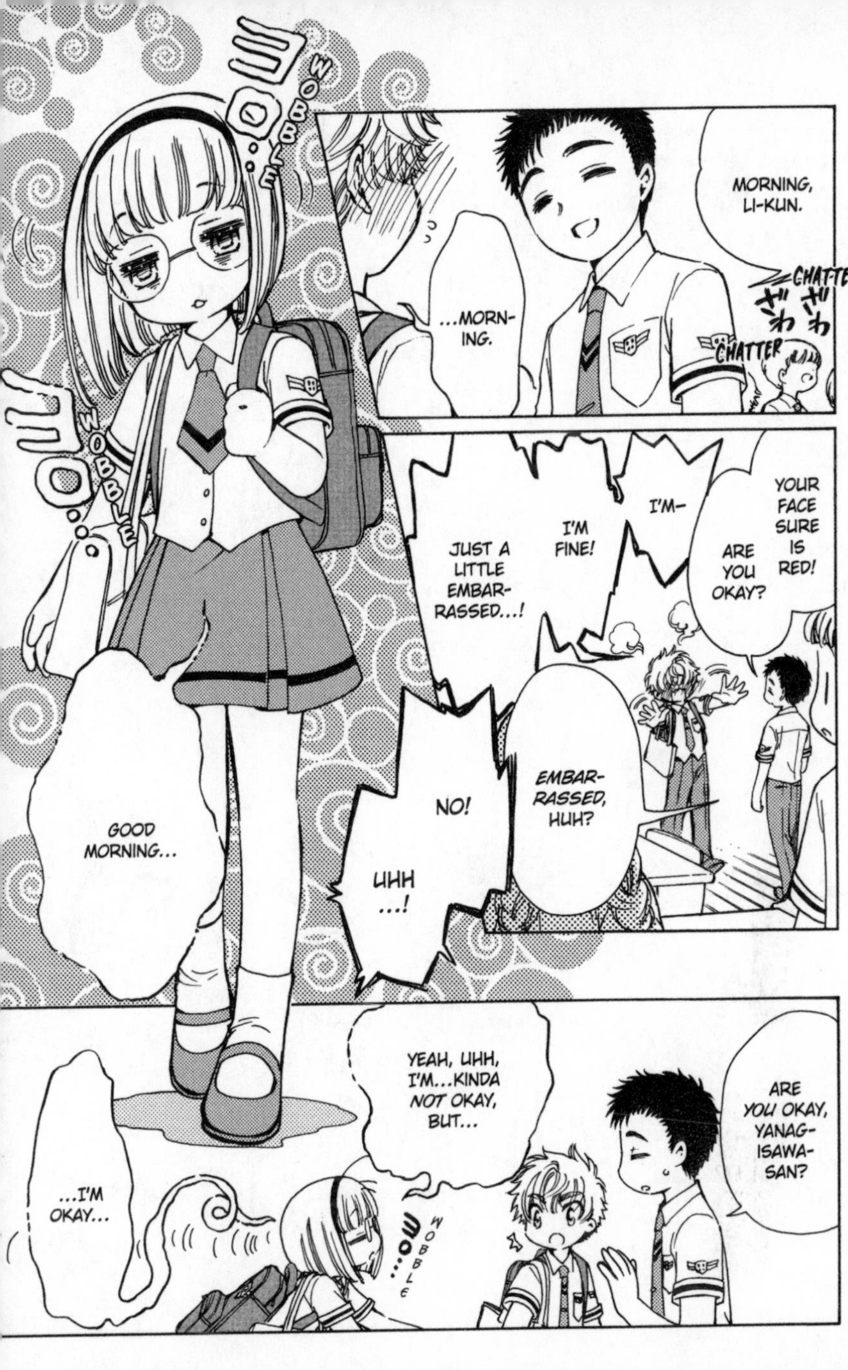

MORNING, LI-KUN.
CHATTER ざわ ざわ CHATTER
...MORNING.
YOUR FACE SURE IS RED!
ARE YOU OKAY?
I'M-
I'M FINE!
JUST A LITTLE EMBARRASSED...!
EMBARRASSED, HUH?
NO!
UHH...!
ヨロ WOBBLE
ヨロ WOBBLE
GOOD MORNING...
ARE YOU OKAY, YANAGISAWA-SAN?
YEAH, UHH, I'M...KINDA *NOT* OKAY, BUT...
ヨロ... WOBBLE
...I'M OKAY...

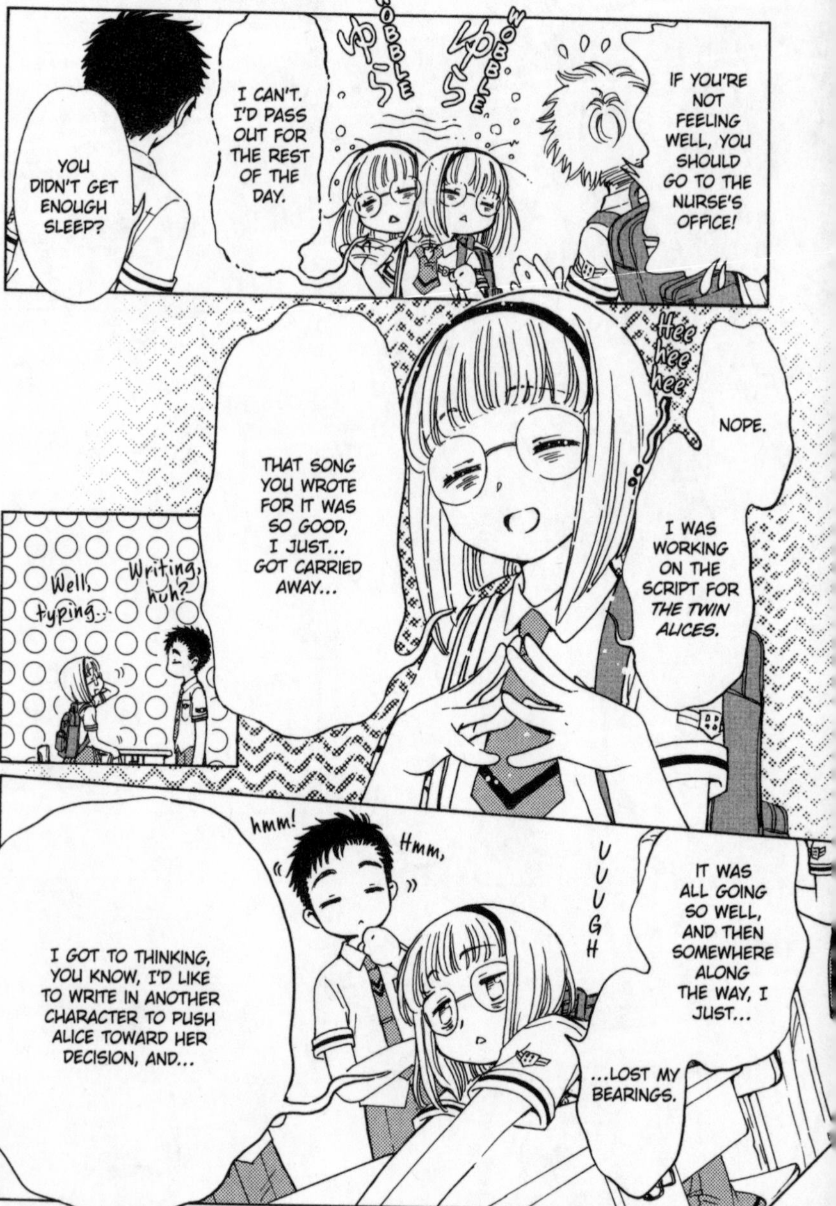
IF YOU'RE NOT FEELING WELL, YOU SHOULD GO TO THE NURSE'S OFFICE!
WOBBLE
WOBBLE
I CAN'T. I'D PASS OUT FOR THE REST OF THE DAY.
YOU DIDN'T GET ENOUGH SLEEP?
Hee hee hee
NOPE.
I WAS WORKING ON THE SCRIPT FOR *THE TWIN ALICES.*
THAT SONG YOU WROTE FOR IT WAS SO GOOD, I JUST... GOT CARRIED AWAY...
Writing, huh?
Well, typing...
UUUGH
IT WAS ALL GOING SO WELL, AND THEN SOMEWHERE ALONG THE WAY, I JUST...
...LOST MY BEARINGS.
Hmm,
hmm!
I GOT TO THINKING, YOU KNOW, I'D LIKE TO WRITE IN ANOTHER CHARACTER TO PUSH ALICE TOWARD HER DECISION, AND...

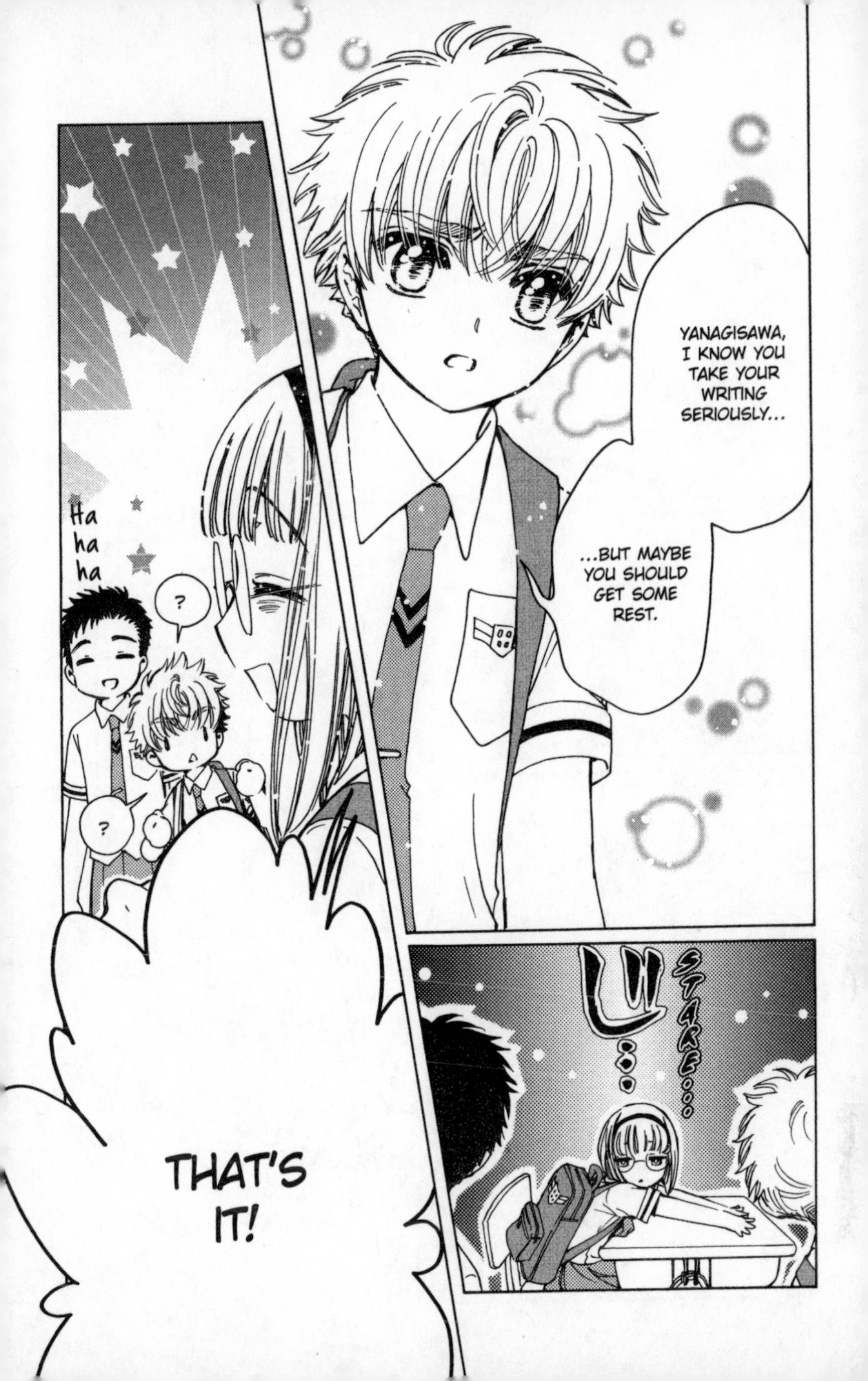

YANAGISAWA, I KNOW YOU TAKE YOUR WRITING SERIOUSLY...
...BUT MAYBE YOU SHOULD GET SOME REST.
Ha ha ha
?
?
STARE...
THAT'S IT!

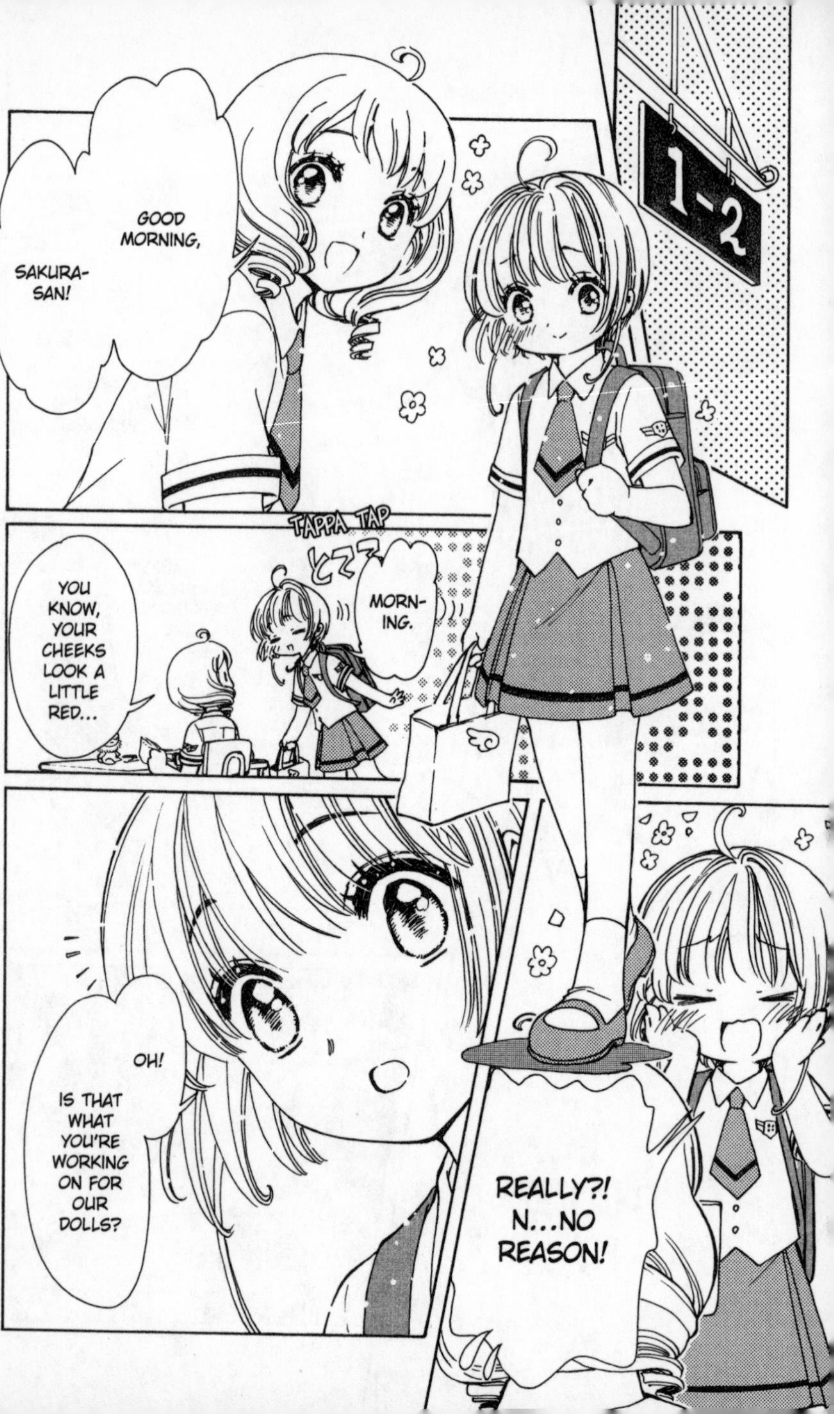
GOOD MORNING,
SAKURA-SAN!
TAPPA TAP
とてて
MORN-ING.
YOU KNOW, YOUR CHEEKS LOOK A LITTLE RED...
REALLY?! N...NO REASON!
OH!
IS THAT WHAT YOU'RE WORKING ON FOR OUR DOLLS?

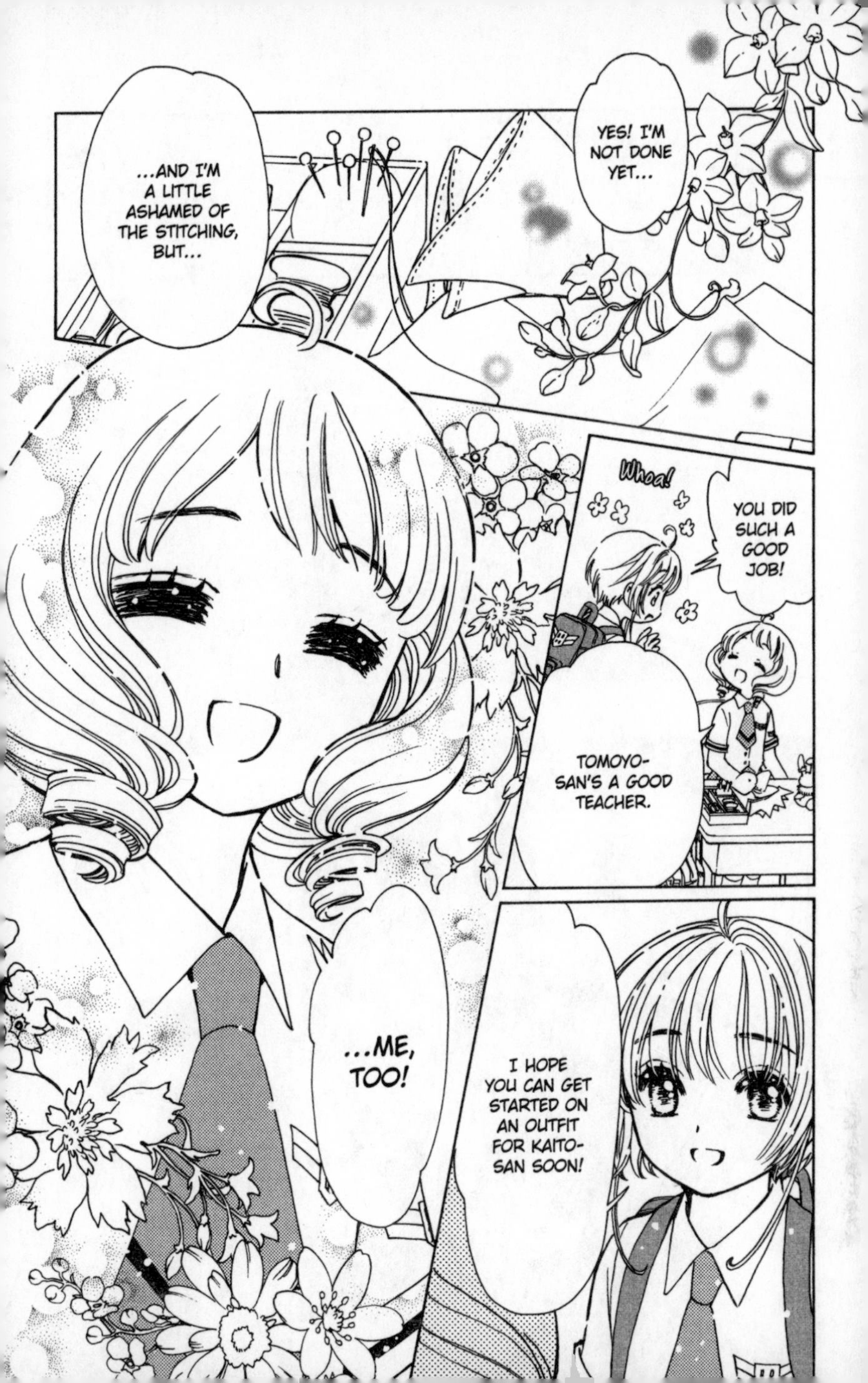
YES! I'M NOT DONE YET...
...AND I'M A LITTLE ASHAMED OF THE STITCHING, BUT...
YOU DID SUCH A GOOD JOB!
Whoa!
TOMOYO-SAN'S A GOOD TEACHER.
I HOPE YOU CAN GET STARTED ON AN OUTFIT FOR KAITO-SAN SOON!
...ME, TOO!

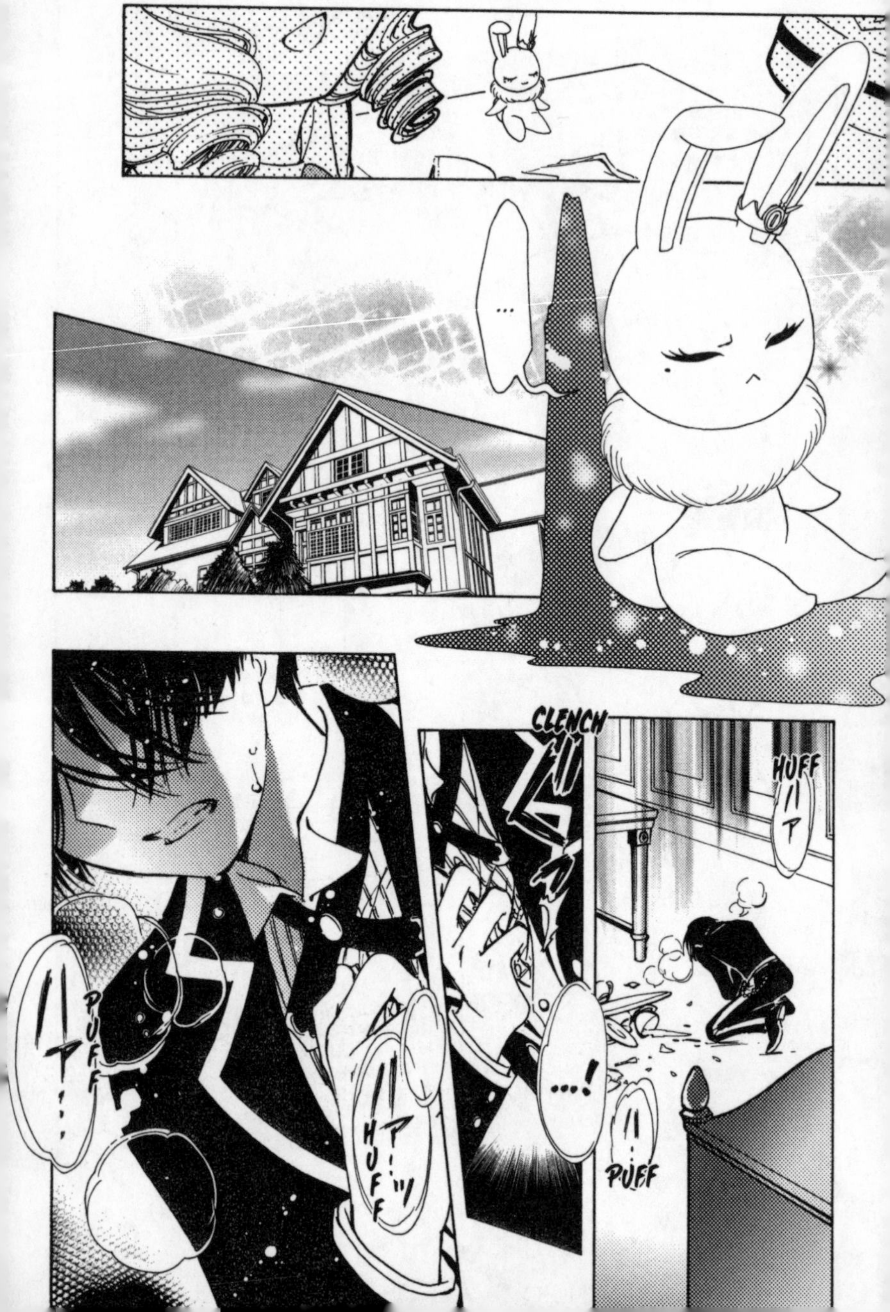
...
HUFF
...!
PUFF
CLENCH
HUFF
PUFF

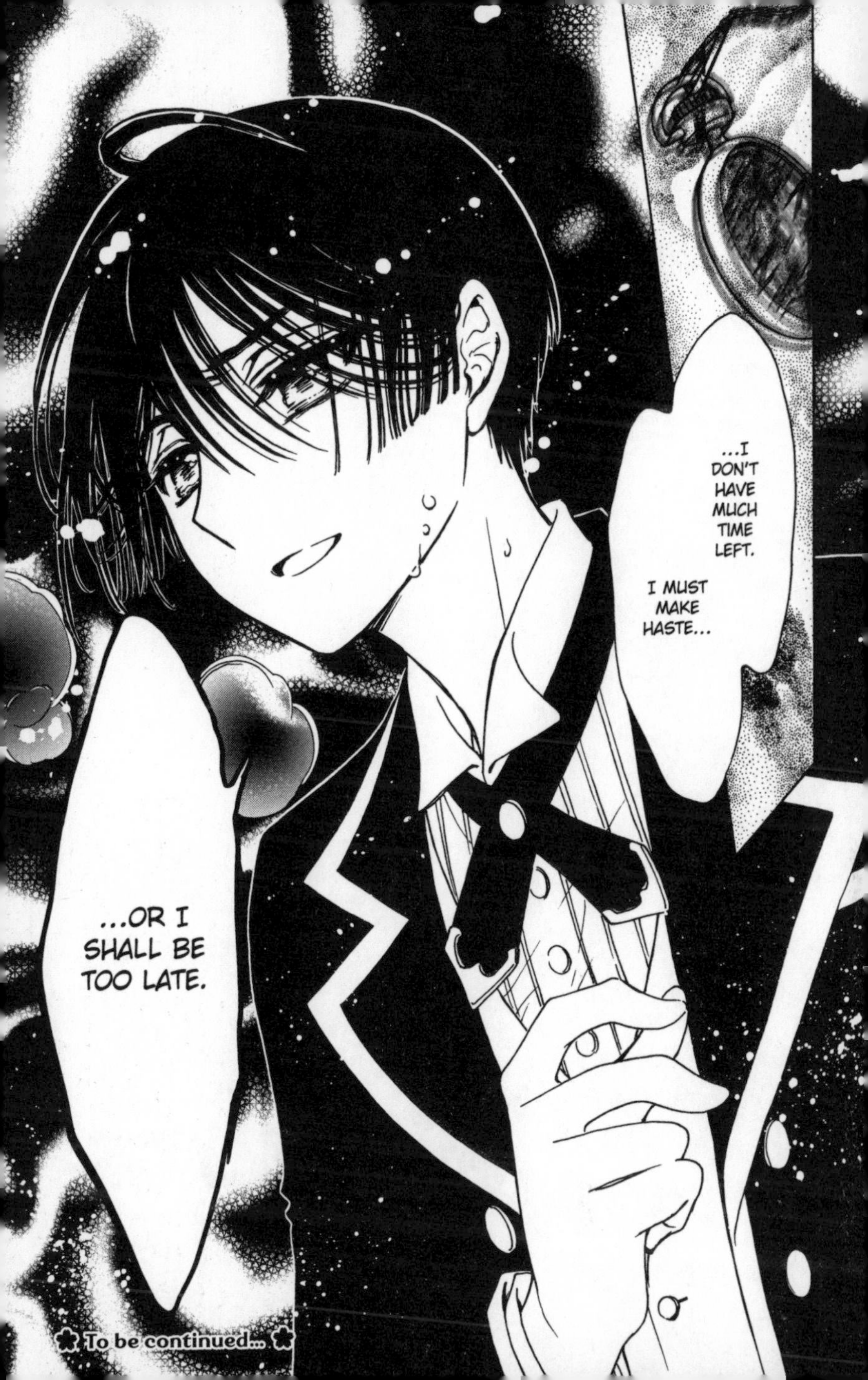
...I DON'T HAVE MUCH TIME LEFT.
I MUST MAKE HASTE...
...OR I SHALL BE TOO LATE.
To be continued...

Cardcaptor Sakura

CLEAR CARD

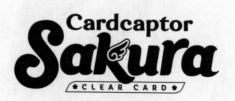

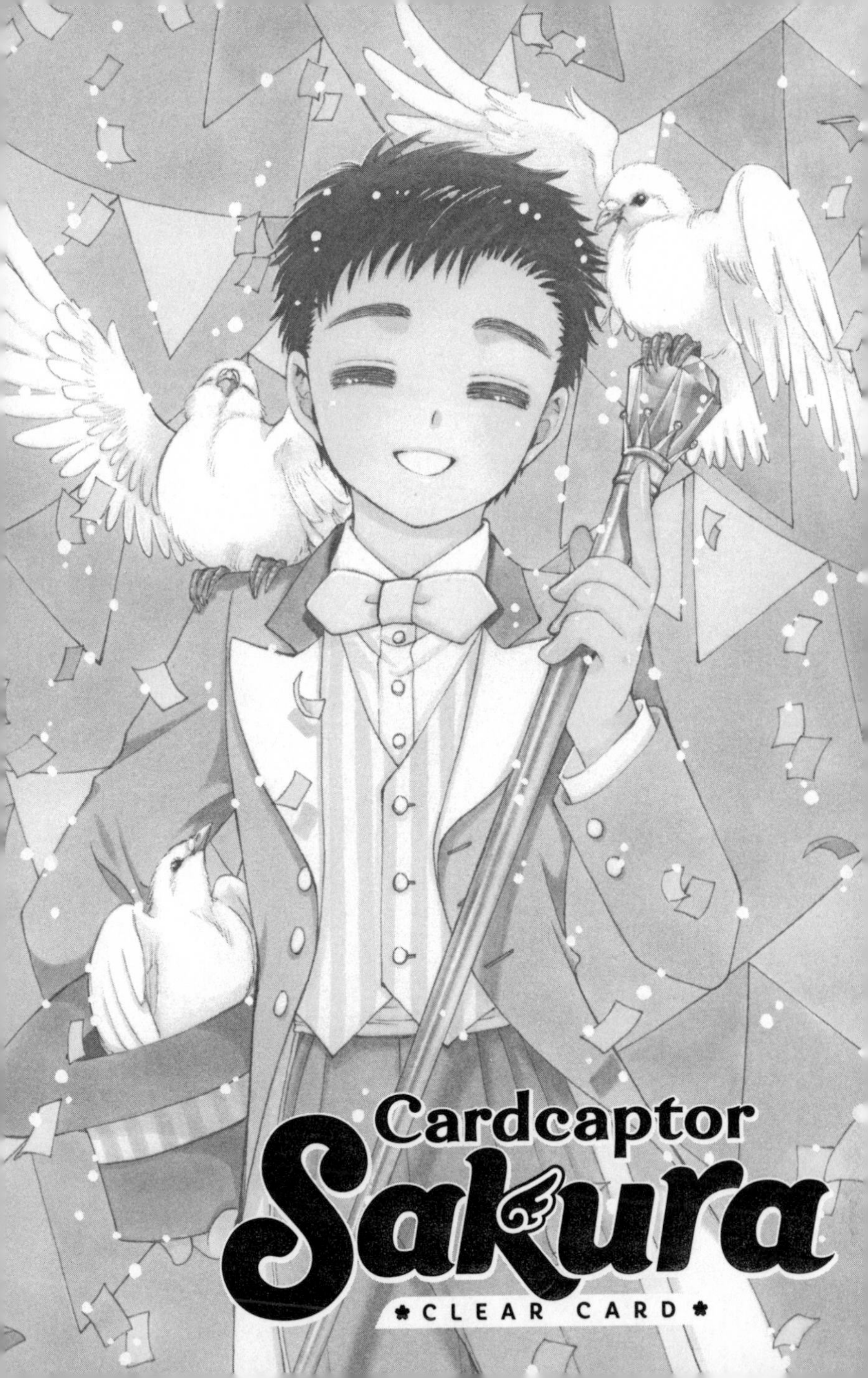
Cardcaptor
Sakura
CLEAR CARD

Cardcaptor Sakura

CLEAR CARD

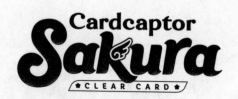

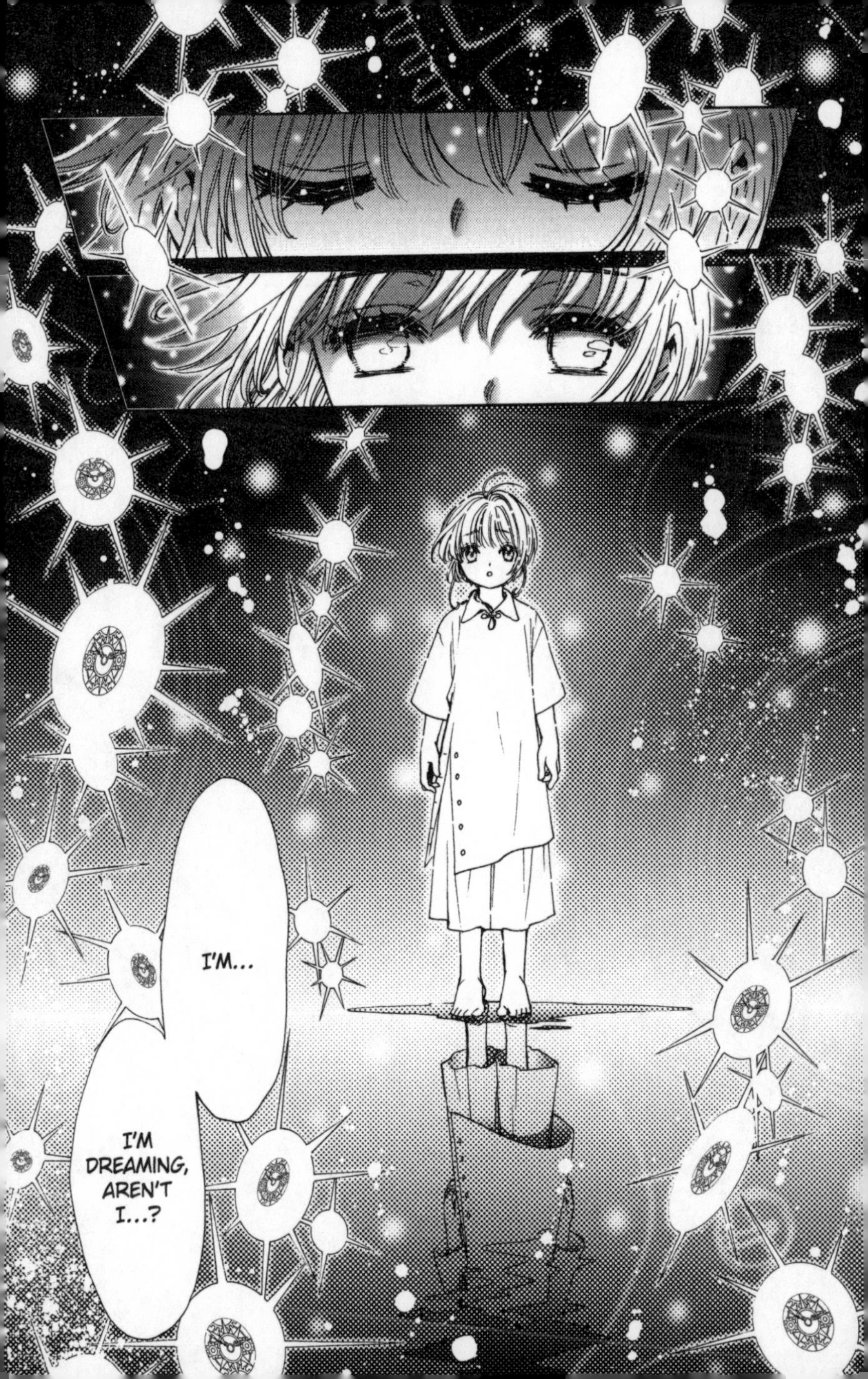
I'M...
I'M DREAMING, AREN'T I...?

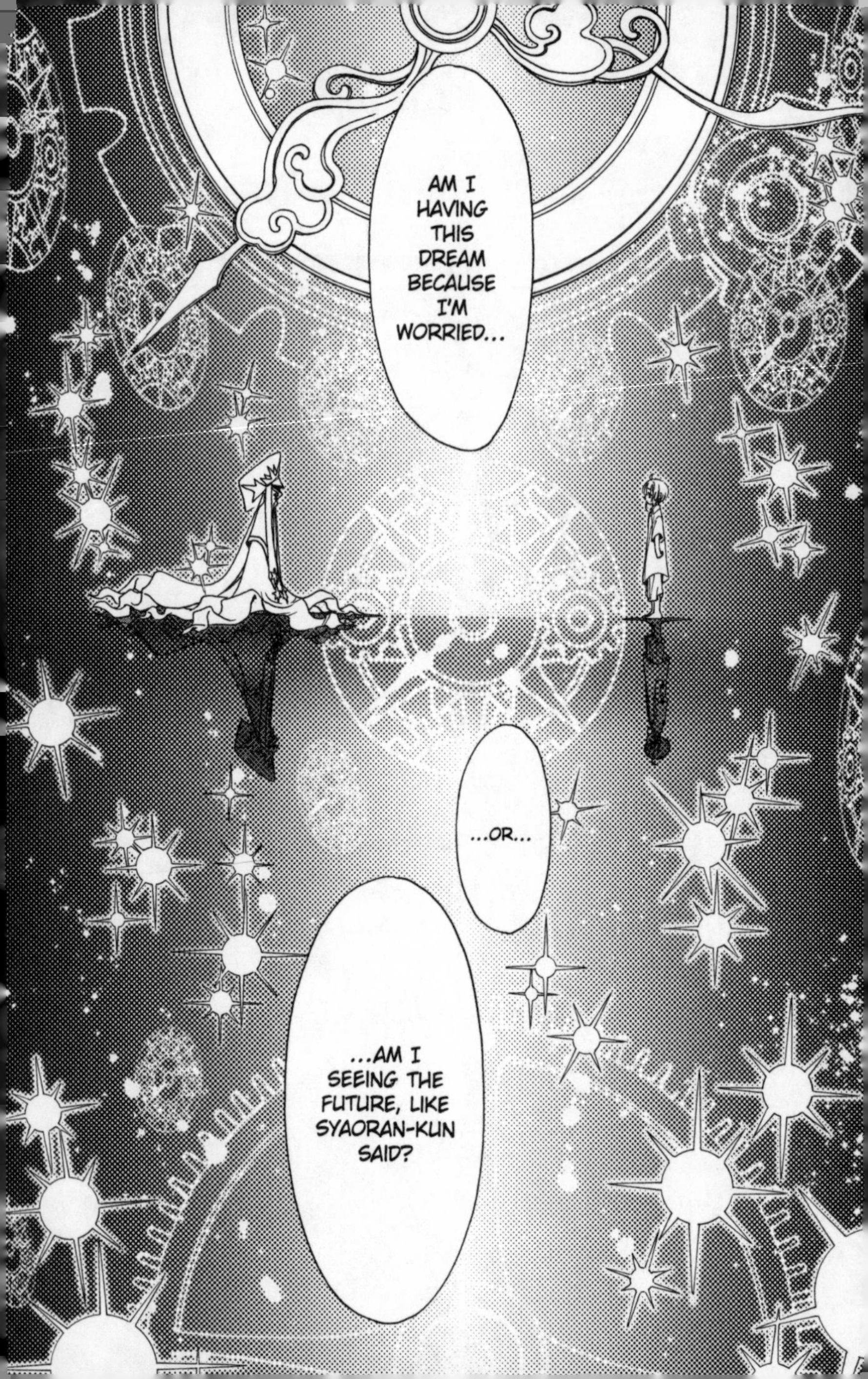
AM I HAVING THIS DREAM BECAUSE I'M WORRIED...
...OR...
...AM I SEEING THE FUTURE, LIKE SYAORAN-KUN SAID?

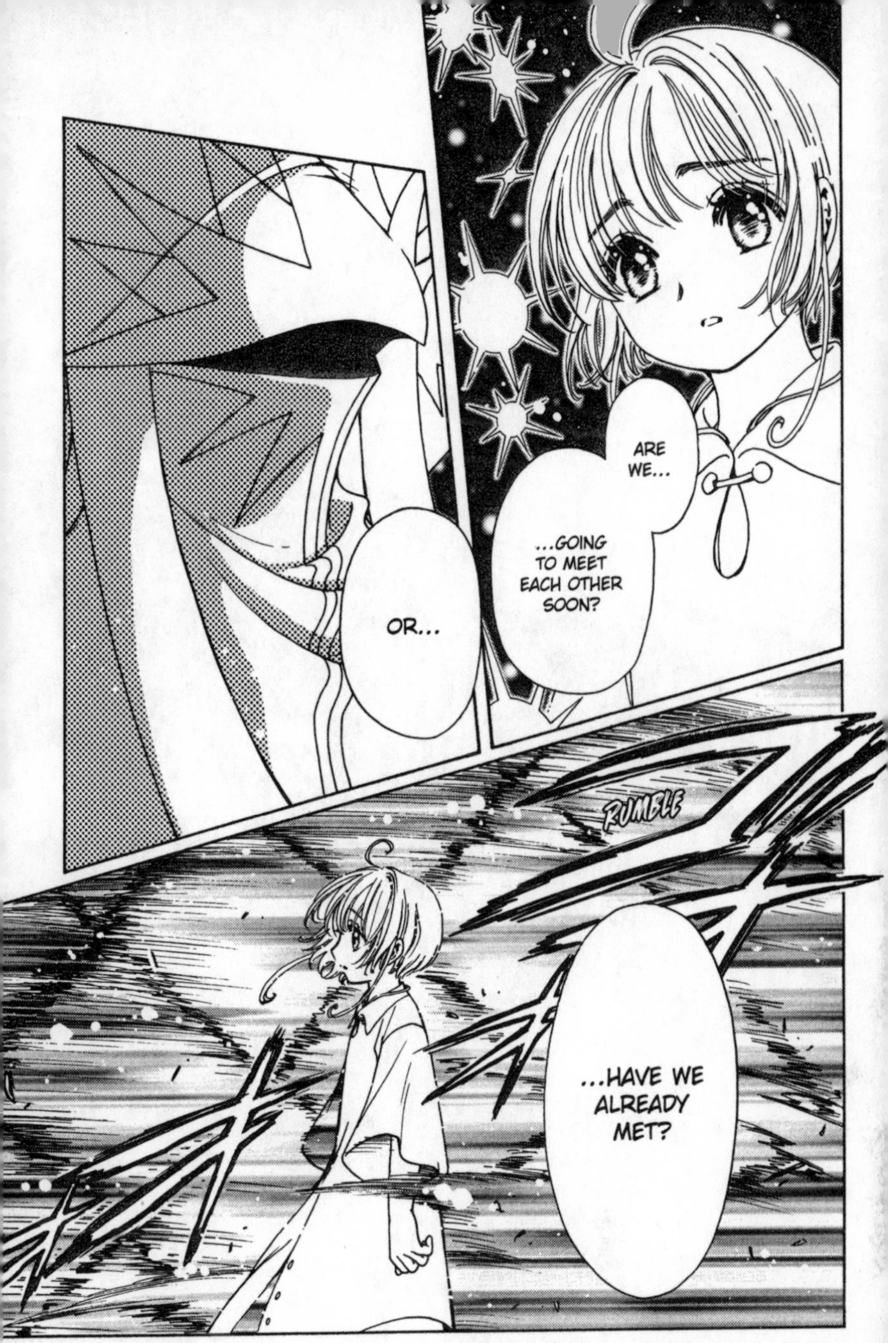
ARE WE...
...GOING TO MEET EACH OTHER SOON?
OR...
RUMBLE
...HAVE WE ALREADY MET?

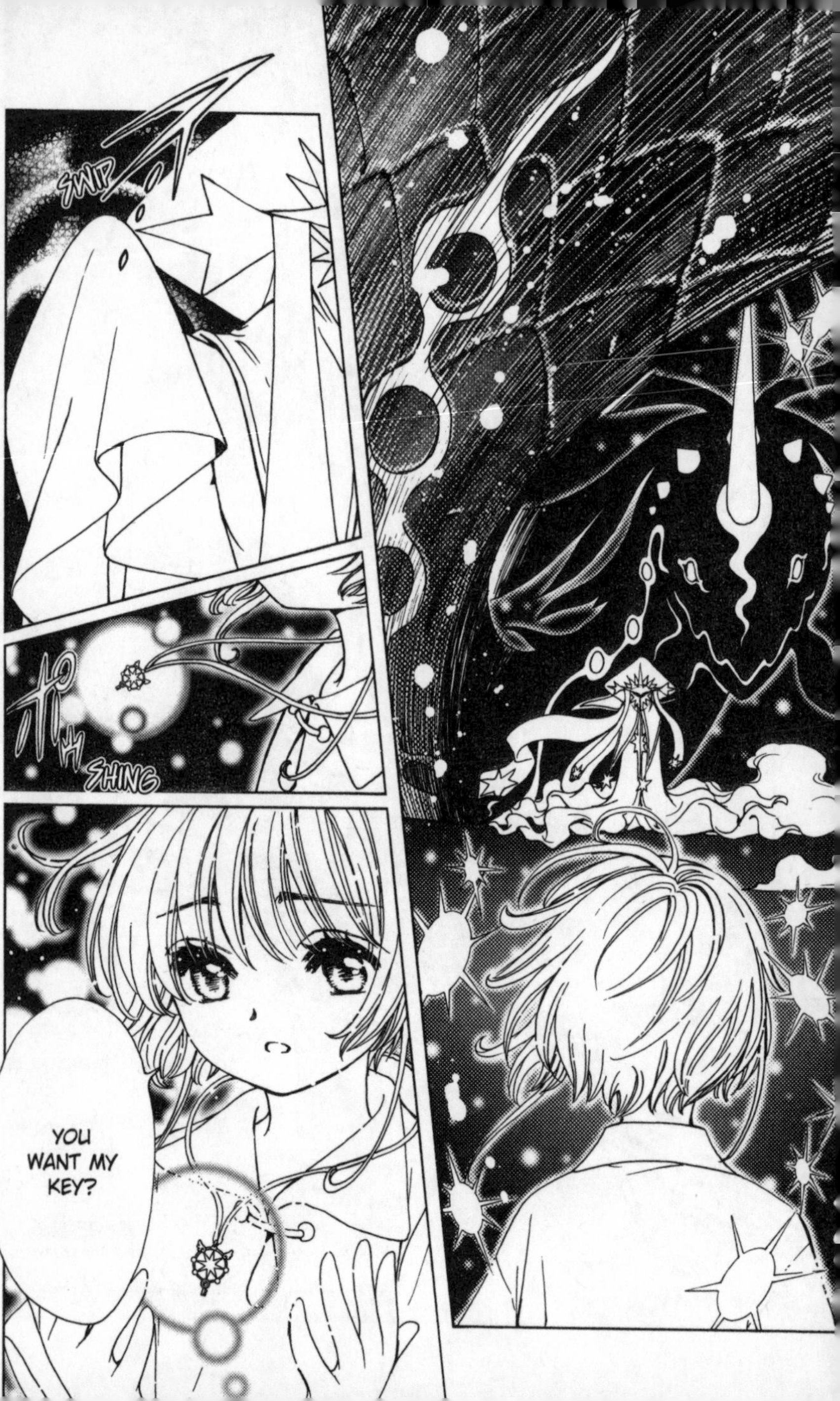
SWIP
SHING
YOU WANT MY KEY?

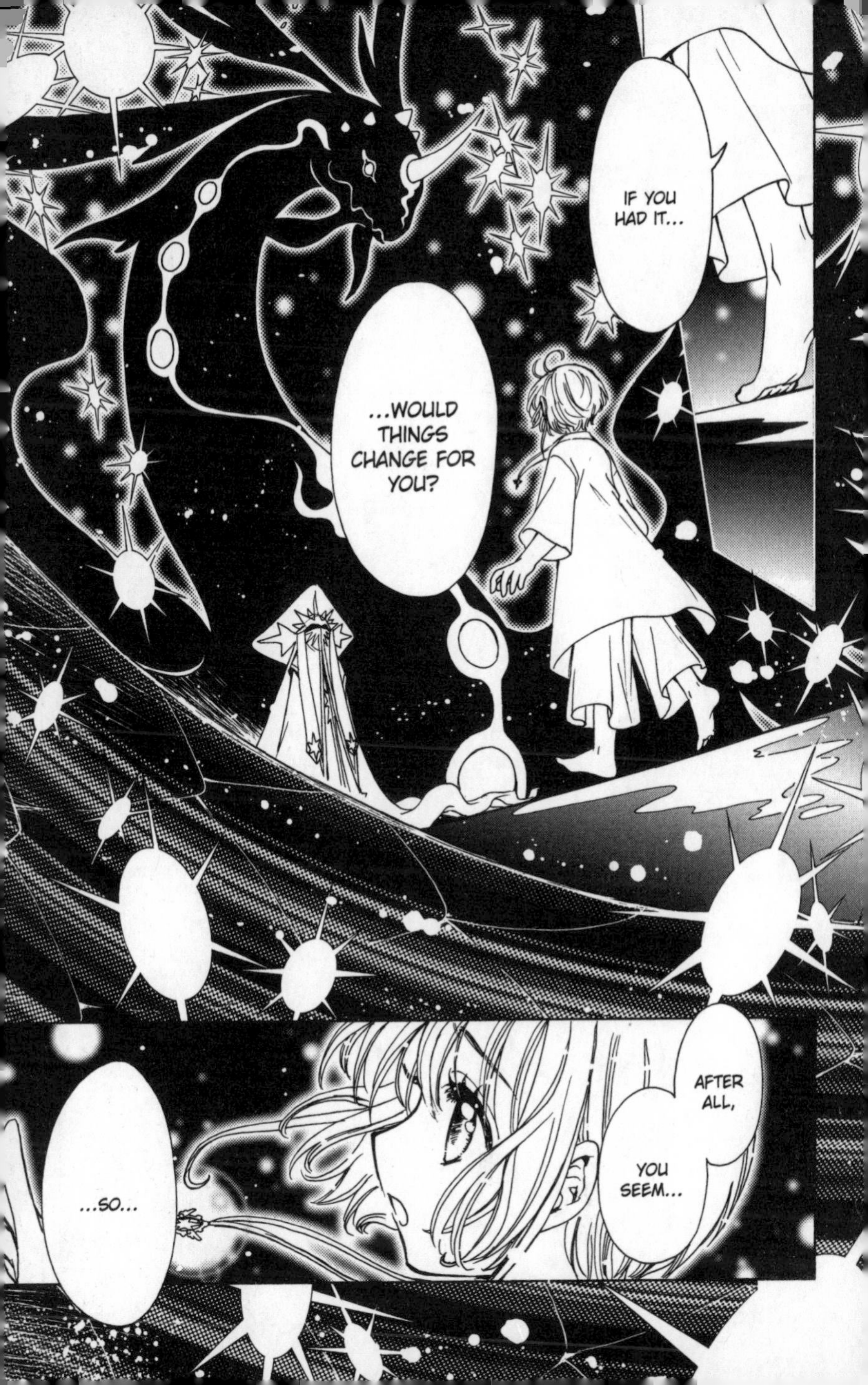
IF YOU HAD IT...
...WOULD THINGS CHANGE FOR YOU?
AFTER ALL,
YOU SEEM...
...SO...

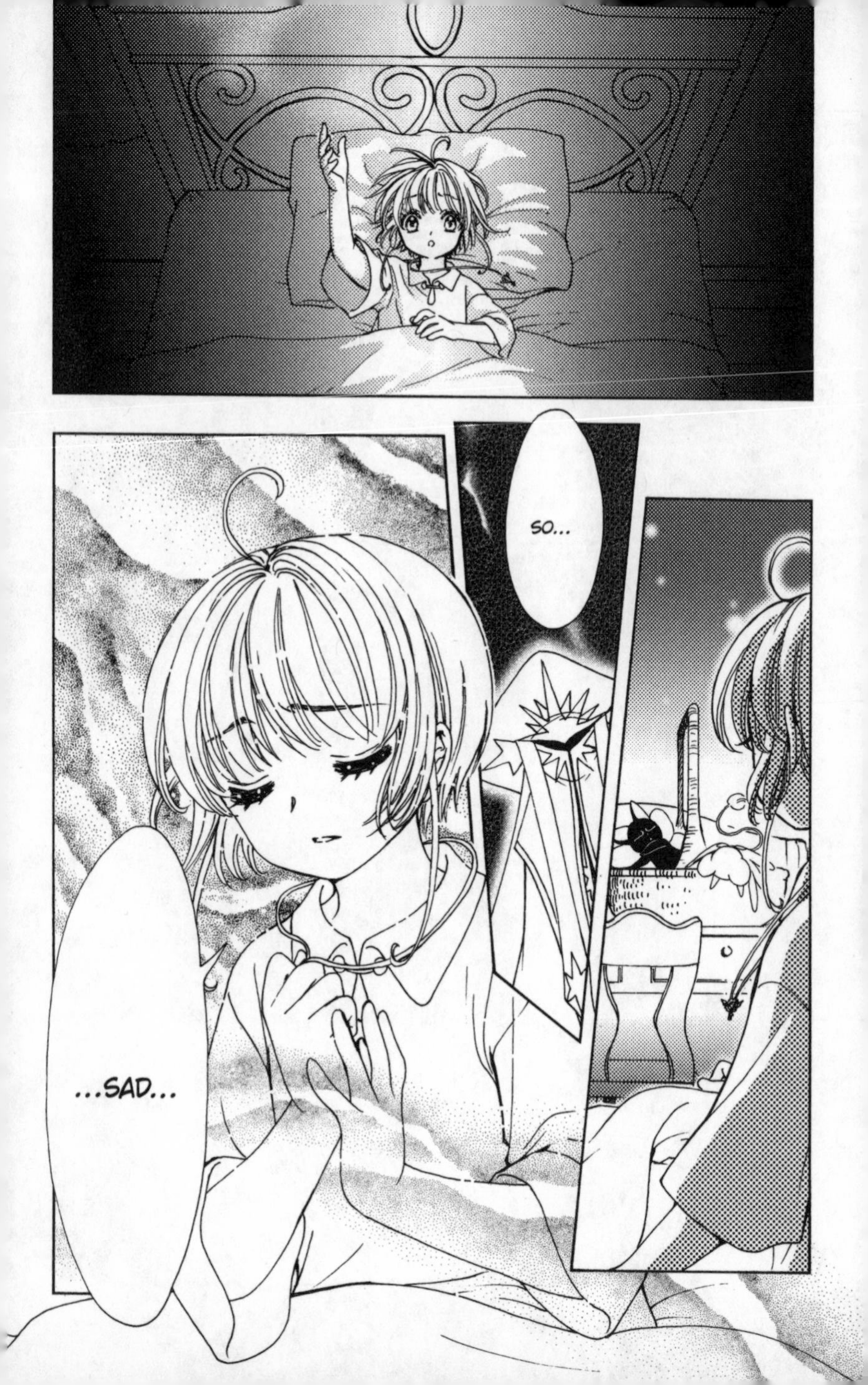
SO...
...SAD...

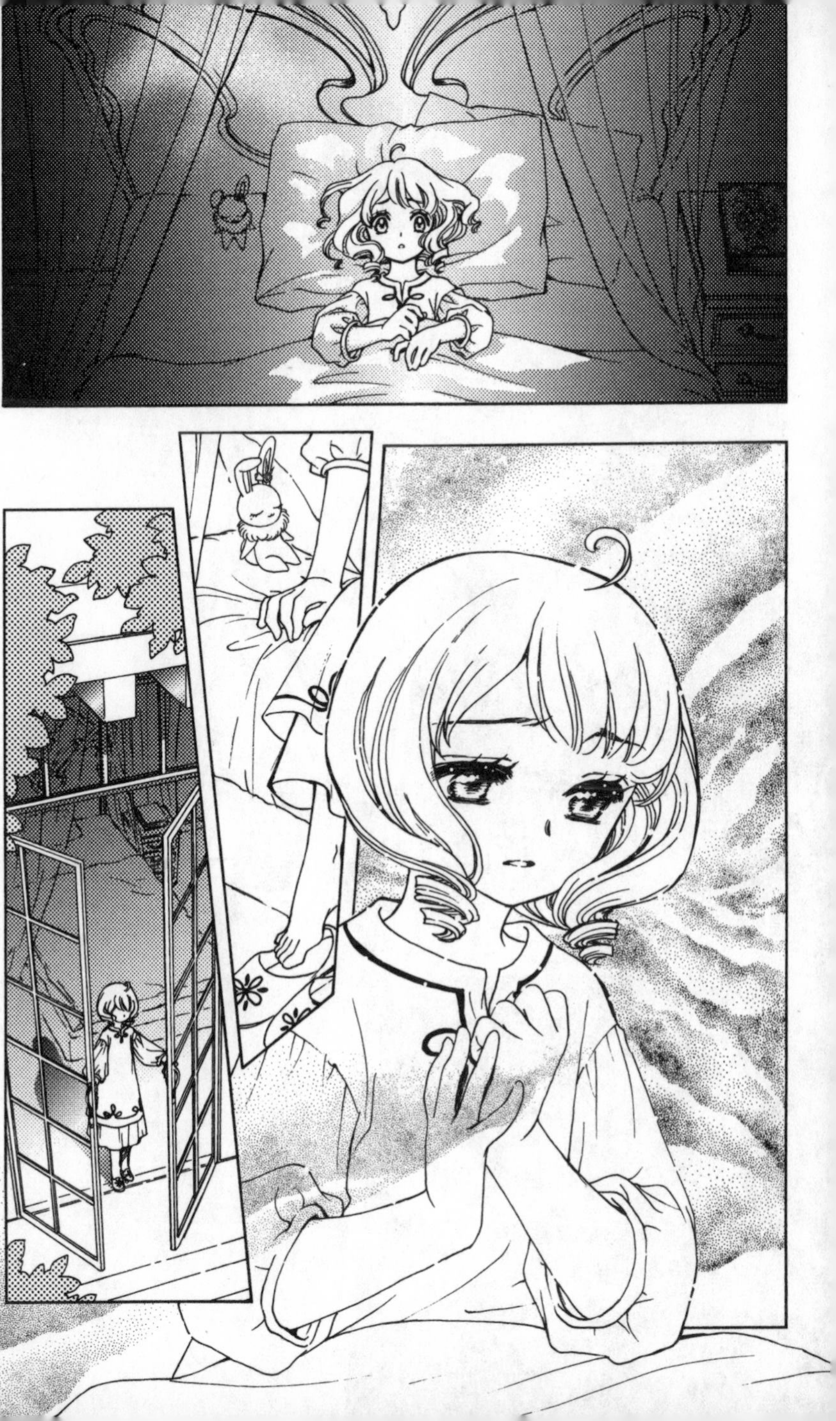

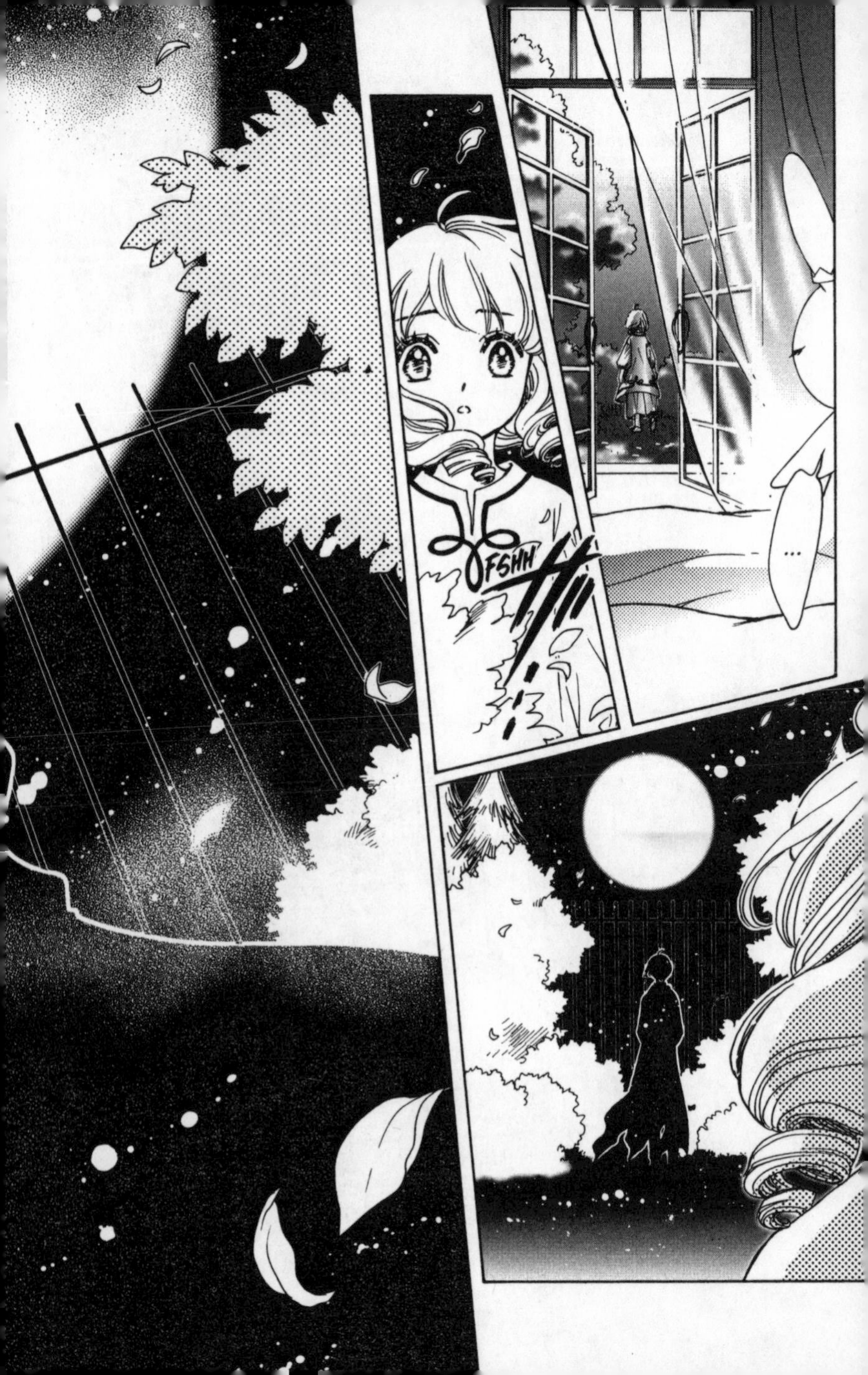
...
FSHH

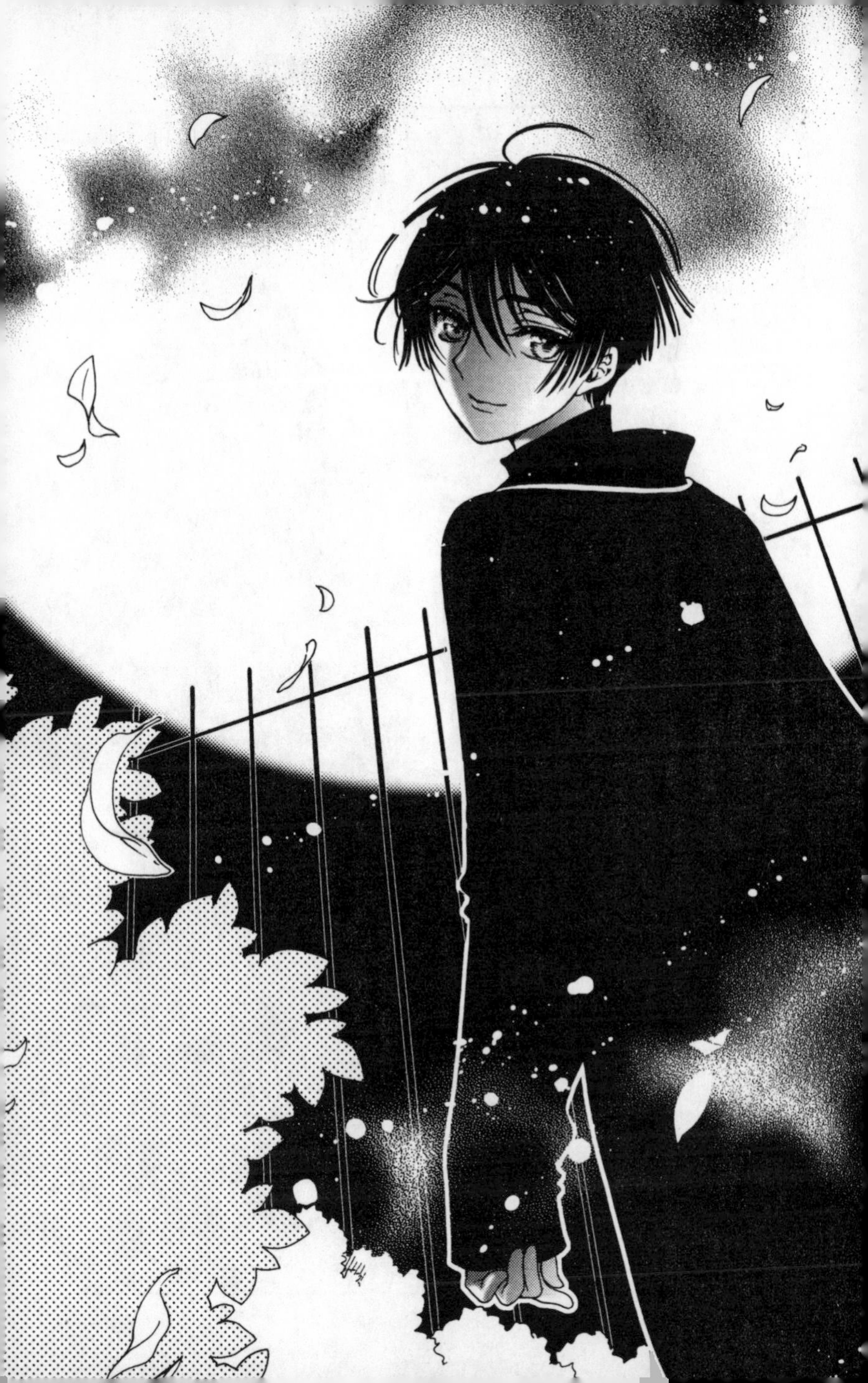

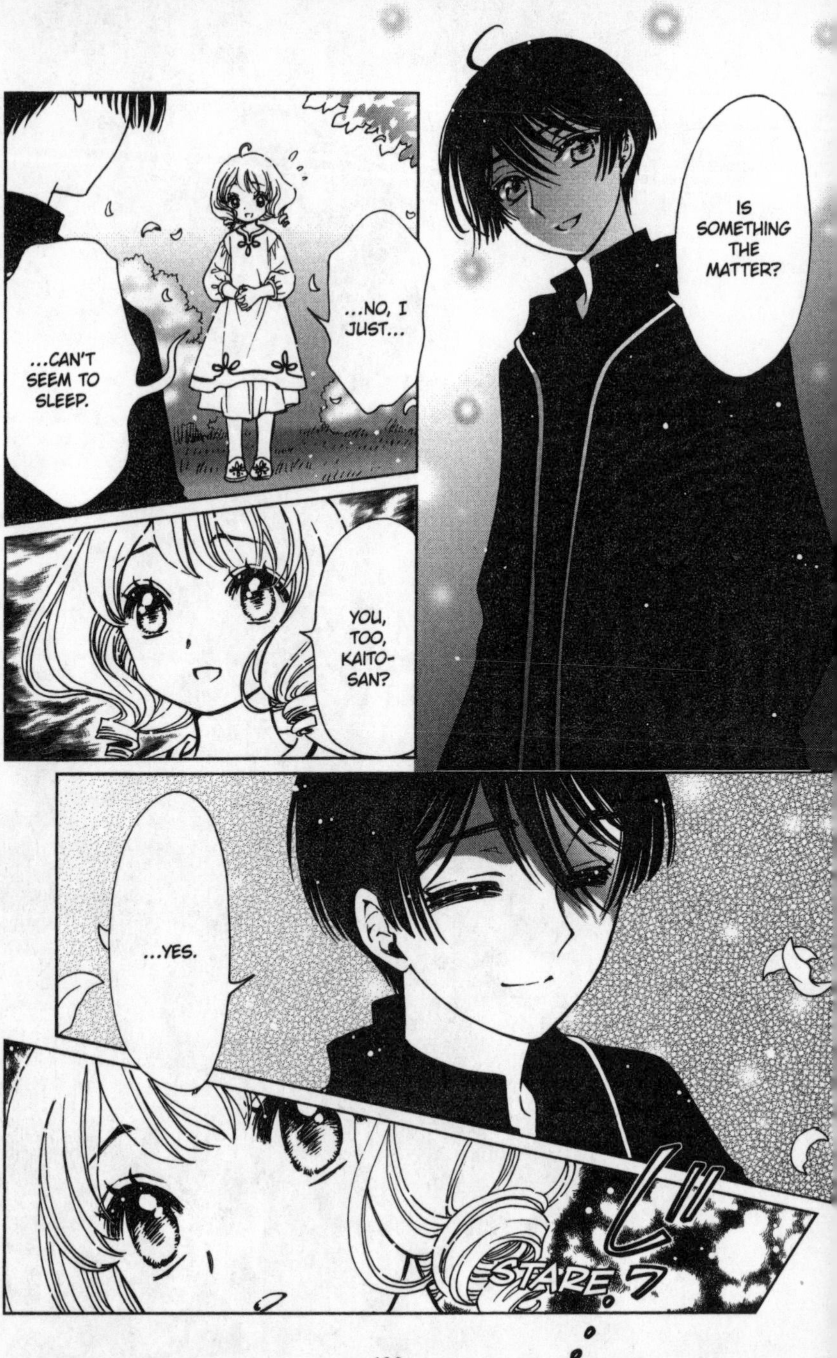
IS SOMETHING THE MATTER?
...NO, I JUST...
...CAN'T SEEM TO SLEEP.
YOU, TOO, KAITO-SAN?
...YES.
STARE

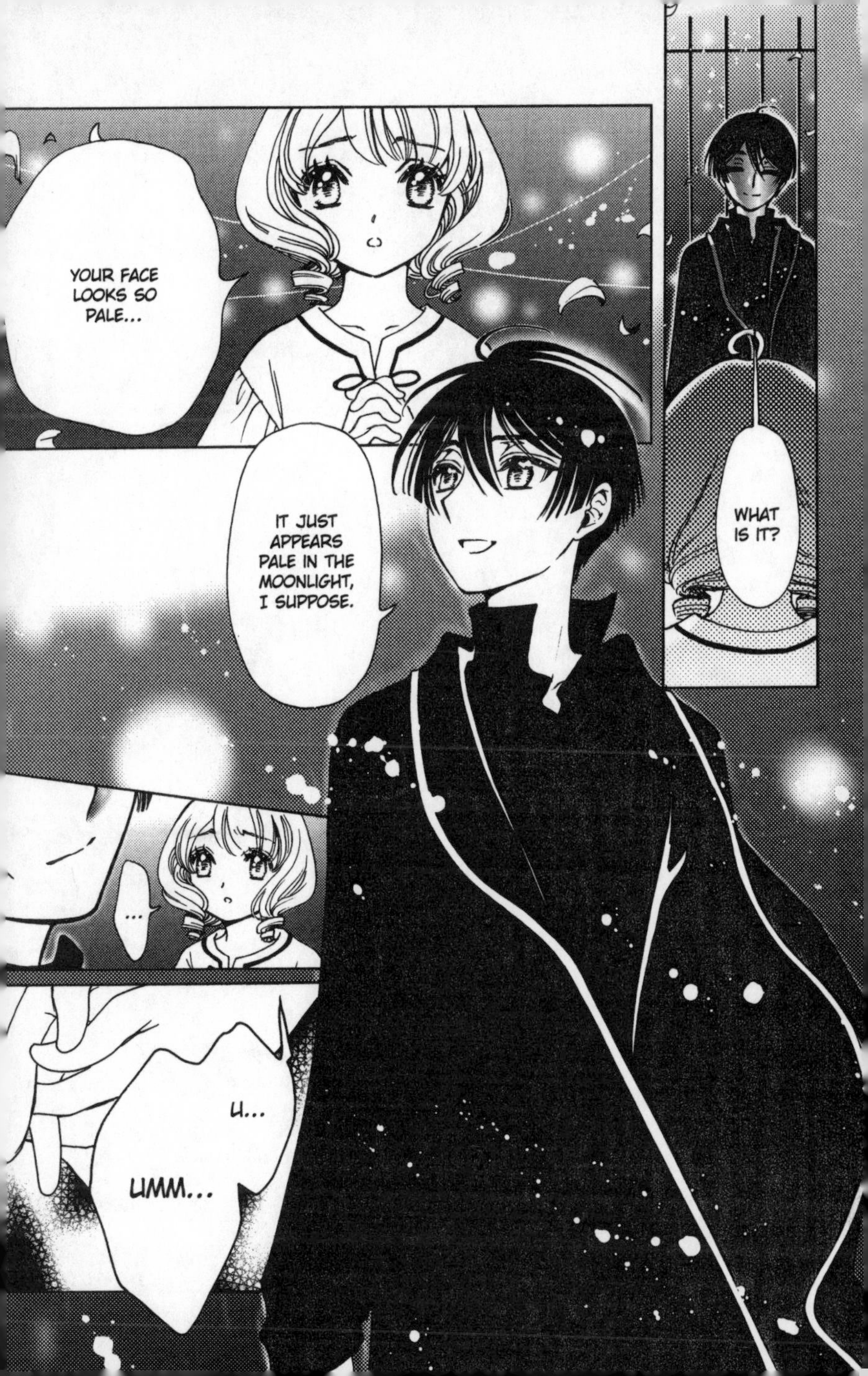
WHAT IS IT?
YOUR FACE LOOKS SO PALE...
IT JUST APPEARS PALE IN THE MOONLIGHT, I SUPPOSE.
...
U...
UMM...

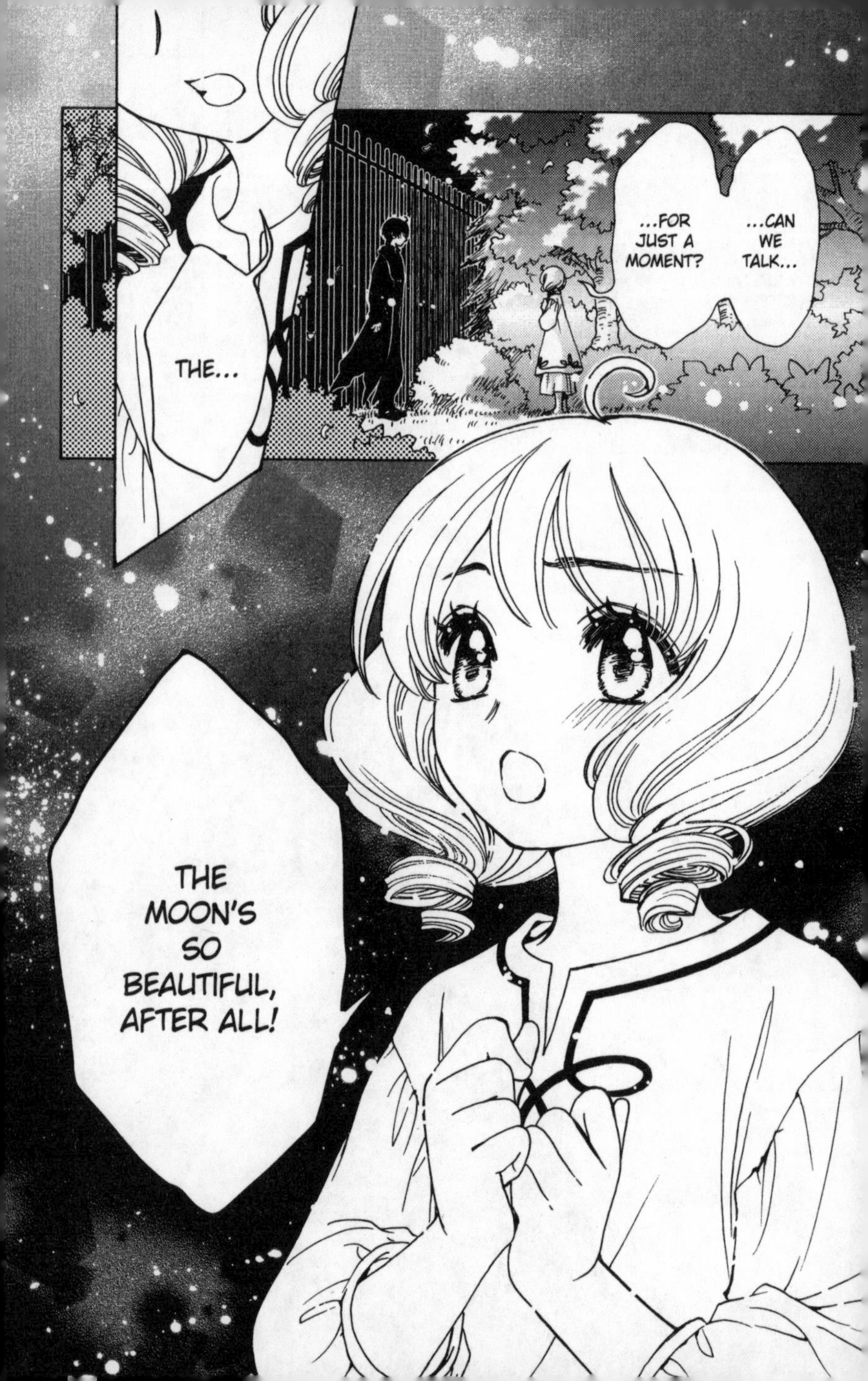
...CAN WE TALK...
...FOR JUST A MOMENT?
THE...
THE MOON'S SO BEAUTIFUL, AFTER ALL!

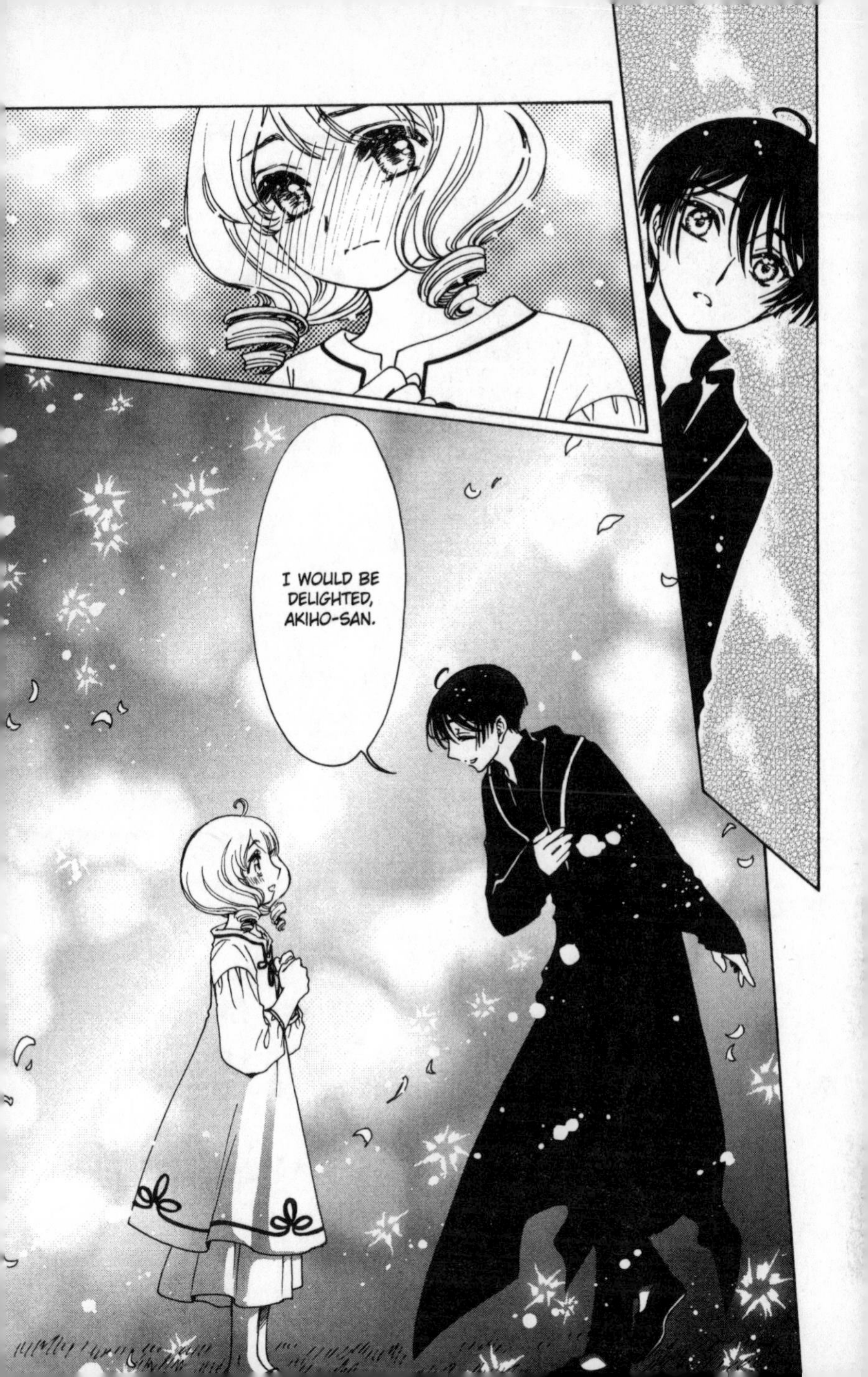
I WOULD BE DELIGHTED, AKIHO-SAN.

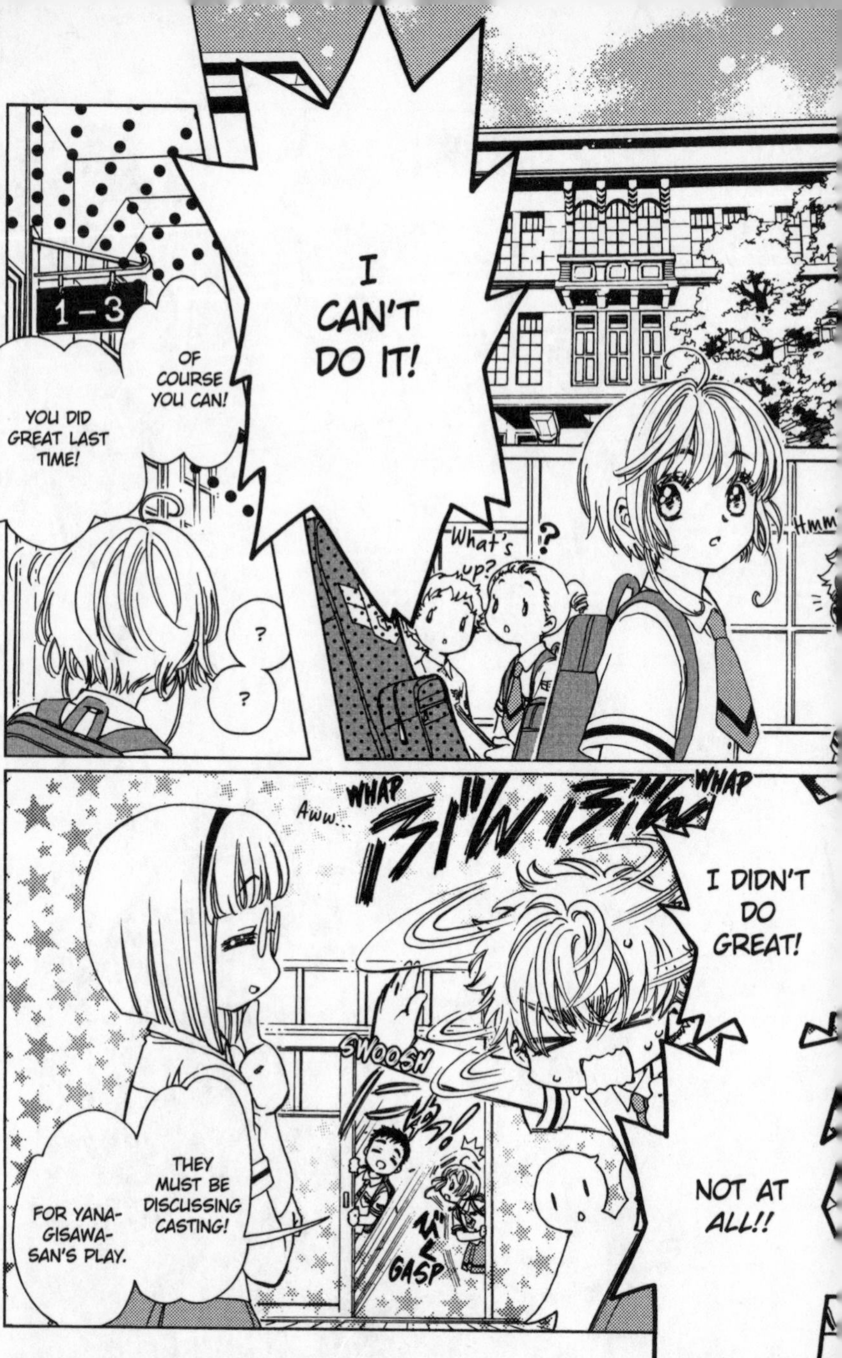
I CAN'T DO IT!
Hmm
What's up?
?
OF COURSE YOU CAN!
YOU DID GREAT LAST TIME!
?
?
WHAP
WHAP
I DIDN'T DO GREAT!
NOT AT ALL!!
Aww...
SWOOSH
GASP
THEY MUST BE DISCUSSING CASTING!
FOR YANA-GISAWA-SAN'S PLAY.

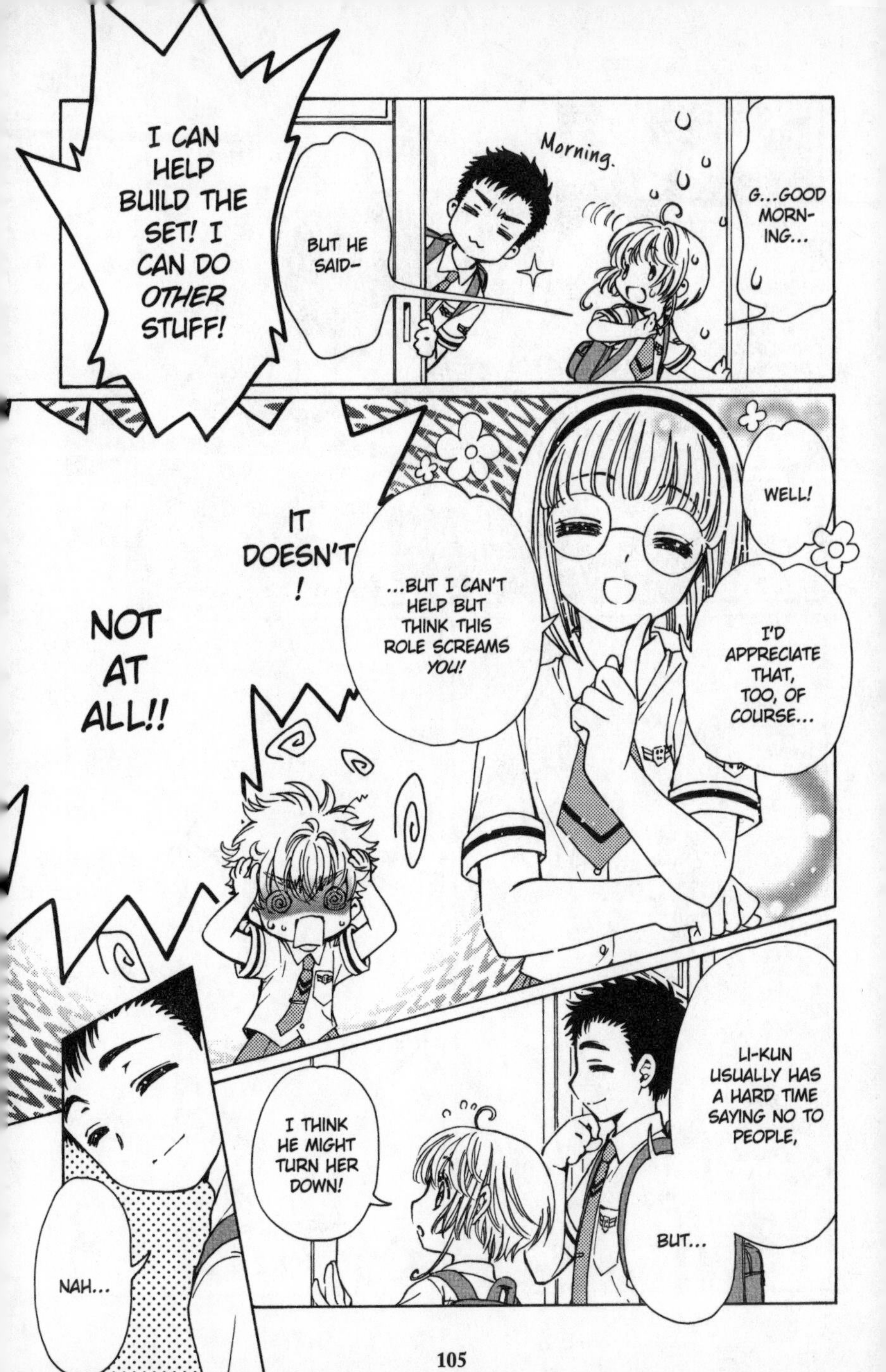
G...GOOD MORNING...
Morning.
BUT HE SAID-
I CAN HELP BUILD THE SET! I CAN DO *OTHER* STUFF!
WELL!
I'D APPRECIATE THAT, TOO, OF COURSE...
...BUT I CAN'T HELP BUT THINK THIS ROLE SCREAMS *YOU!*
IT DOESN'T!
NOT AT ALL!!
LI-KUN USUALLY HAS A HARD TIME SAYING NO TO PEOPLE,
BUT...
I THINK HE MIGHT TURN HER DOWN!
NAH...

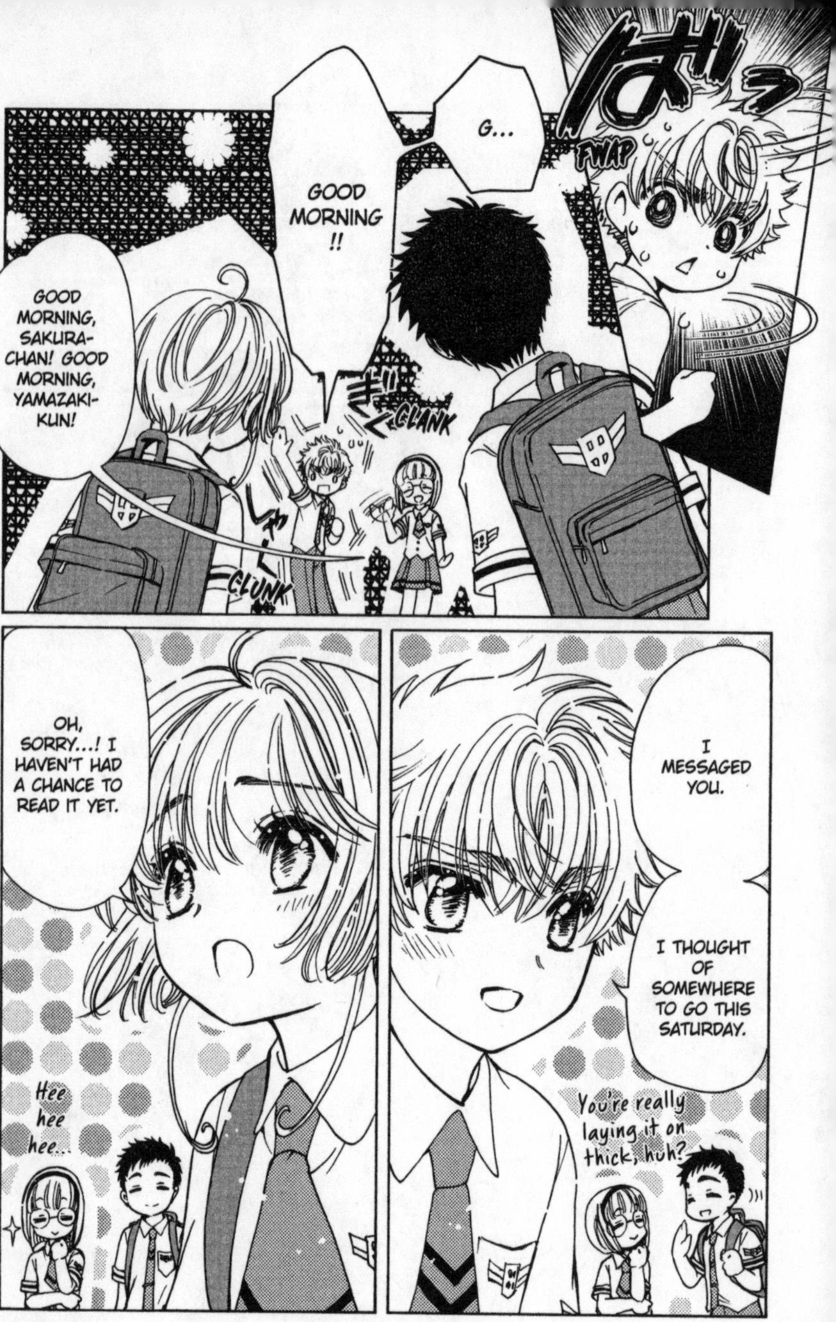
FWAP
G...
GOOD MORNING !!
GOOD MORNING, SAKURA-CHAN! GOOD MORNING, YAMAZAKI-KUN!
CLANK
CLANK
I MESSAGED YOU.
I THOUGHT OF SOMEWHERE TO GO THIS SATURDAY.
You're really laying it on thick, huh?
OH, SORRY...! I HAVEN'T HAD A CHANCE TO READ IT YET.
Hee hee hee...

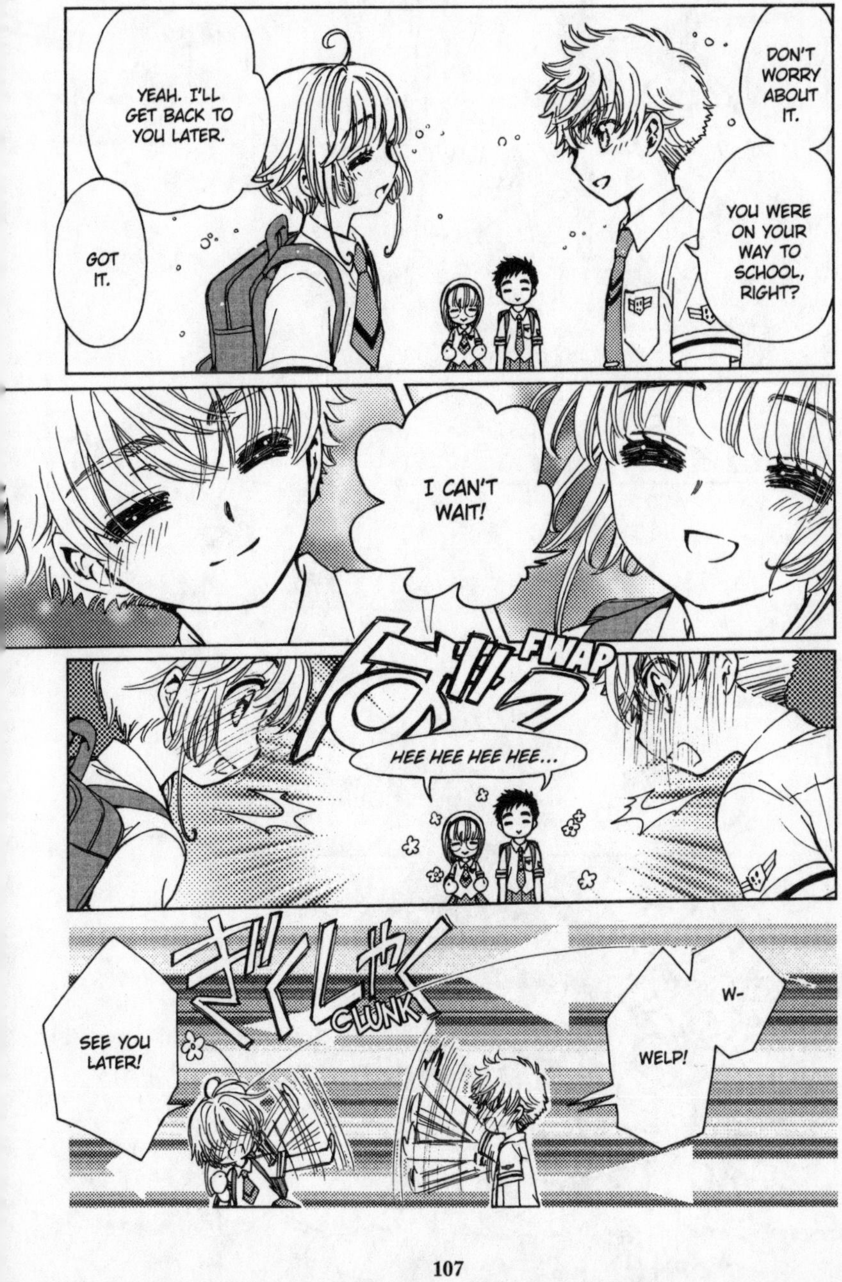
DON'T WORRY ABOUT IT.
YOU WERE ON YOUR WAY TO SCHOOL, RIGHT?
YEAH. I'LL GET BACK TO YOU LATER.
GOT IT.
I CAN'T WAIT!
FWAP
HEE HEE HEE HEE...
W-
WELP!
CLUNK
SEE YOU LATER!

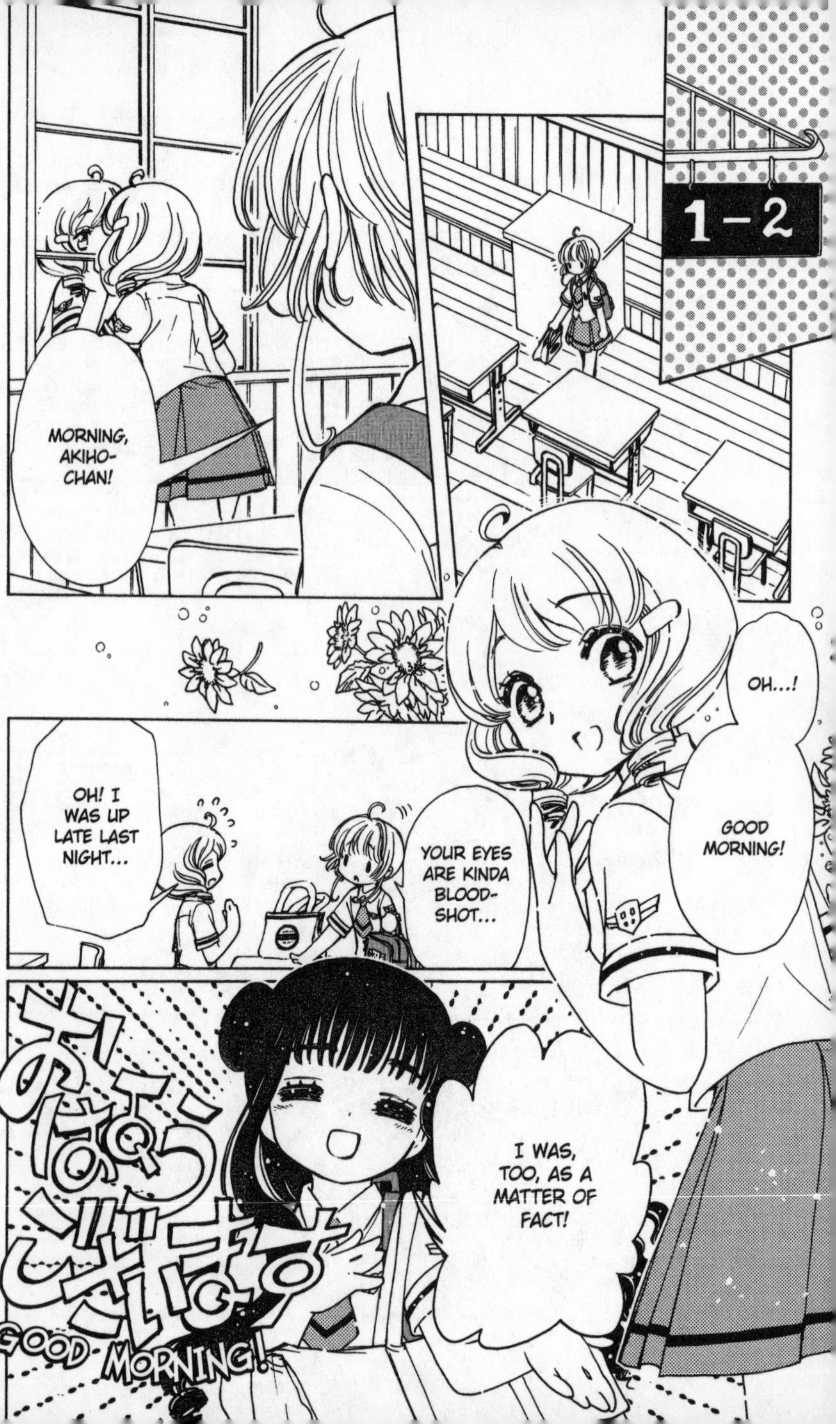
1-2
MORNING, AKIHO-CHAN!
OH...!
GOOD MORNING!
YOUR EYES ARE KINDA BLOODSHOT...
OH! I WAS UP LATE LAST NIGHT...
I WAS, TOO, AS A MATTER OF FACT!
おはようございます
GOOD MORNING!

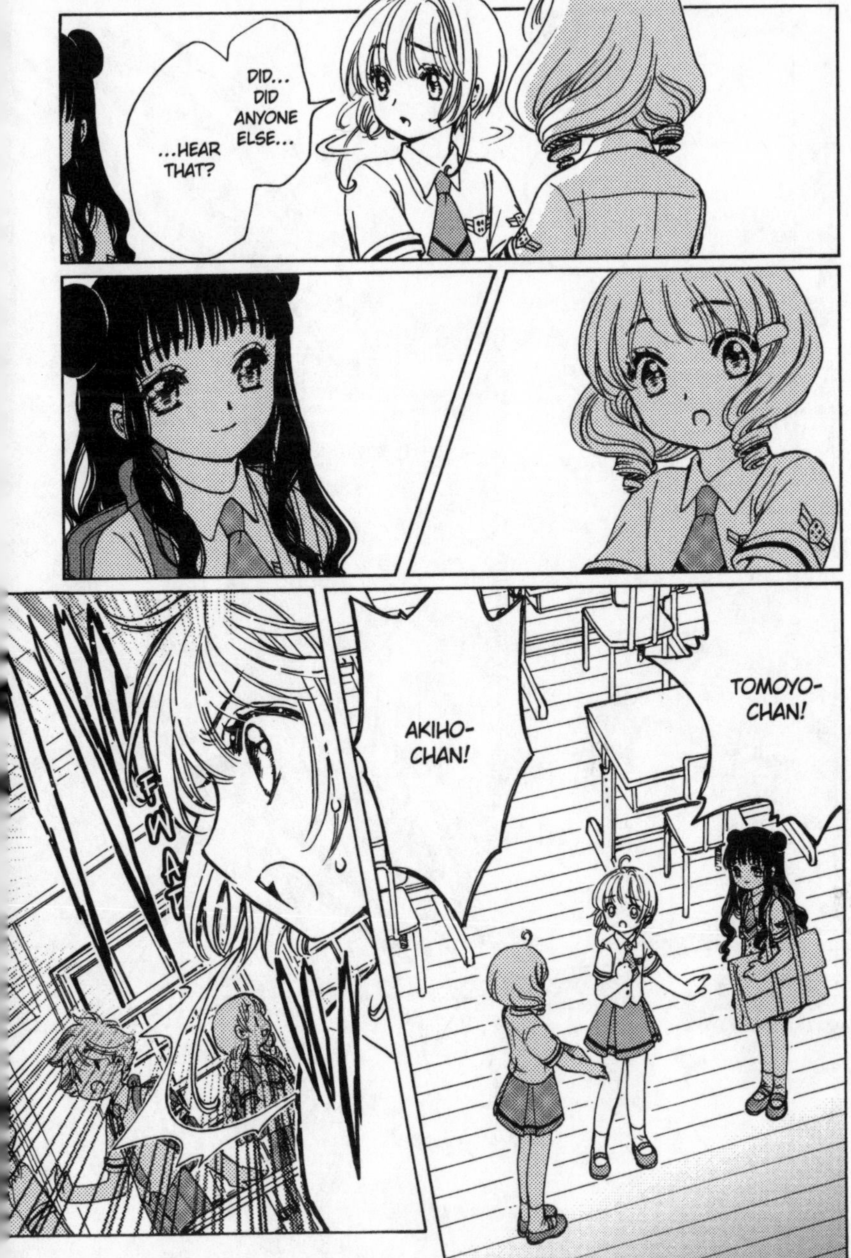
DID... DID ANYONE ELSE... ...HEAR THAT?
TOMOYO-CHAN!
AKIHO-CHAN!
FWAP

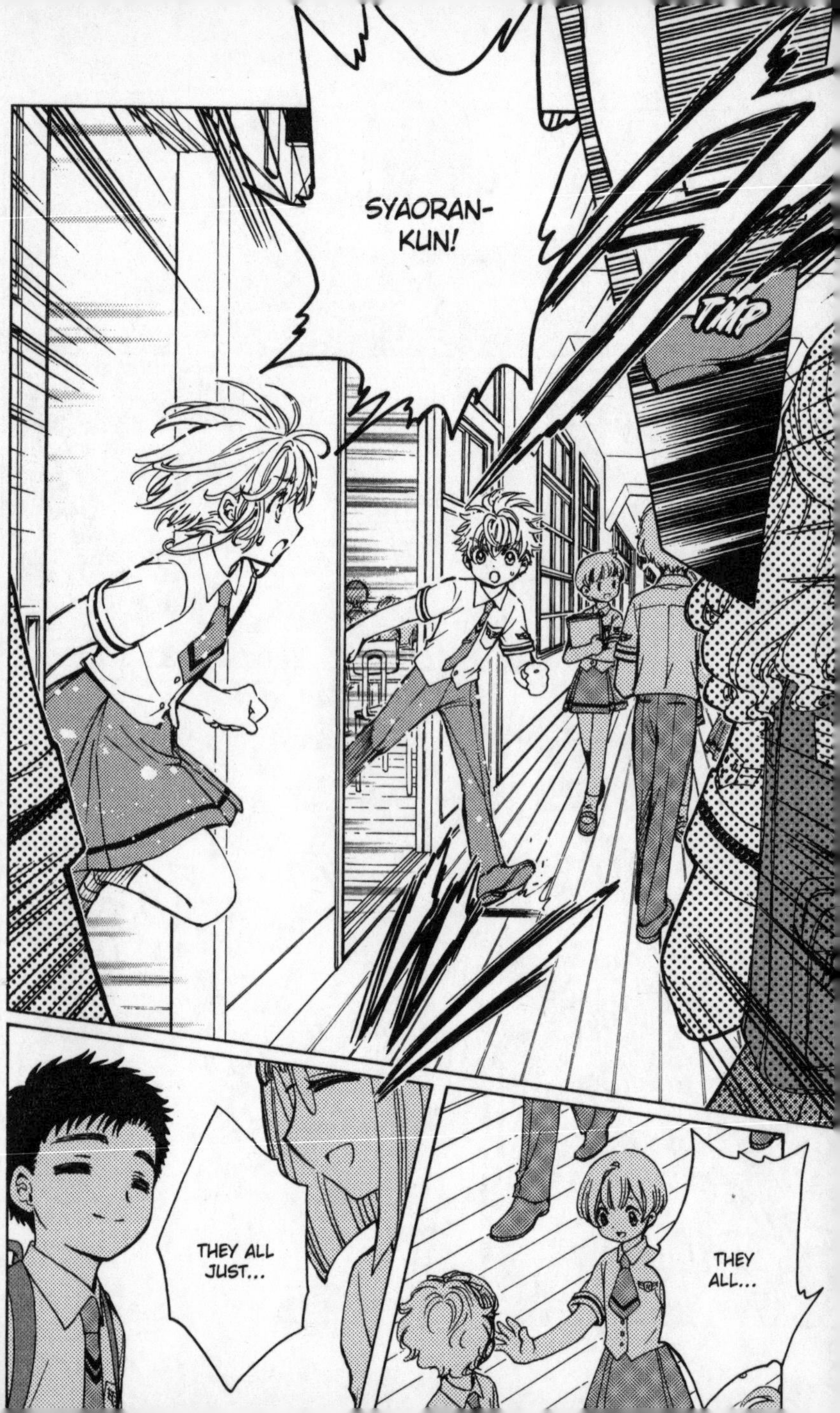
SYAORAN-KUN!
TMP
THEY ALL...
THEY ALL JUST...

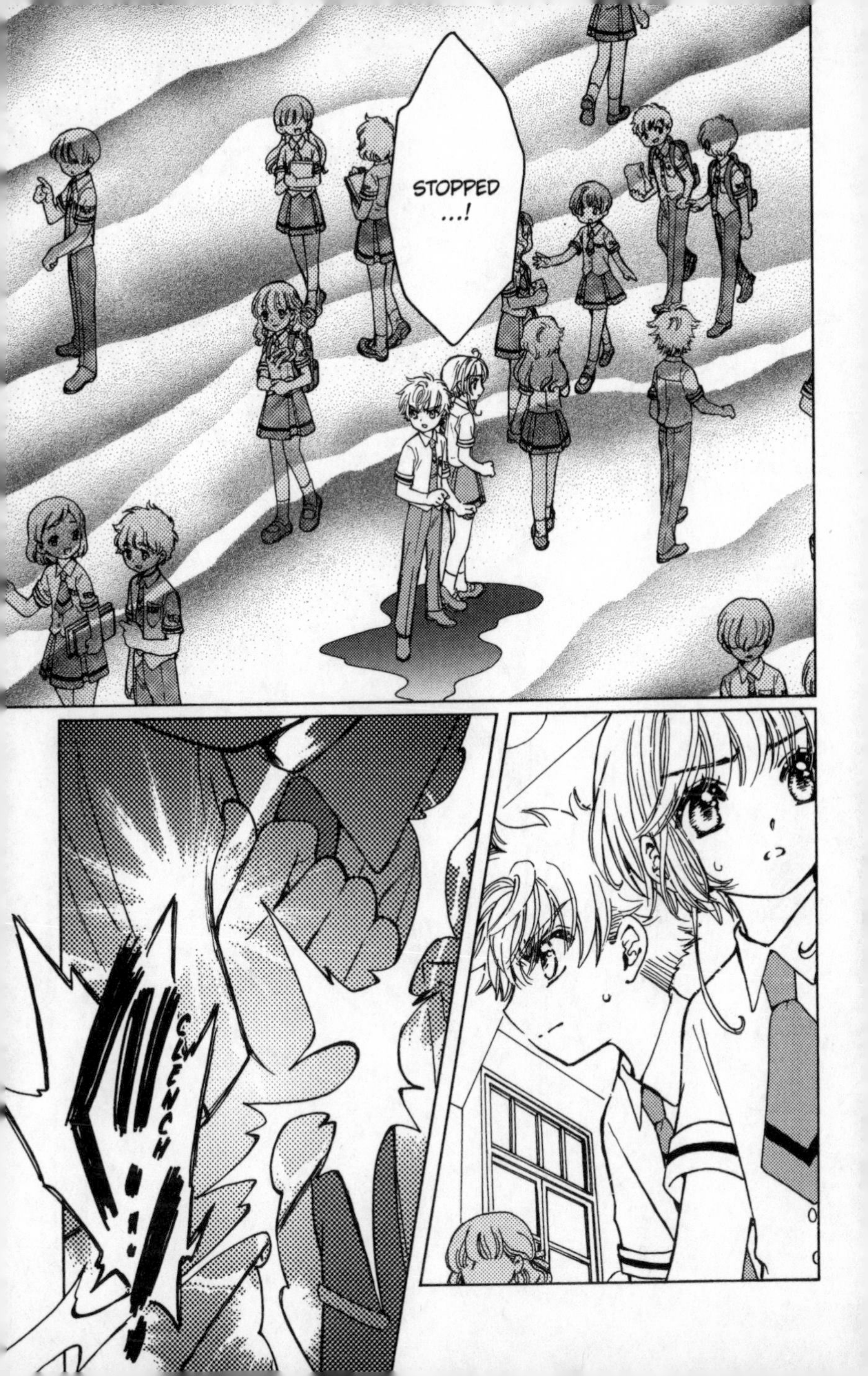
STOPPED ...!
CLENCH

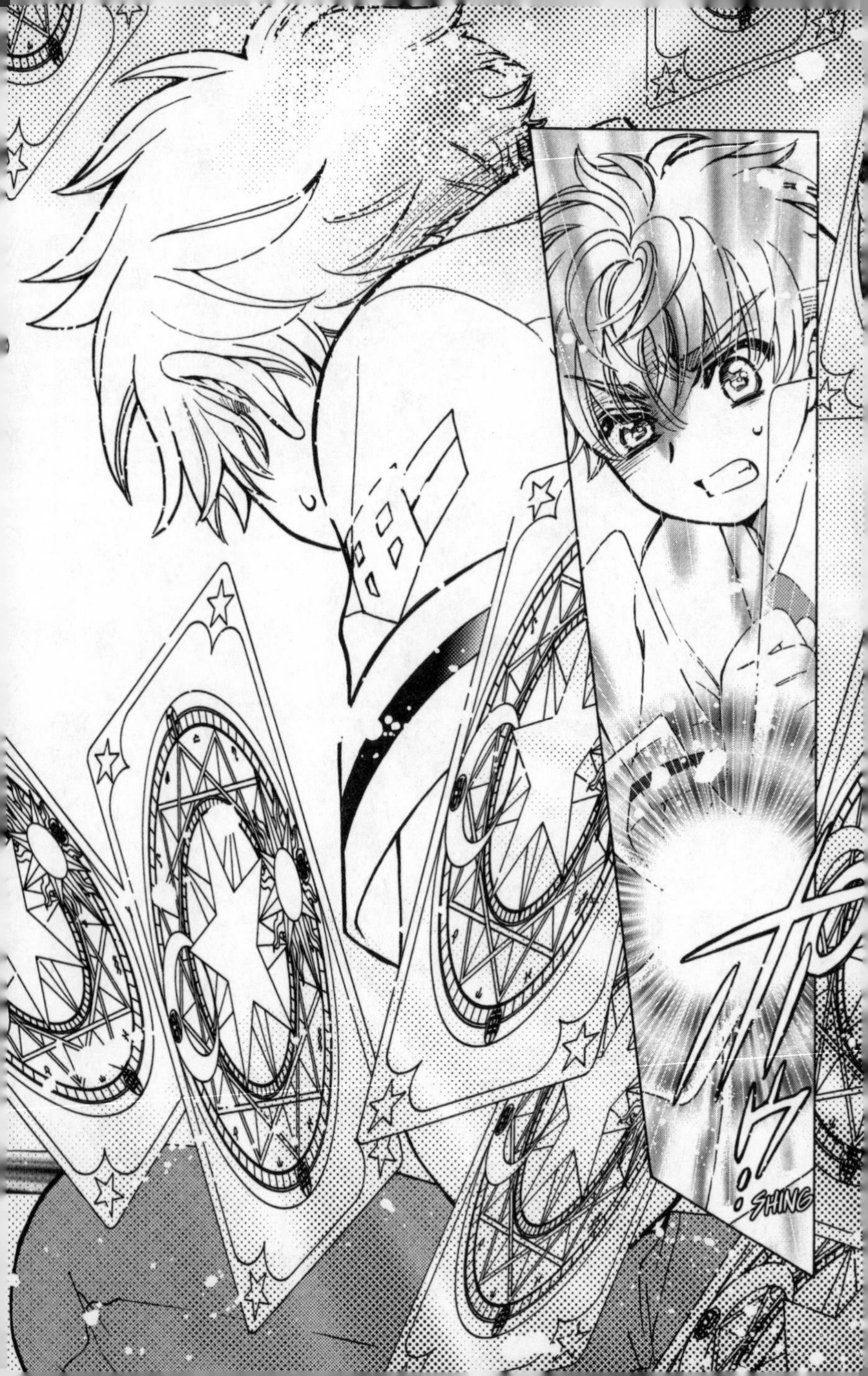
SHING

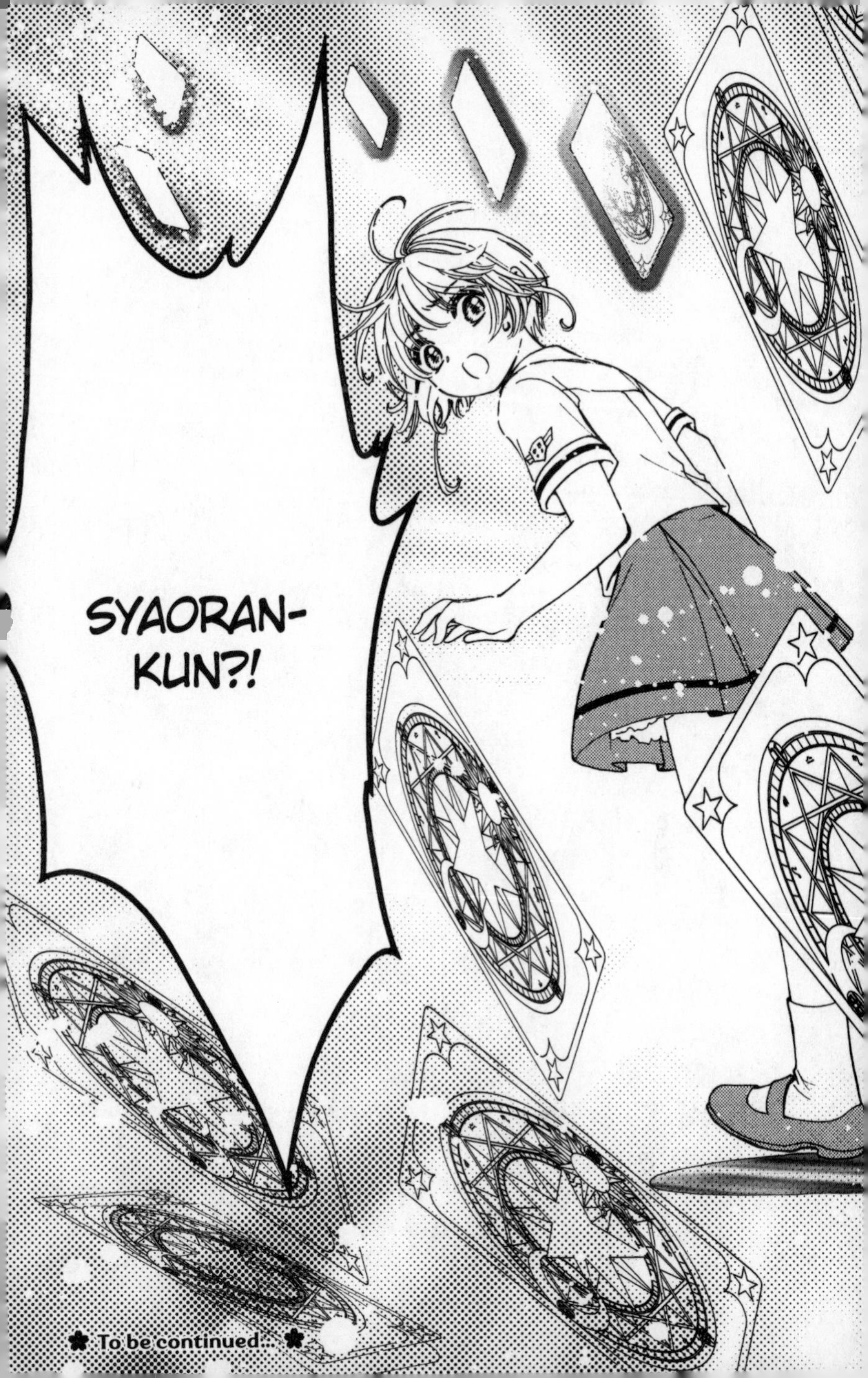
SYAORAN-KUN?!
To be continued...

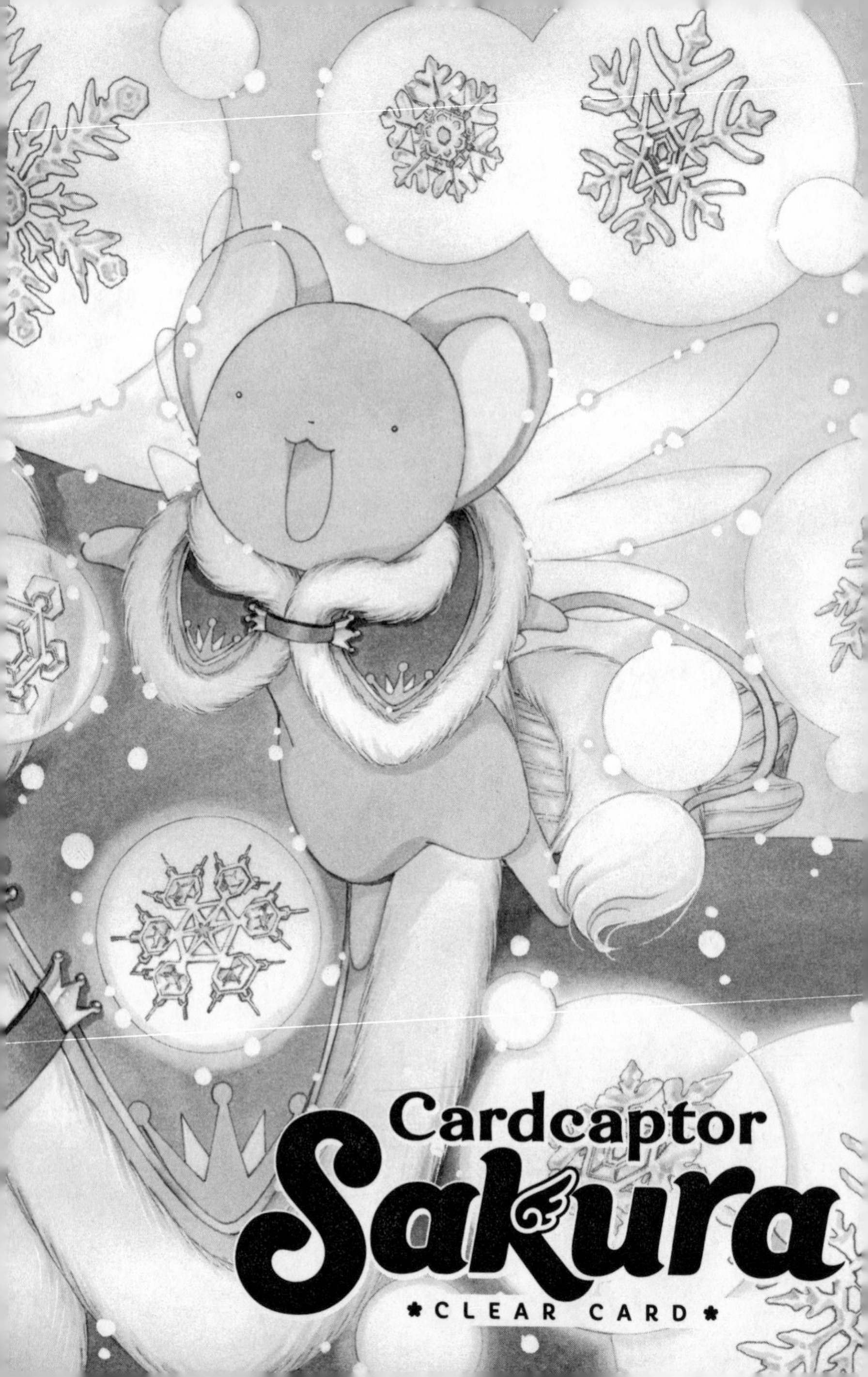
Cardcaptor
Sakura
CLEAR CARD

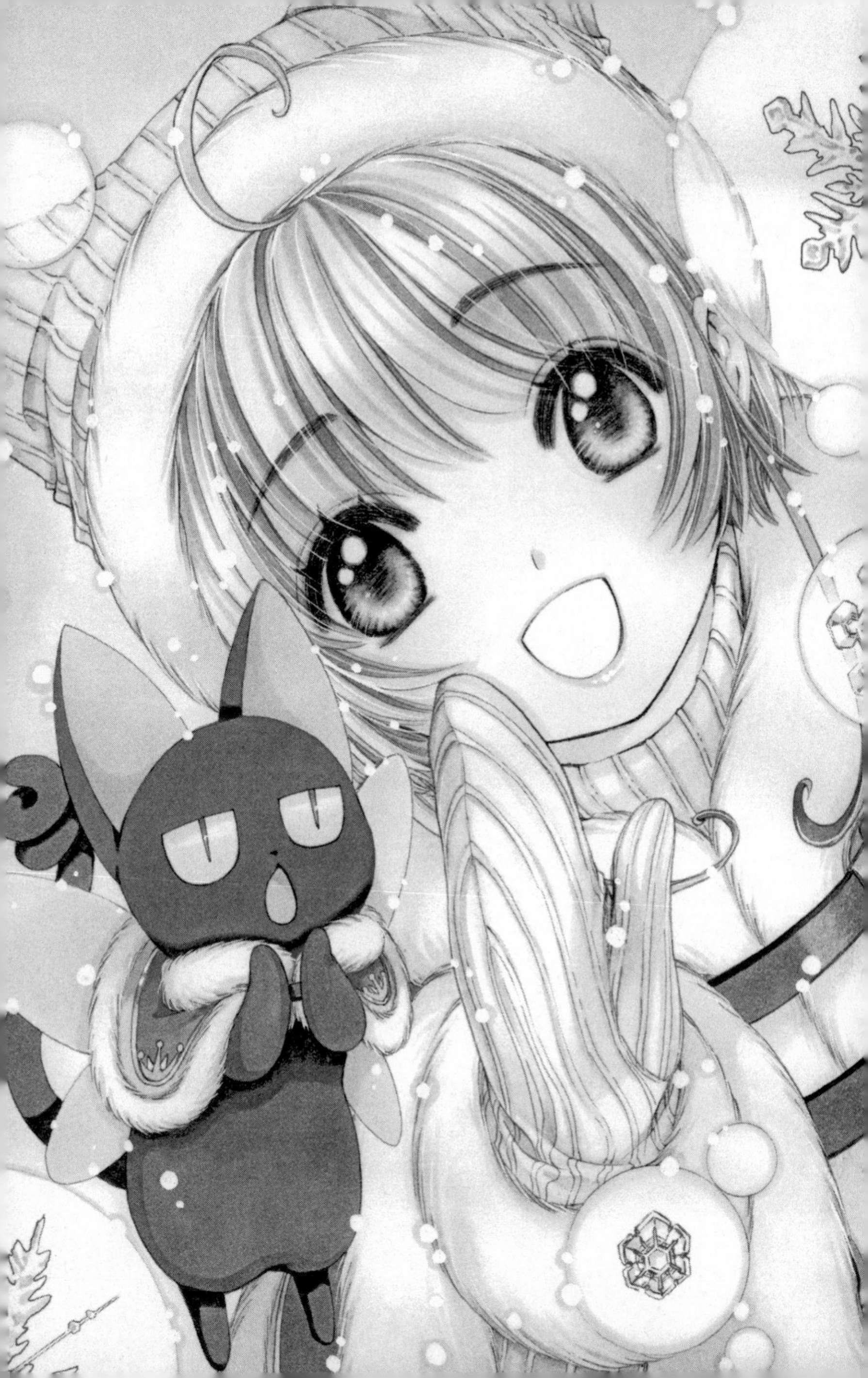

Cardcaptor Sakura

CLEAR CARD

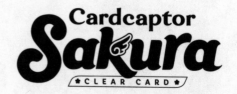

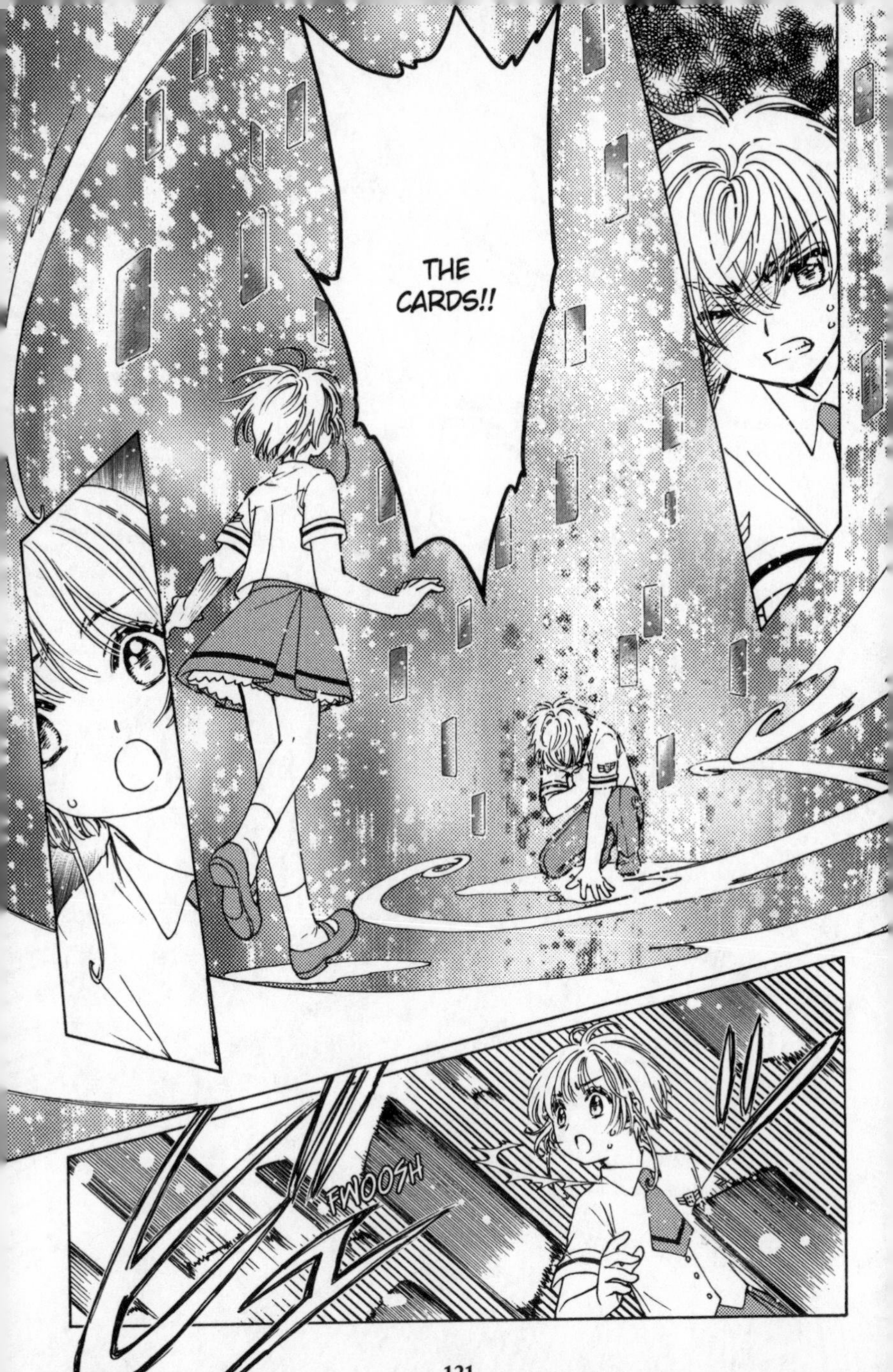
THE
CARDS!!
FWOOSH

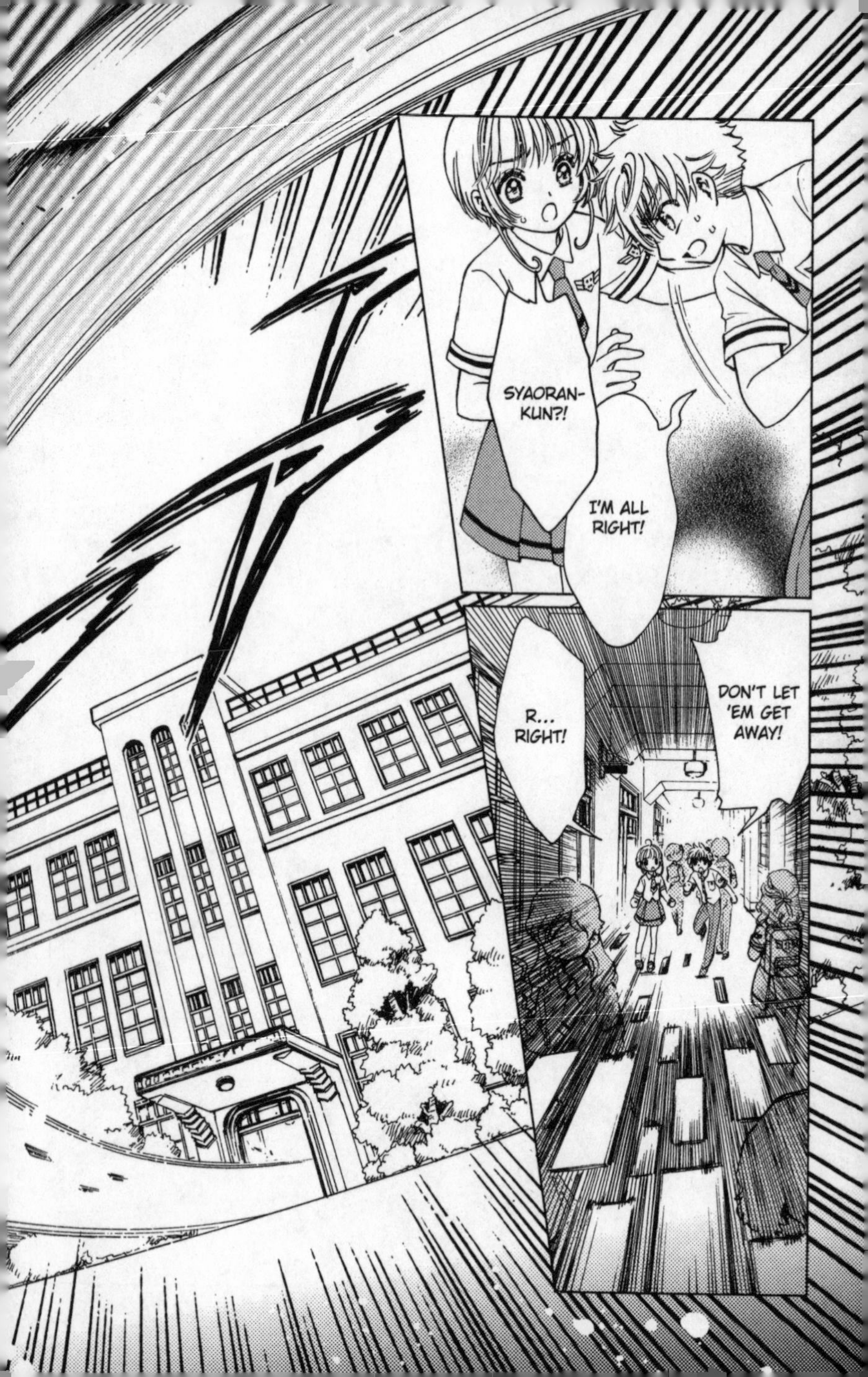
SYAORAN-KUN?!
I'M ALL RIGHT!
DON'T LET 'EM GET AWAY!
R... RIGHT!

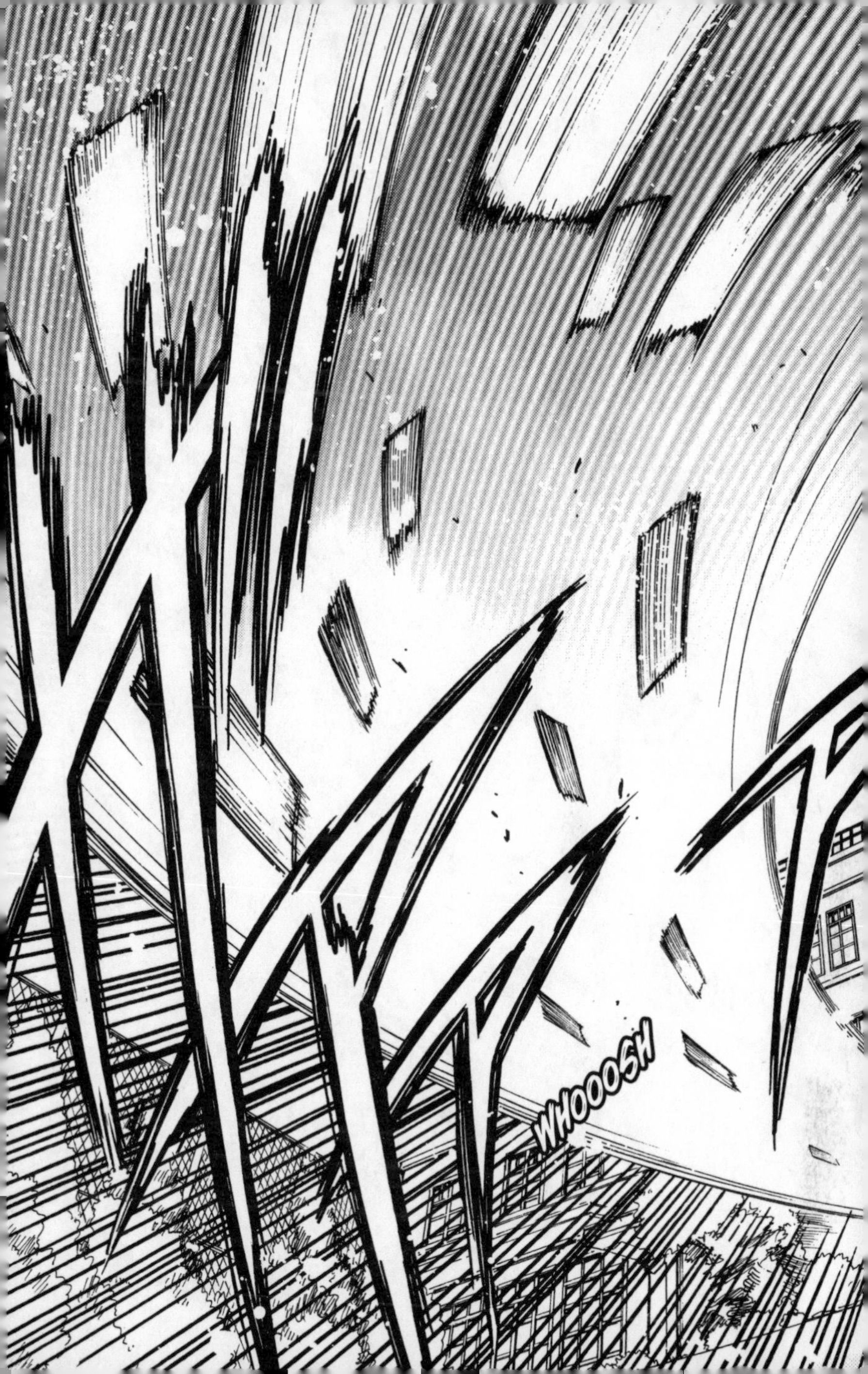
WHOOOSH

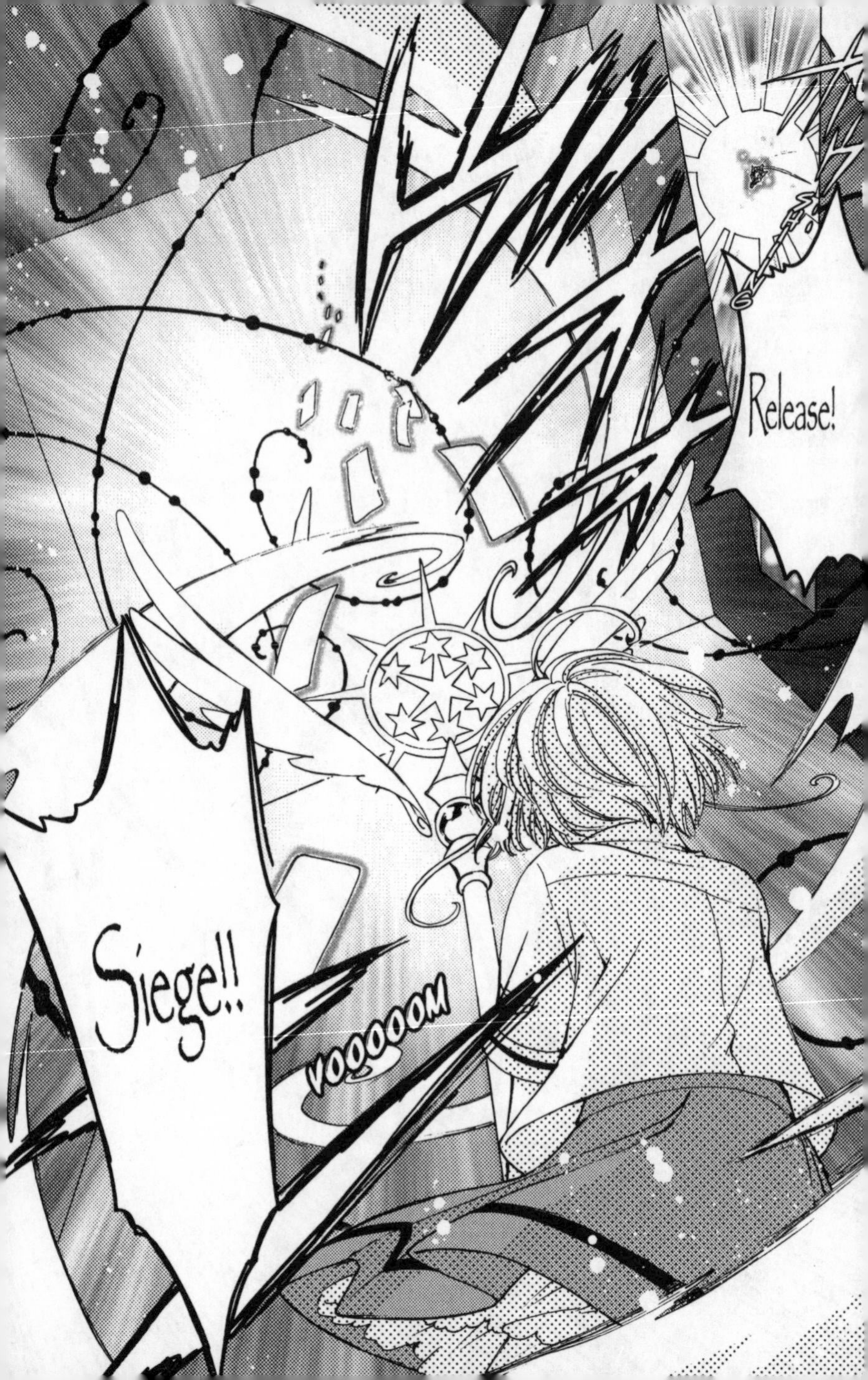
Release!
VOOOOOM
Siege!!

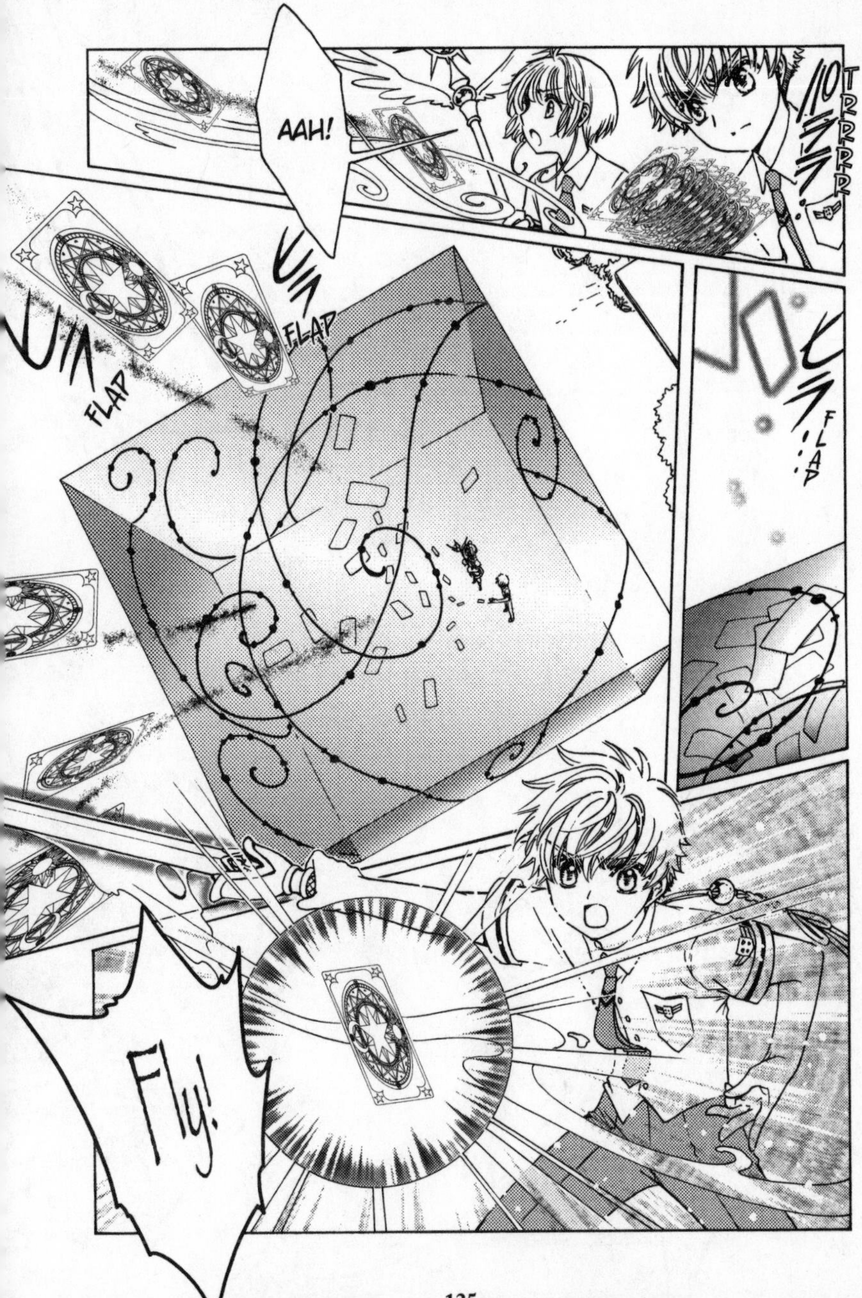
TRRRR
AAH!
FLAP
FLAP
FLAP
Fly!

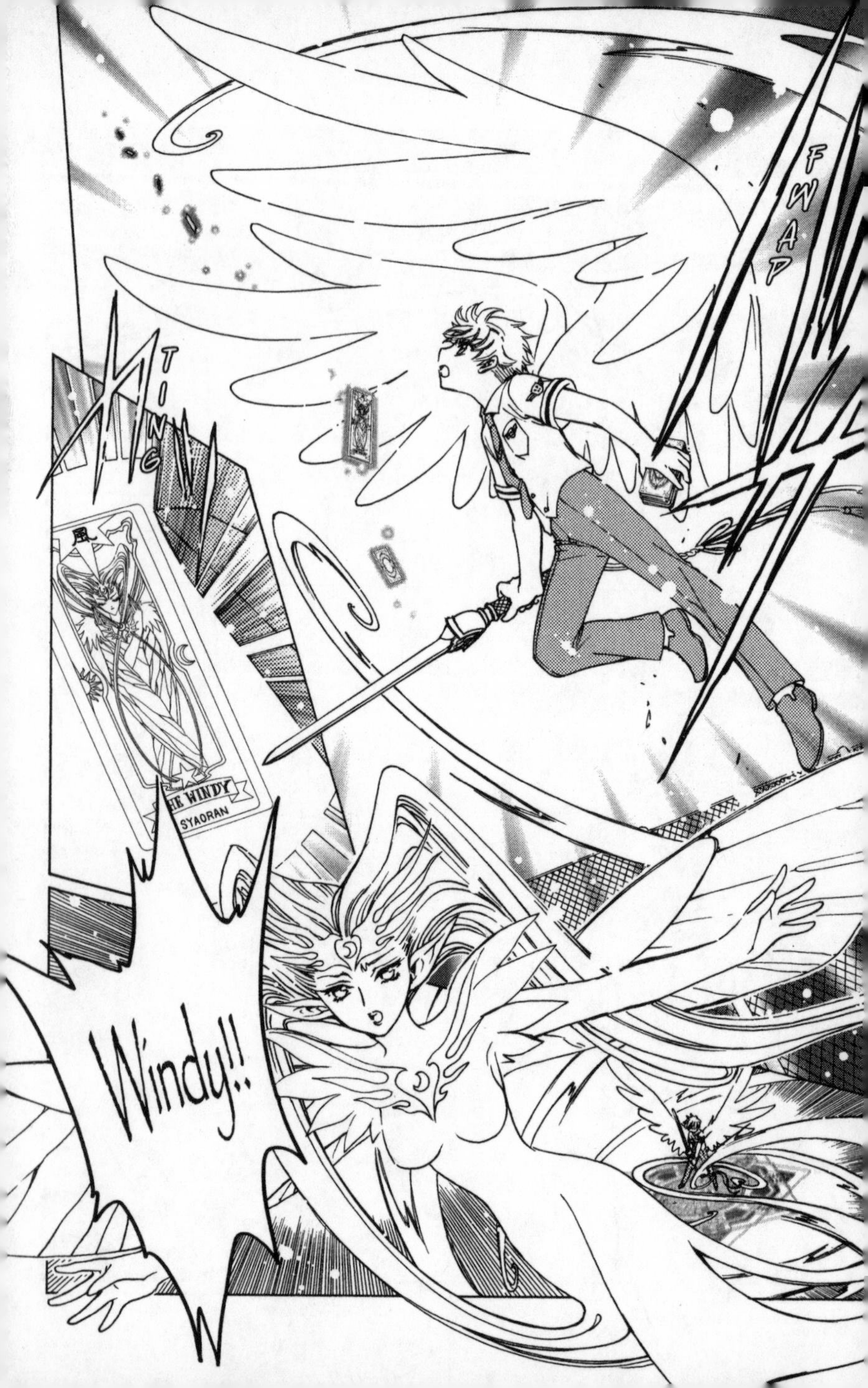
FWAP
TING
風
THE WINDY
SYAORAN
Windy!!

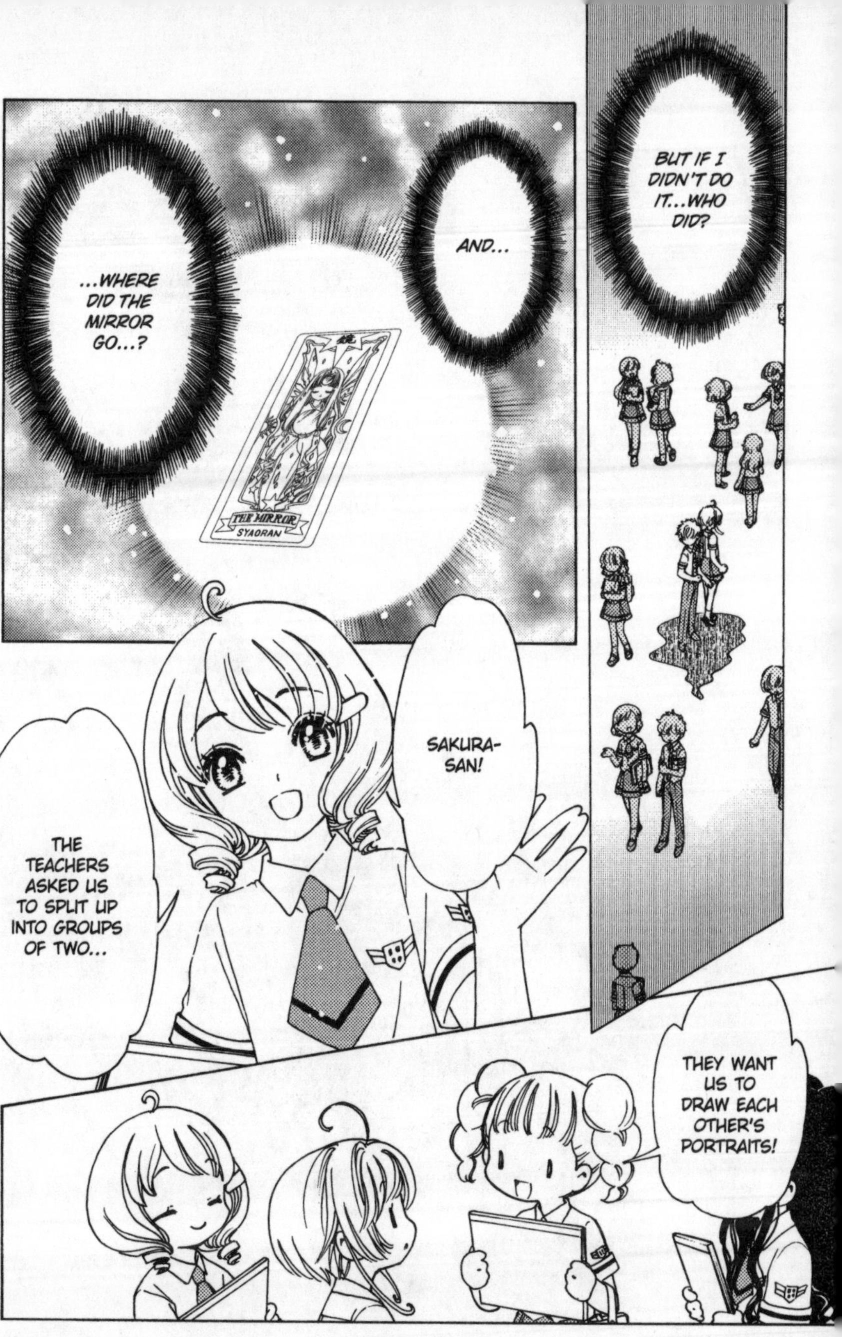
BUT IF I DIDN'T DO IT...WHO DID?
AND...
...WHERE DID THE MIRROR GO...?
THE MIRROR
SYAORAN
SAKURA-SAN!
THE TEACHERS ASKED US TO SPLIT UP INTO GROUPS OF TWO...
THEY WANT US TO DRAW EACH OTHER'S PORTRAITS!

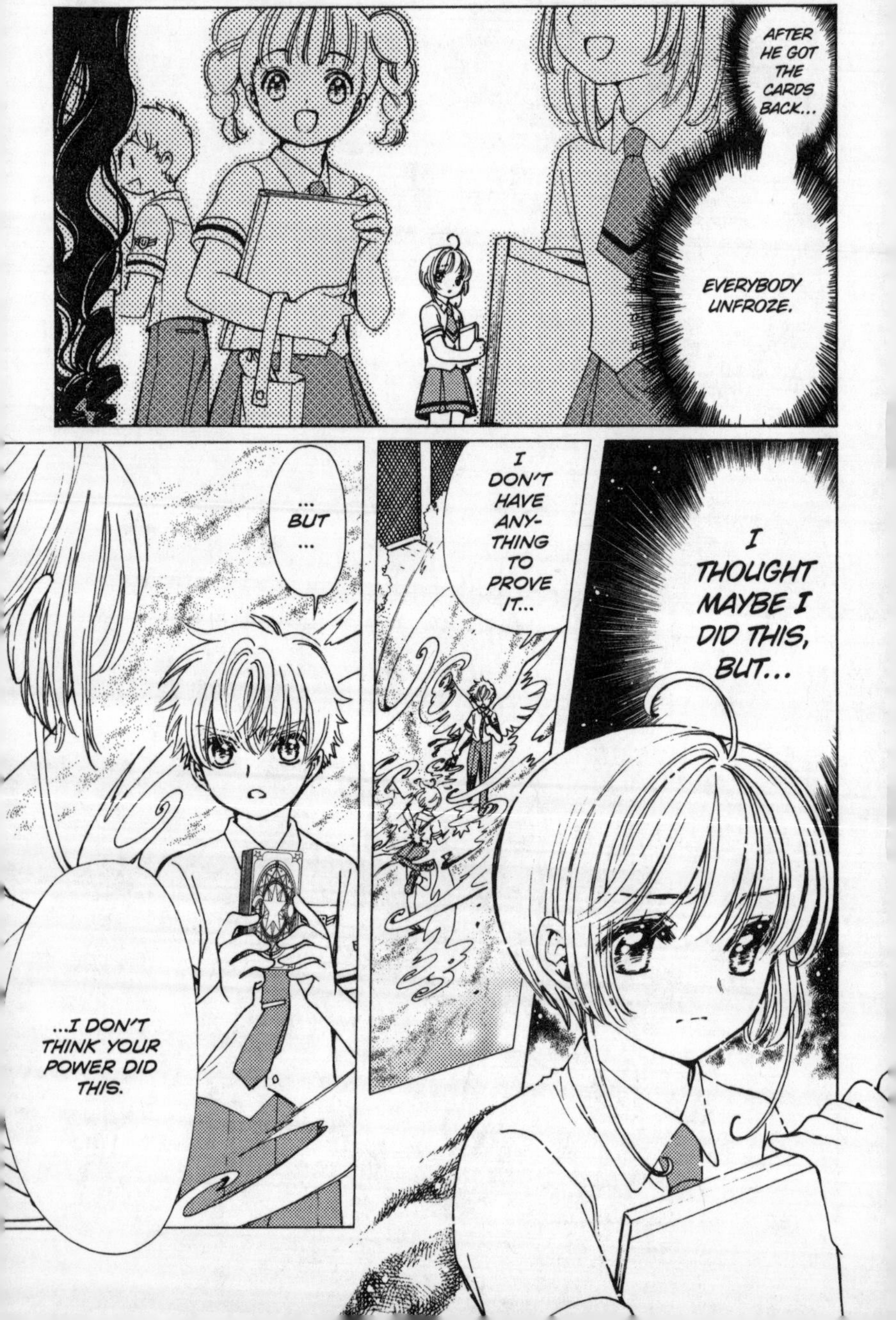
AFTER HE GOT THE CARDS BACK...
EVERYBODY UNFROZE.
I THOUGHT MAYBE I DID THIS, BUT...
I DON'T HAVE ANY-THING TO PROVE IT...
...BUT...
...I DON'T THINK YOUR POWER DID THIS.

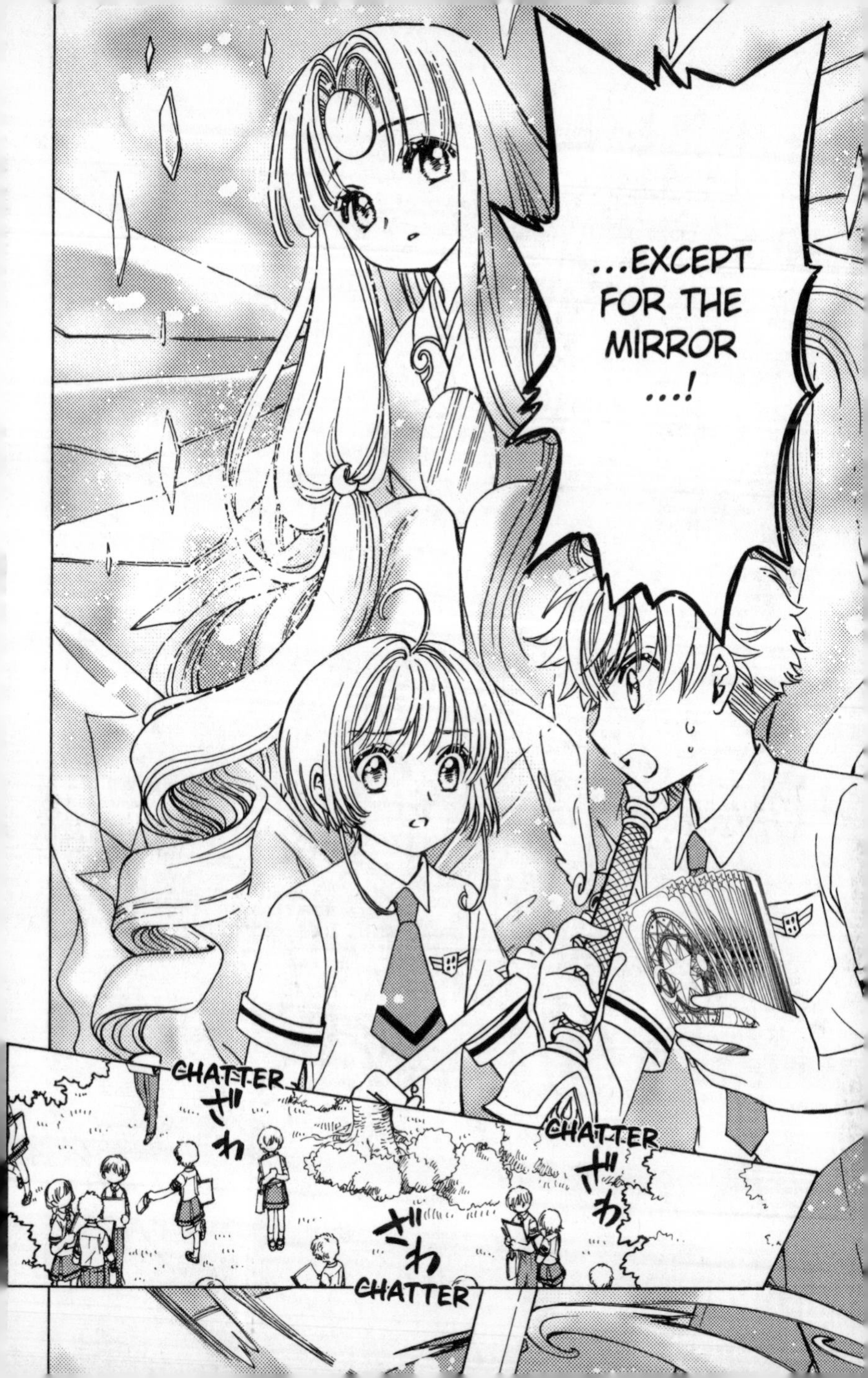
...EXCEPT FOR THE MIRROR ...!
CHATTER
ざわ
CHATTER
ざわ
ざわ
CHATTER

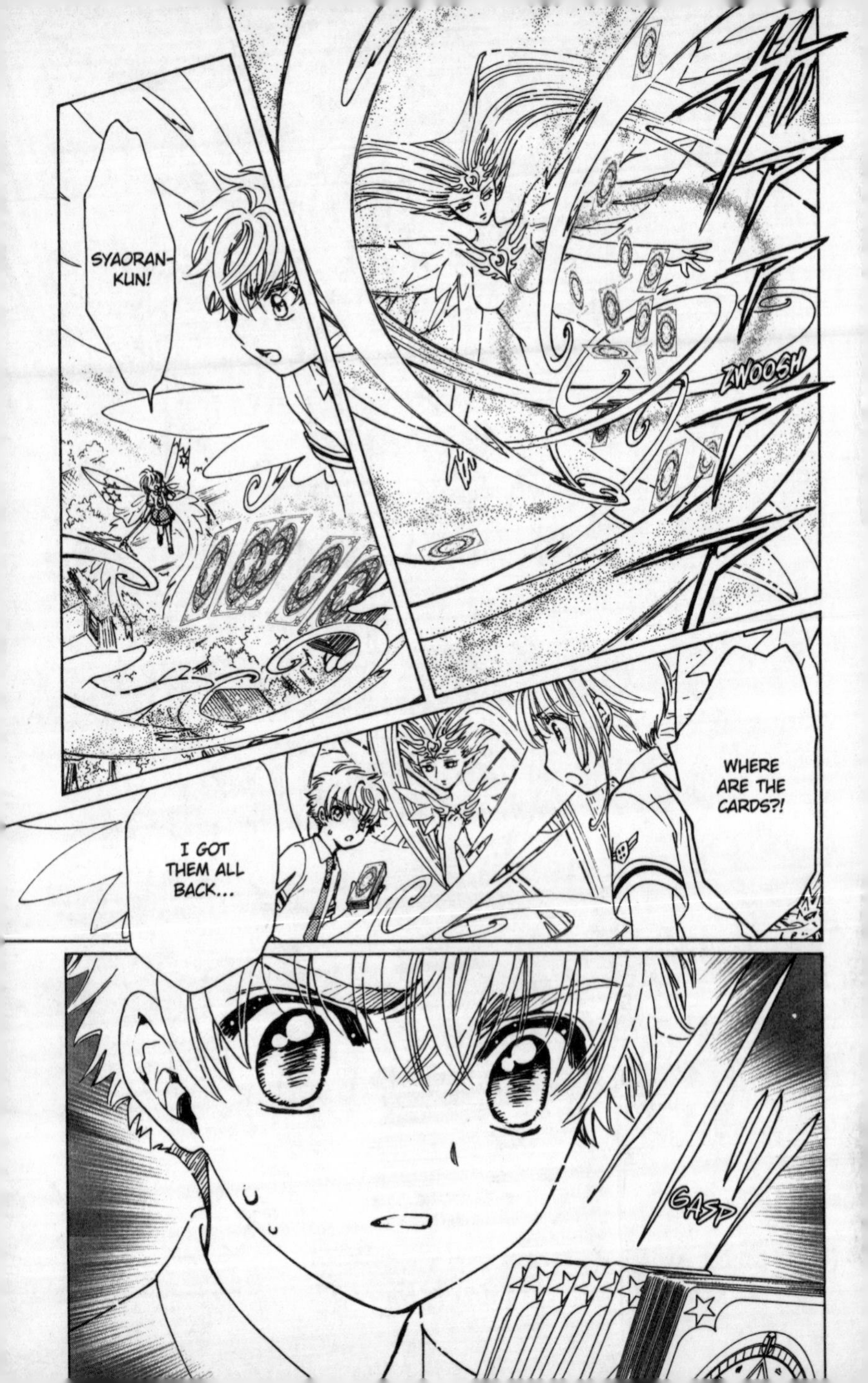
ZWOOSH
SYAORAN-KUN!
WHERE ARE THE CARDS?!
I GOT THEM ALL BACK...
GASP

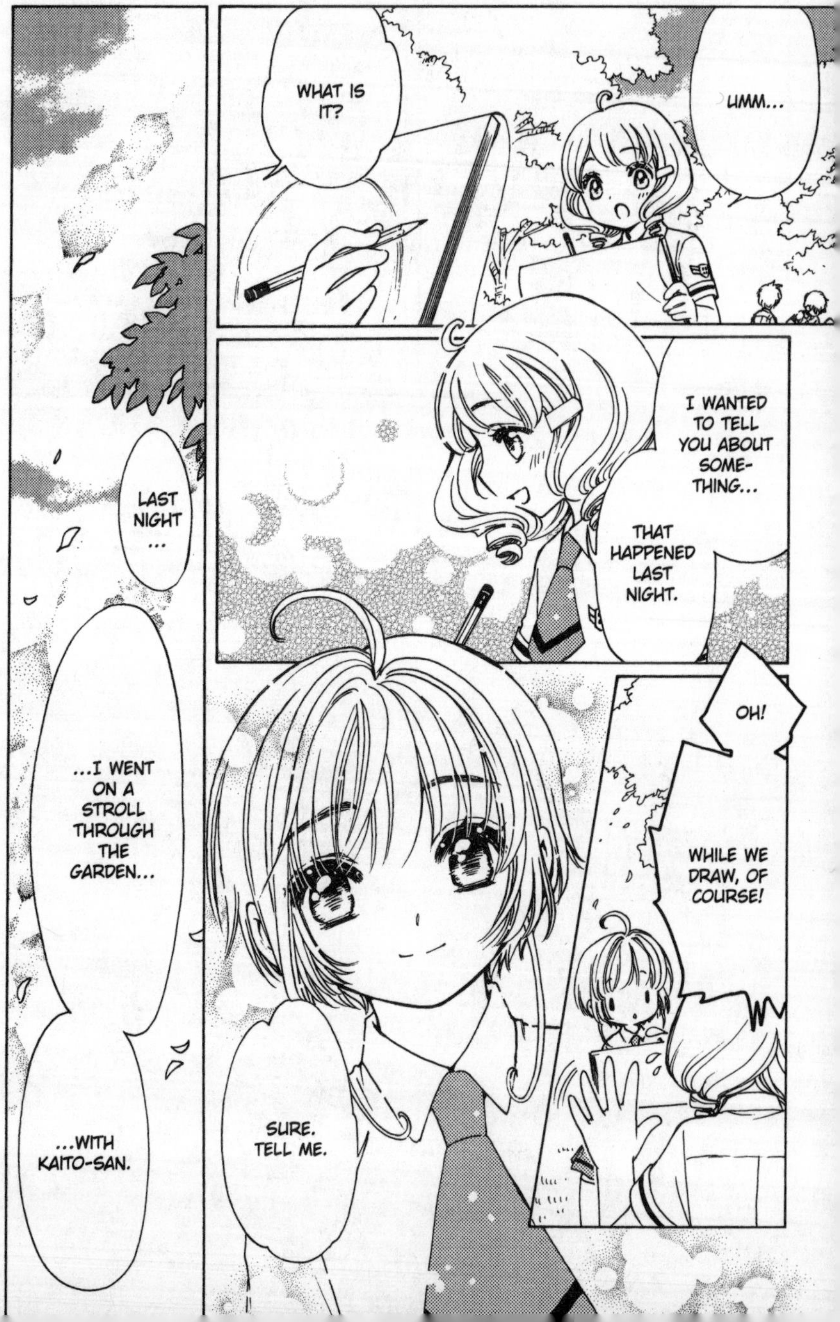
UMM...
WHAT IS IT?
I WANTED TO TELL YOU ABOUT SOME-THING...
THAT HAPPENED LAST NIGHT.
OH!
WHILE WE DRAW, OF COURSE!
SURE. TELL ME.
LAST NIGHT...
...I WENT ON A STROLL THROUGH THE GARDEN...
...WITH KAITO-SAN.

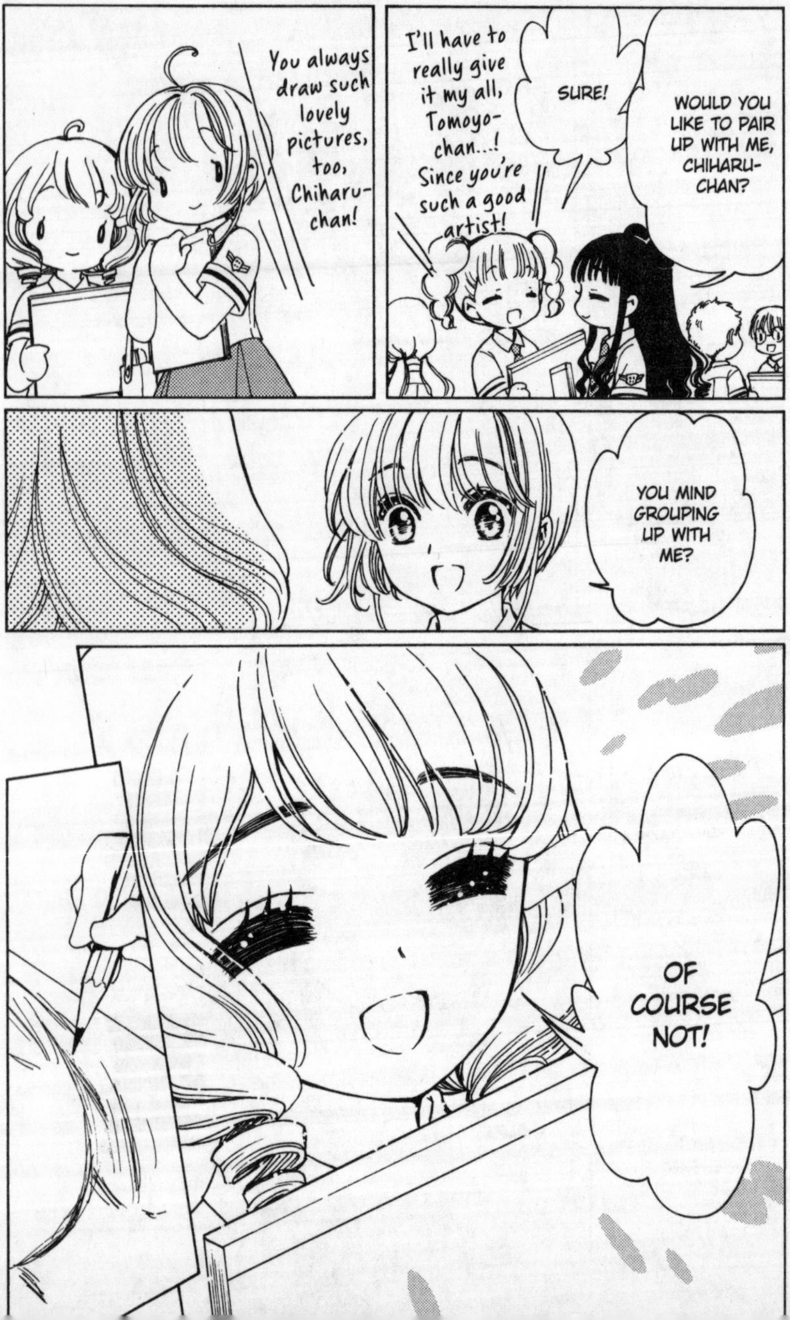
WOULD YOU LIKE TO PAIR UP WITH ME, CHIHARU-CHAN?
SURE!
I'll have to really give it my all, Tomoyo-chan...! Since you're such a good artist!
You always draw such lovely pictures, too, Chiharu-chan!
YOU MIND GROUPING UP WITH ME?
OF COURSE NOT!

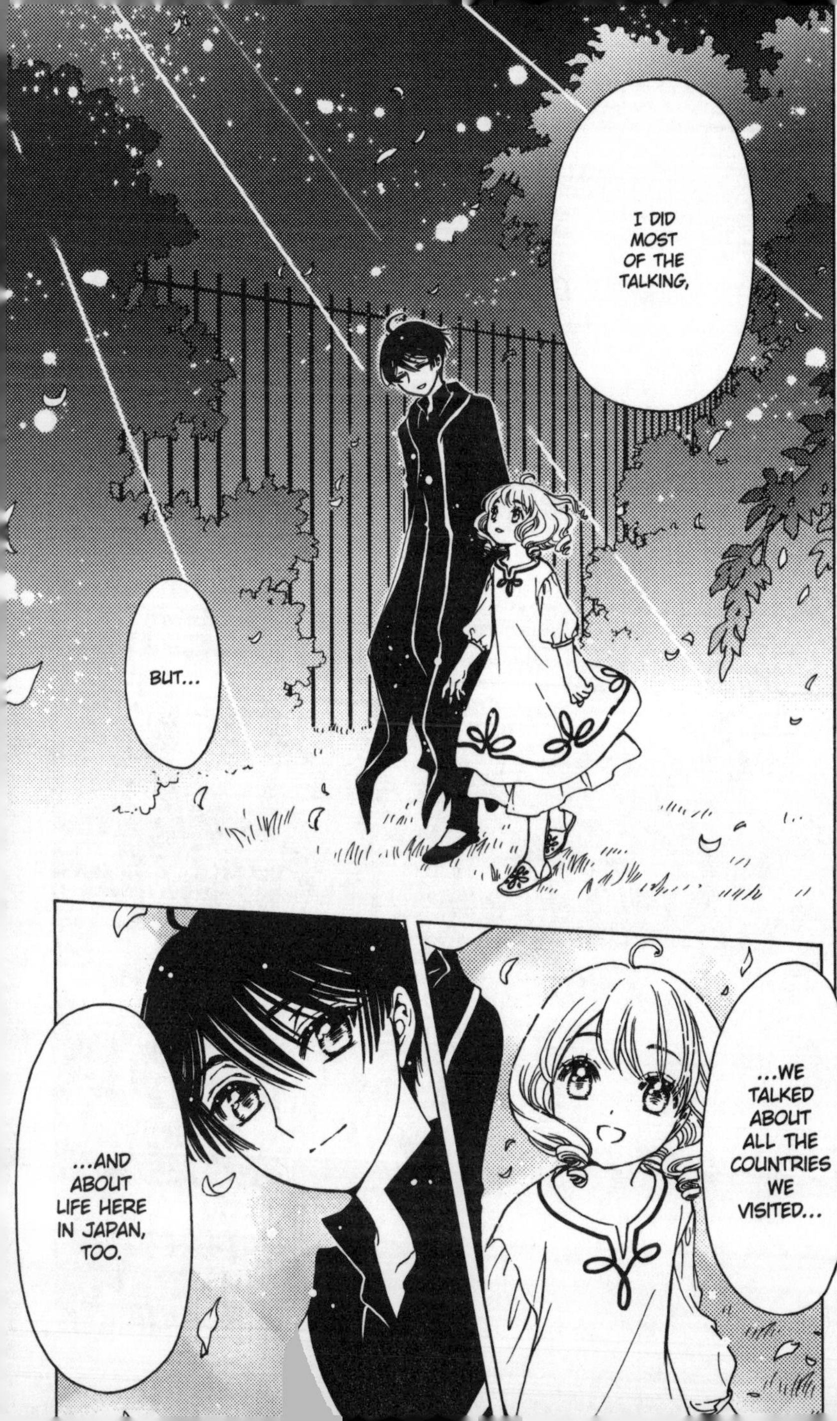
I DID MOST OF THE TALKING,
BUT...
...WE TALKED ABOUT ALL THE COUNTRIES WE VISITED...
...AND ABOUT LIFE HERE IN JAPAN, TOO.

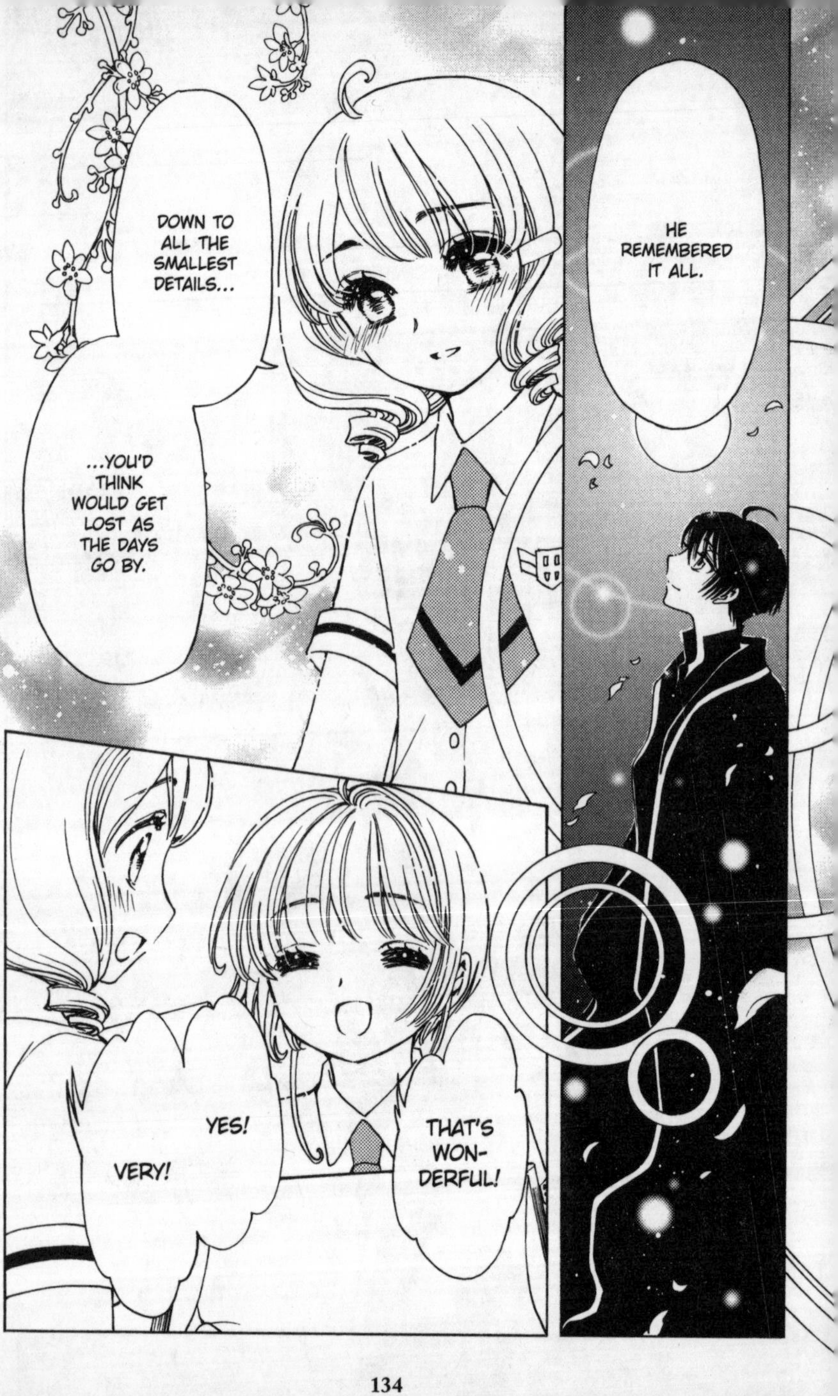
HE REMEMBERED IT ALL.
DOWN TO ALL THE SMALLEST DETAILS...
...YOU'D THINK WOULD GET LOST AS THE DAYS GO BY.
THAT'S WON-DERFUL!
YES!
VERY!

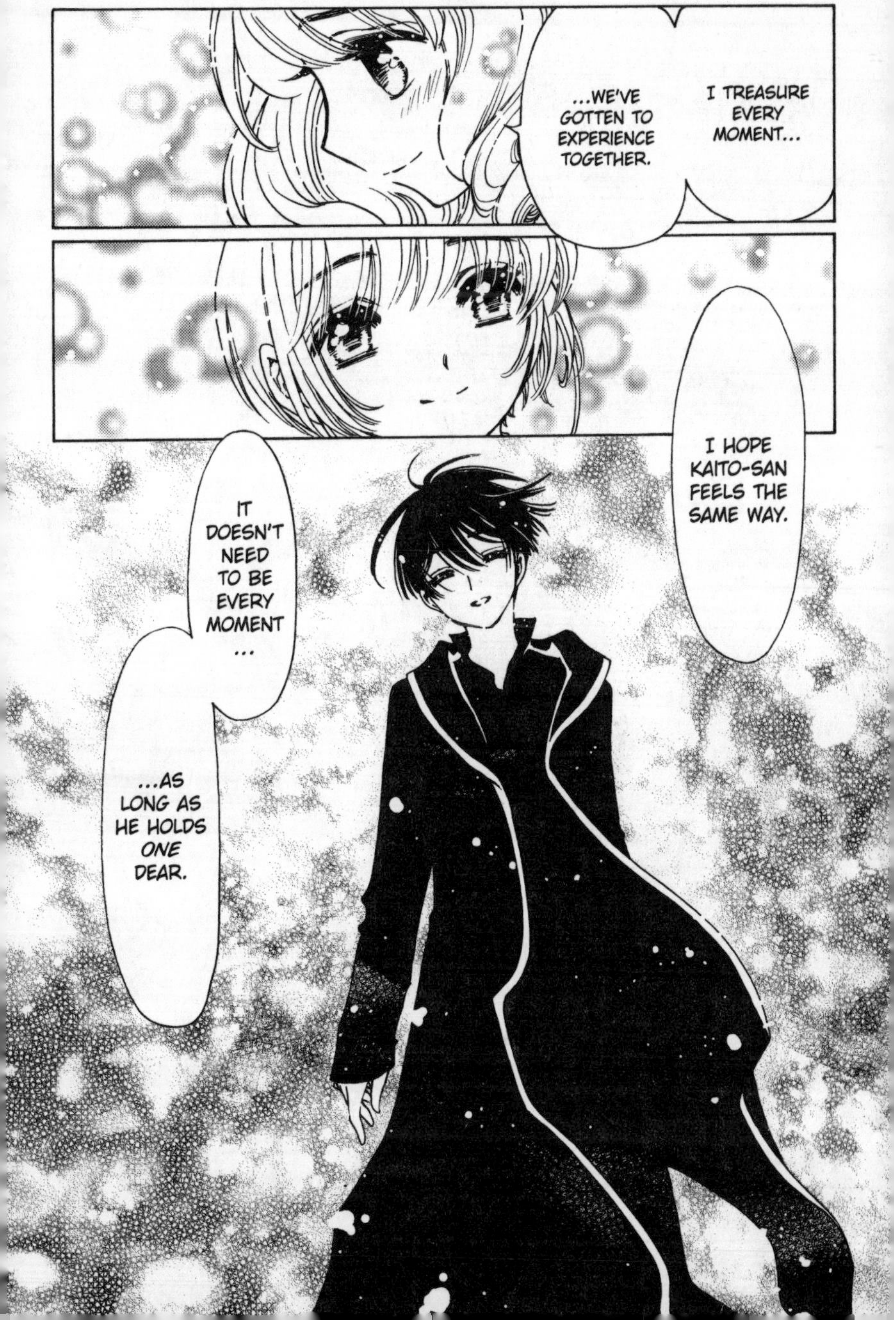
I TREASURE EVERY MOMENT...
...WE'VE GOTTEN TO EXPERIENCE TOGETHER.
I HOPE KAITO-SAN FEELS THE SAME WAY.
IT DOESN'T NEED TO BE EVERY MOMENT ...
...AS LONG AS HE HOLDS ONE DEAR.

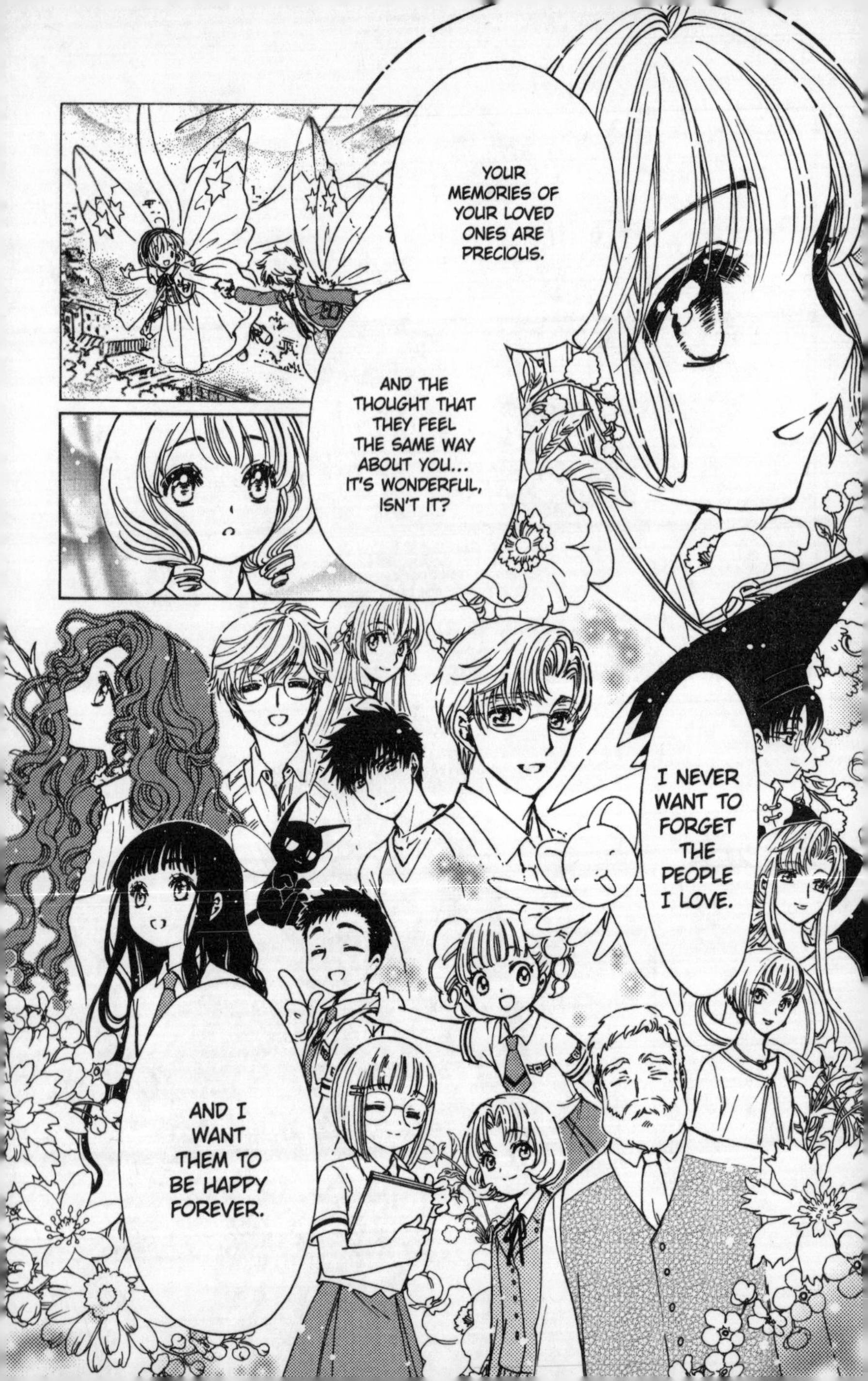
YOUR MEMORIES OF YOUR LOVED ONES ARE PRECIOUS.
AND THE THOUGHT THAT THEY FEEL THE SAME WAY ABOUT YOU... IT'S WONDERFUL, ISN'T IT?
I NEVER WANT TO FORGET THE PEOPLE I LOVE.
AND I WANT THEM TO BE HAPPY FOREVER.

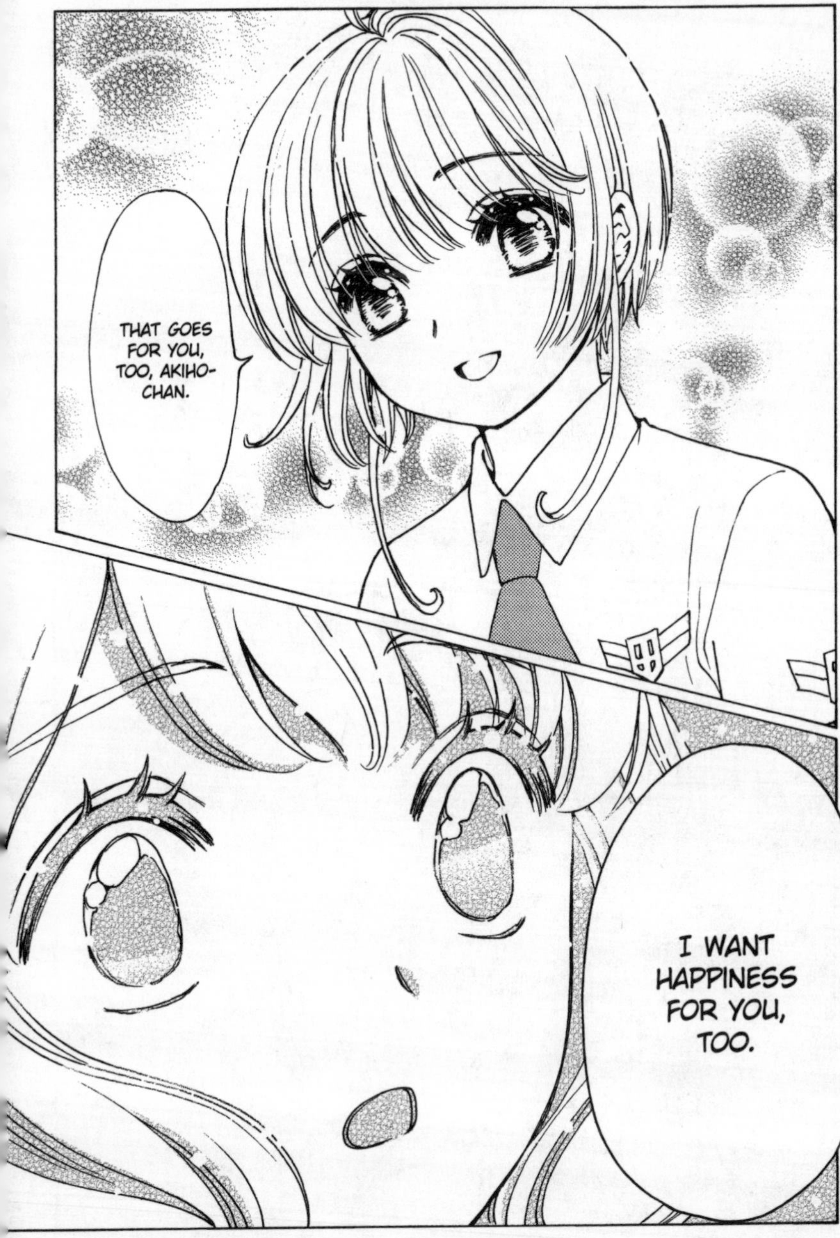
THAT GOES FOR YOU, TOO, AKIHO-CHAN.
I WANT HAPPINESS FOR YOU, TOO.

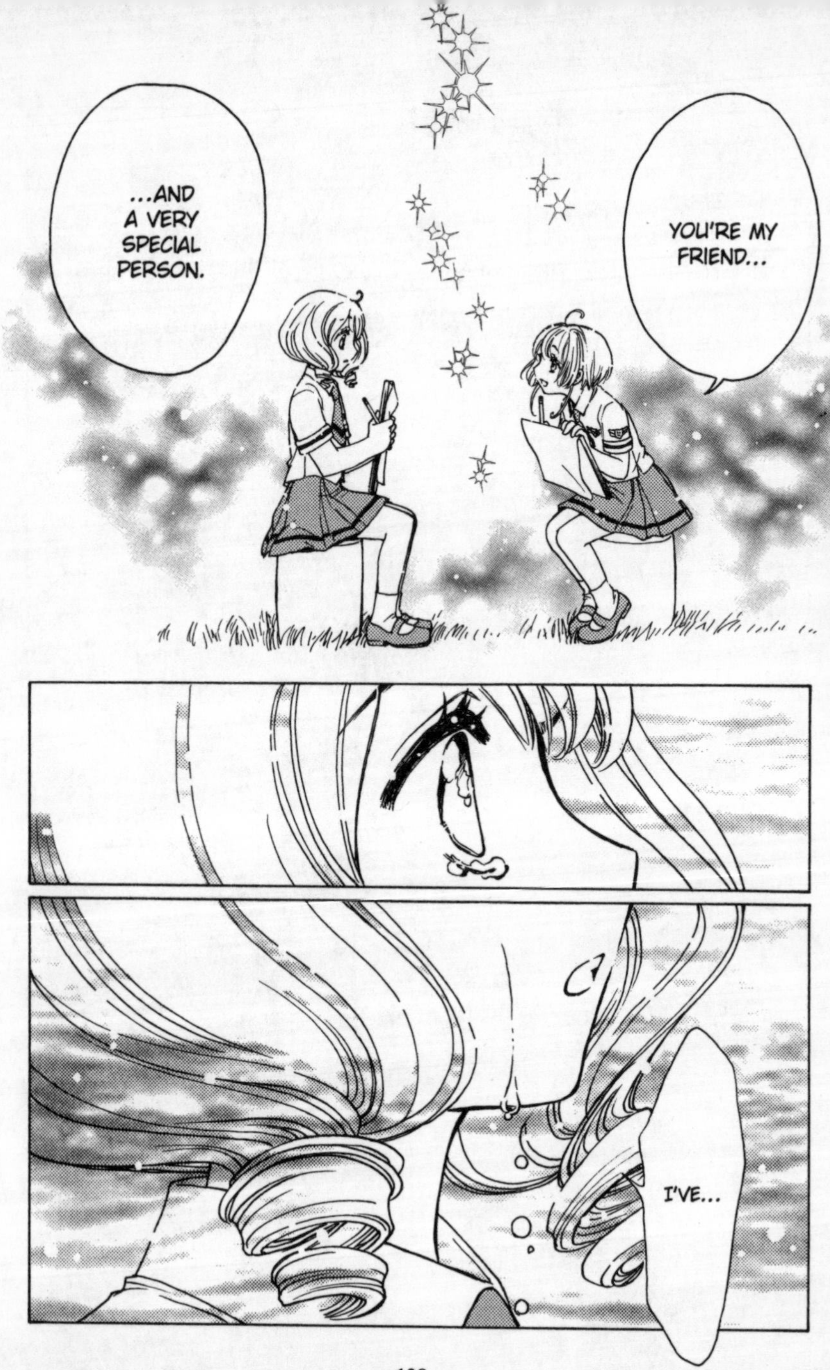
YOU'RE MY FRIEND...
...AND A VERY SPECIAL PERSON.
I'VE...

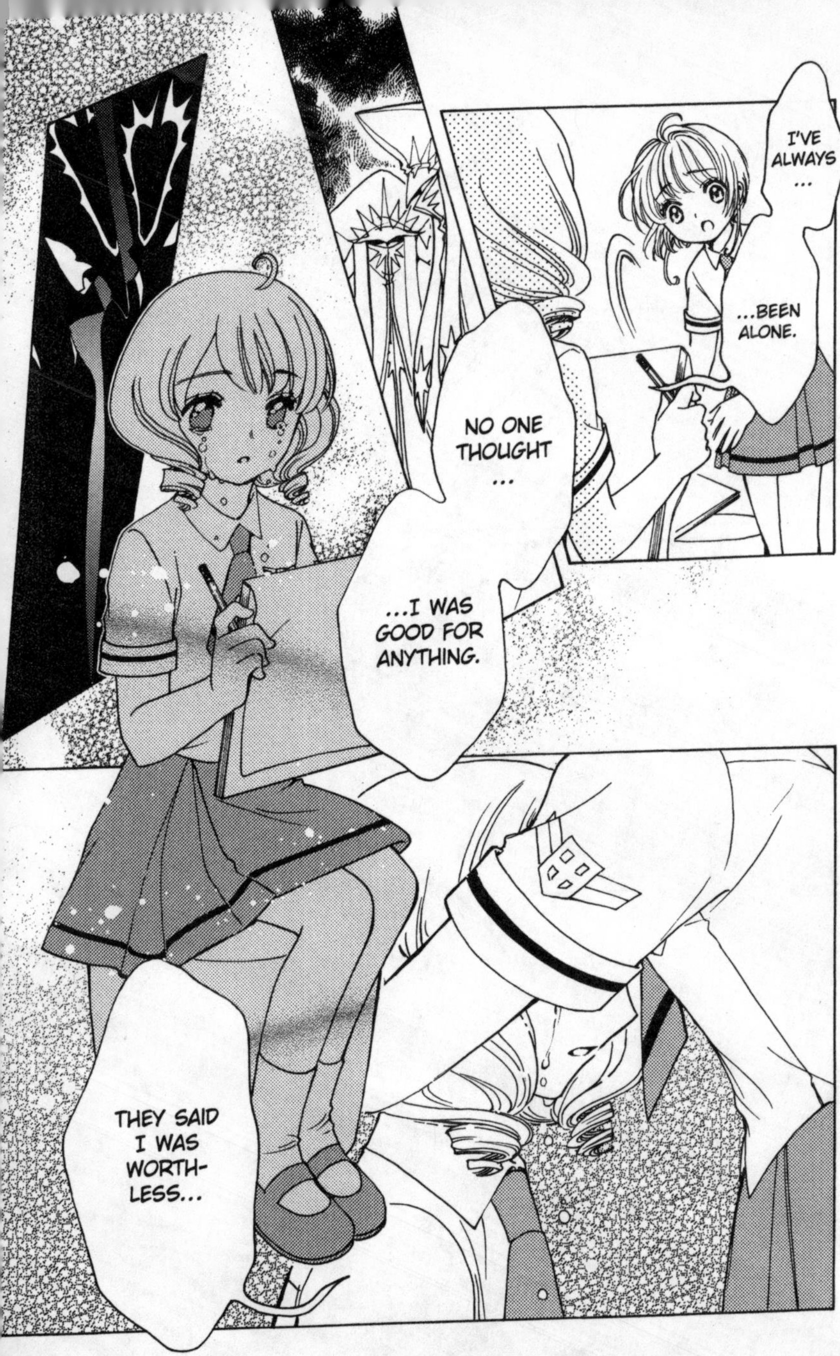
I'VE ALWAYS ...
...BEEN ALONE.
NO ONE THOUGHT ...
...I WAS GOOD FOR ANYTHING.
THEY SAID I WAS WORTH-LESS...

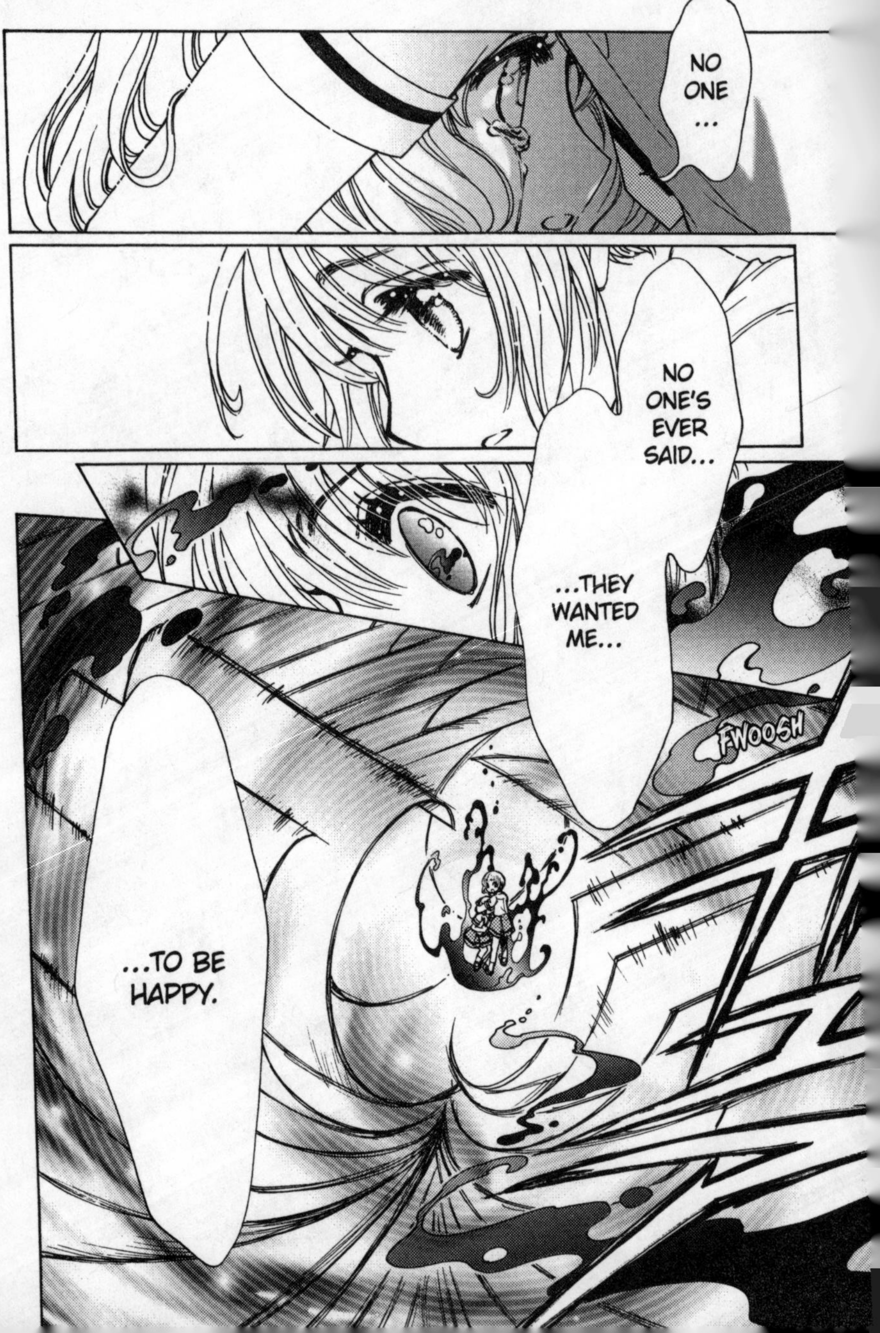
NO ONE ...
NO ONE'S EVER SAID...
...THEY WANTED ME...
FWOOSH
...TO BE HAPPY.

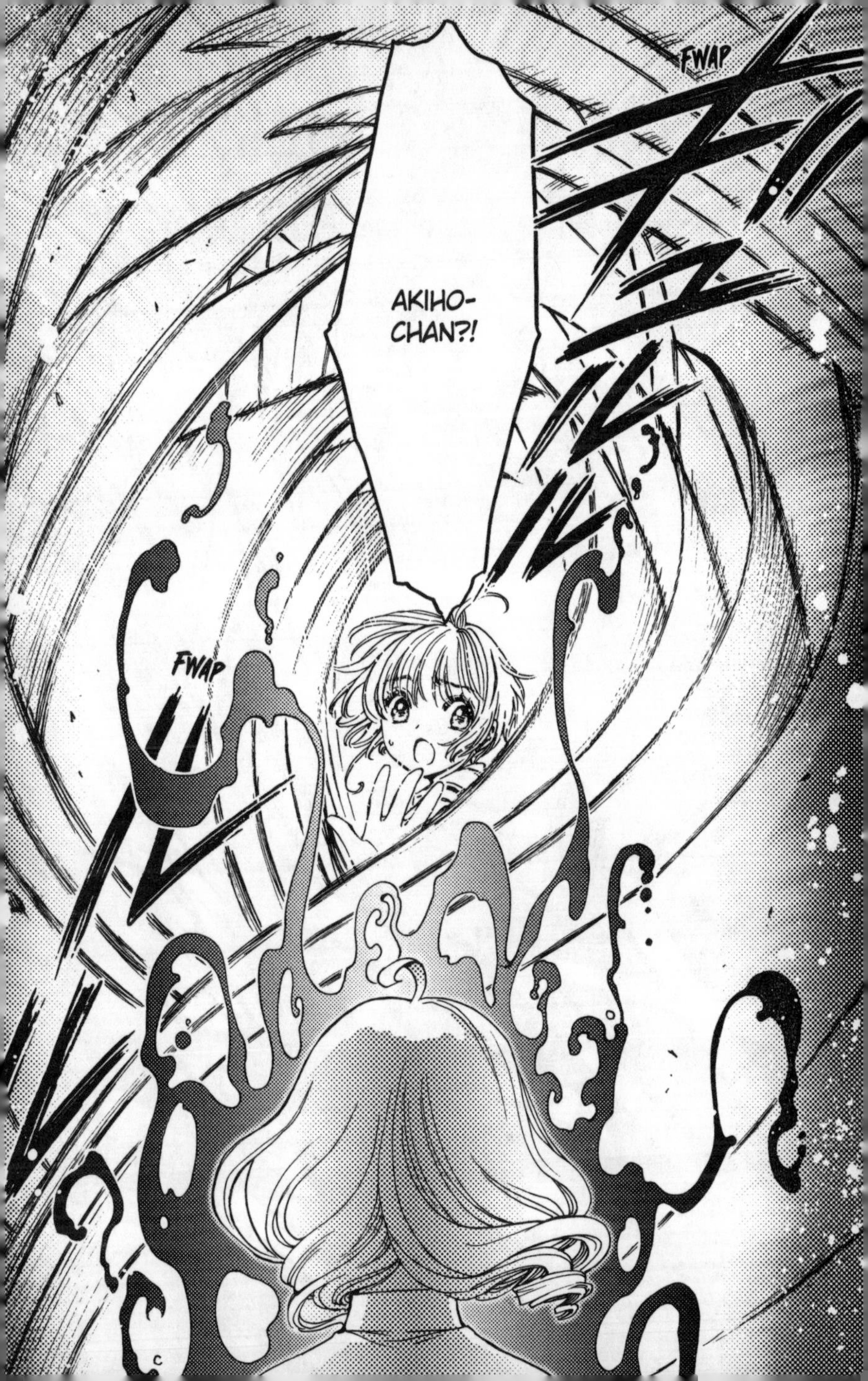
FWAP
AKIHO-CHAN?!
FWAP

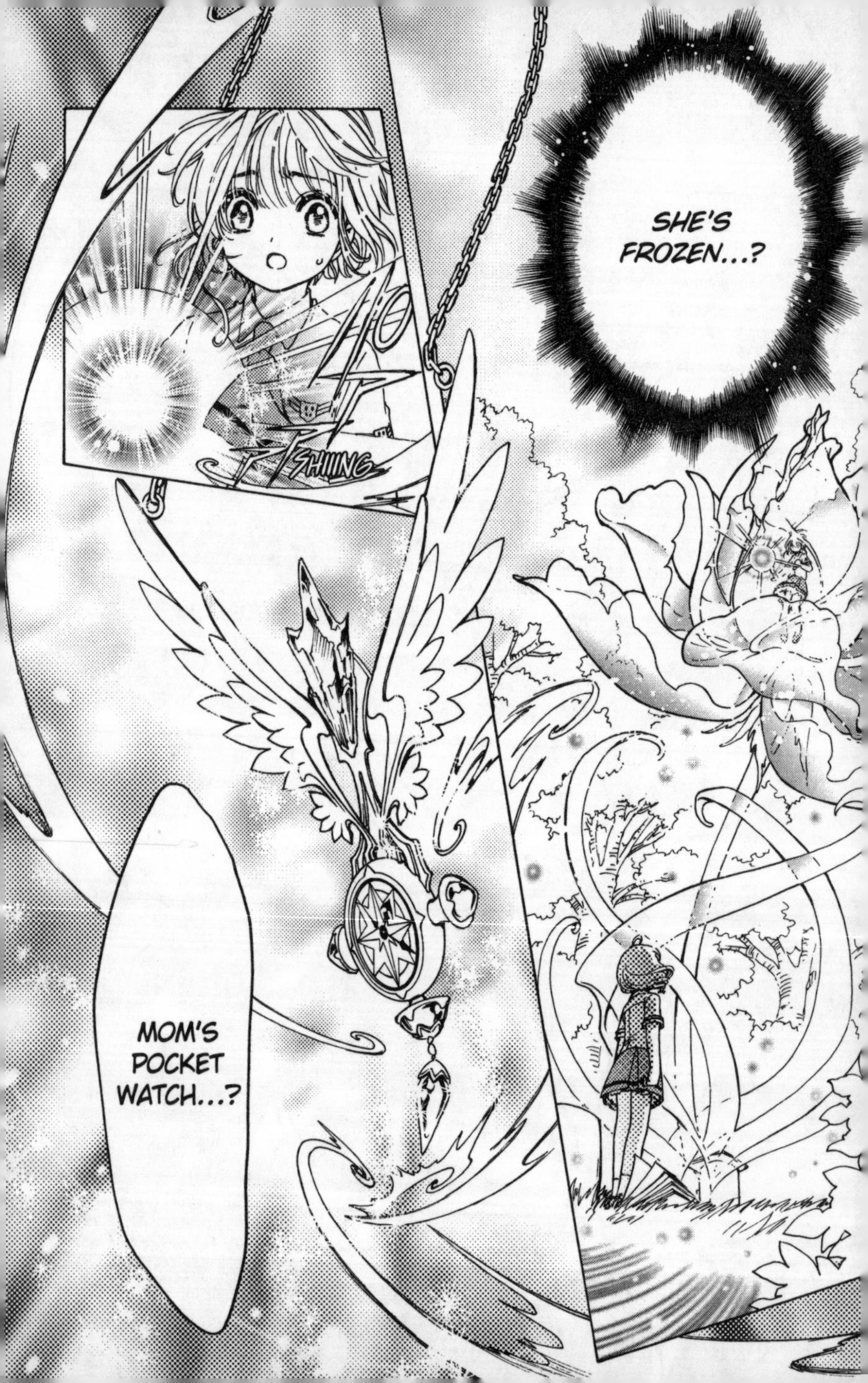
SHE'S FROZEN...?
SHIIING
MOM'S POCKET WATCH...?

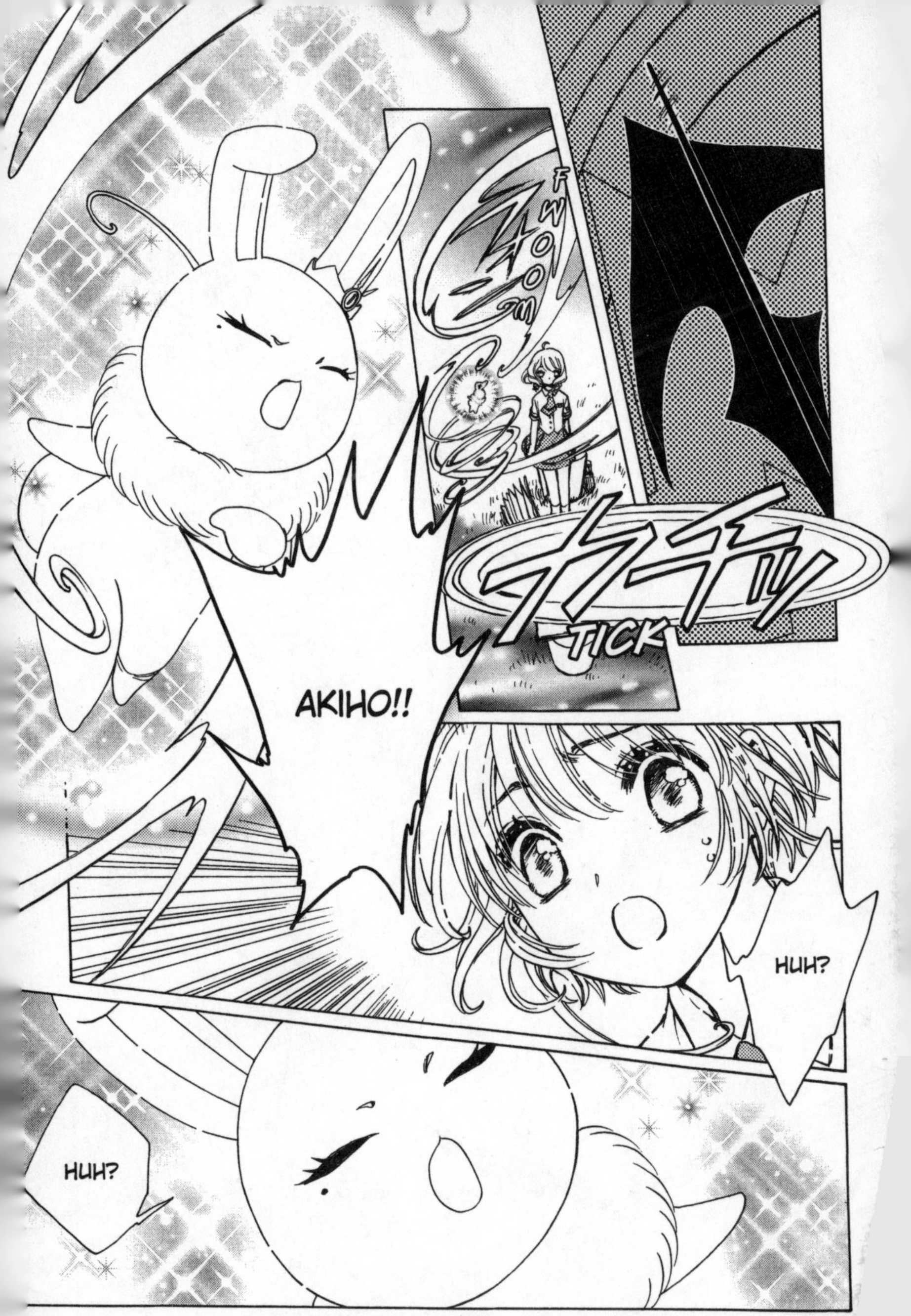
FWOOOM
カチッ
TICK
AKIHO!!
HUH?
HUH?

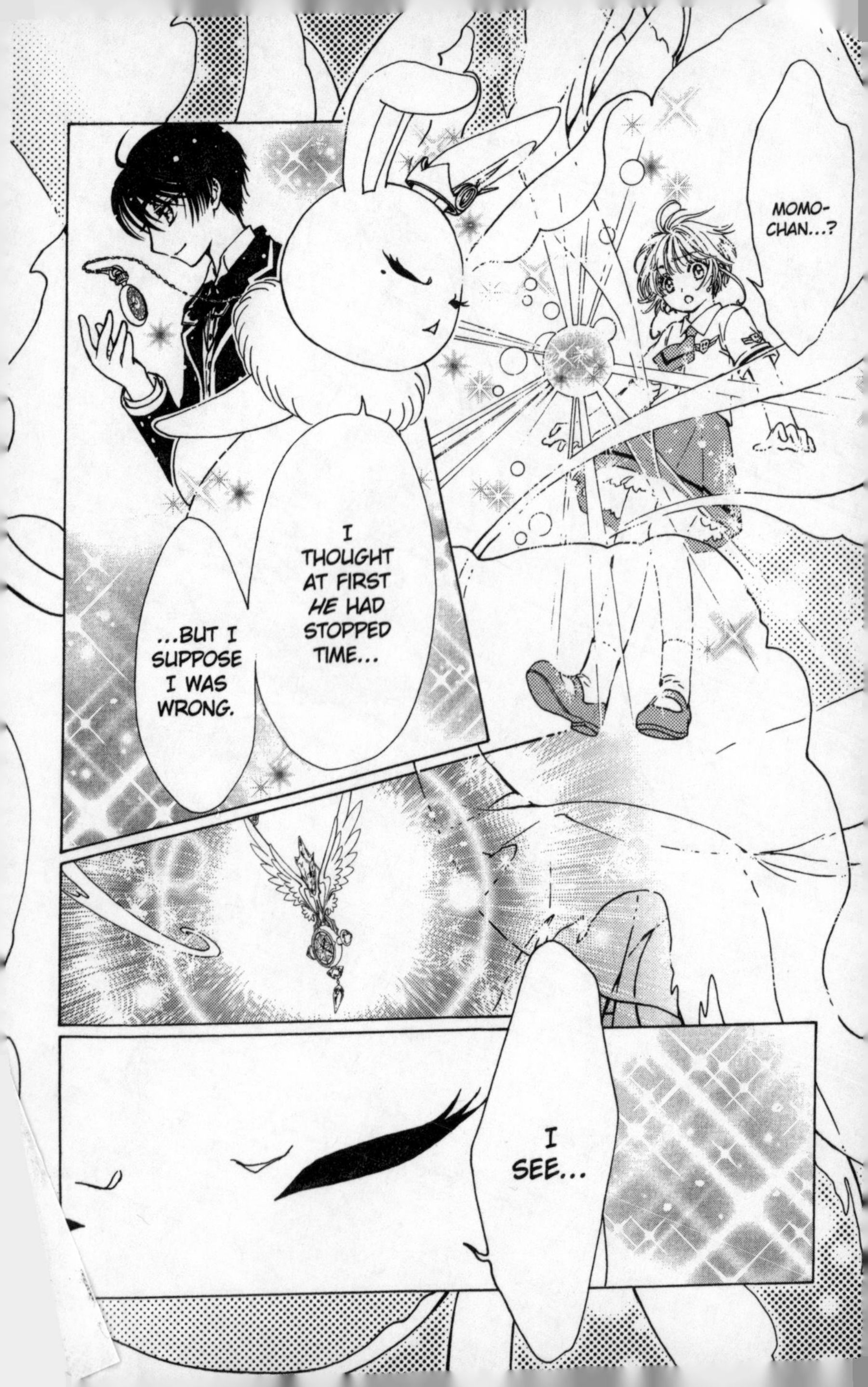
MOMO-CHAN...?
I THOUGHT AT FIRST *HE* HAD STOPPED TIME...
...BUT I SUPPOSE I WAS WRONG.
I SEE...

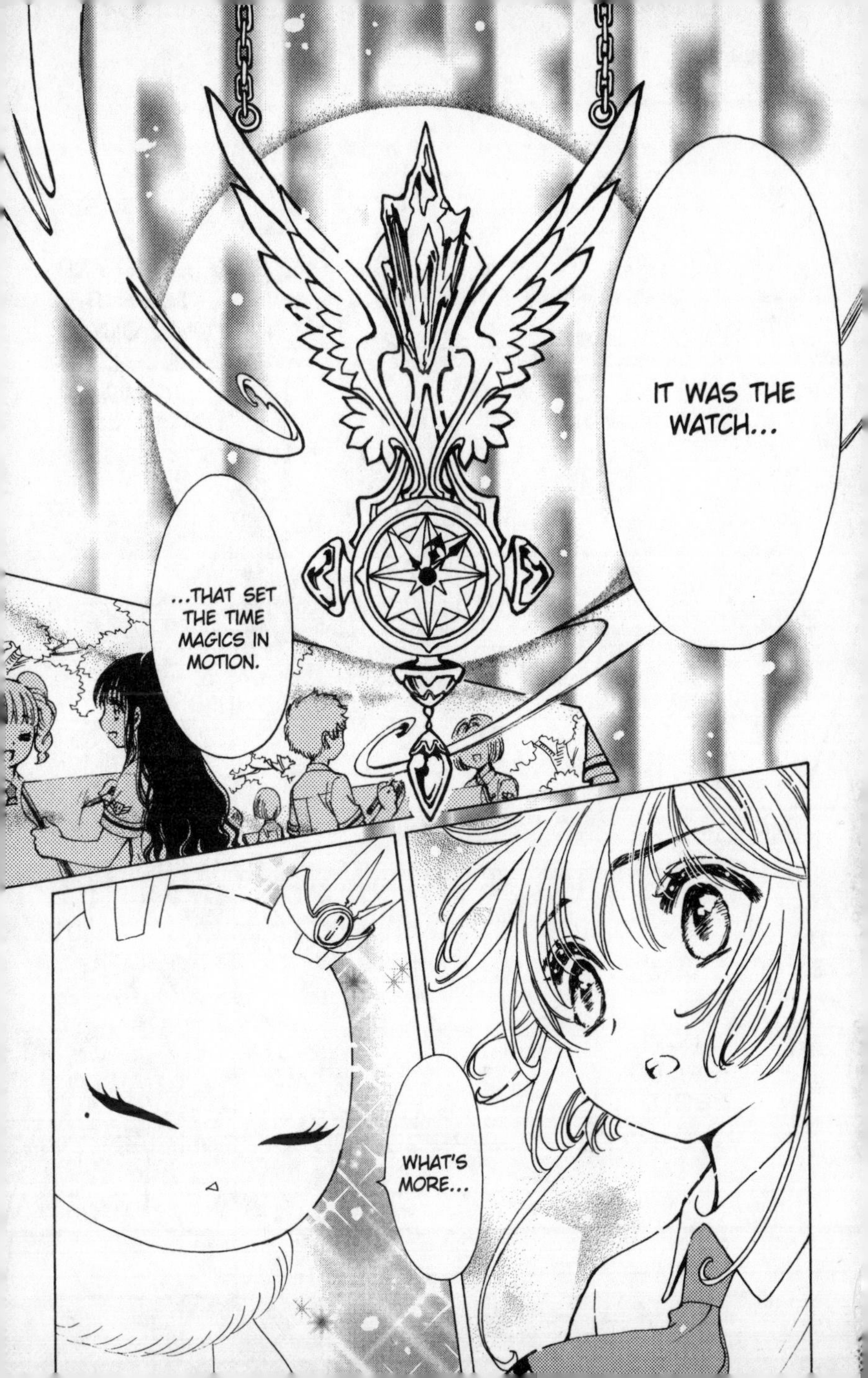
IT WAS THE WATCH...
...THAT SET THE TIME MAGICS IN MOTION.
WHAT'S MORE...

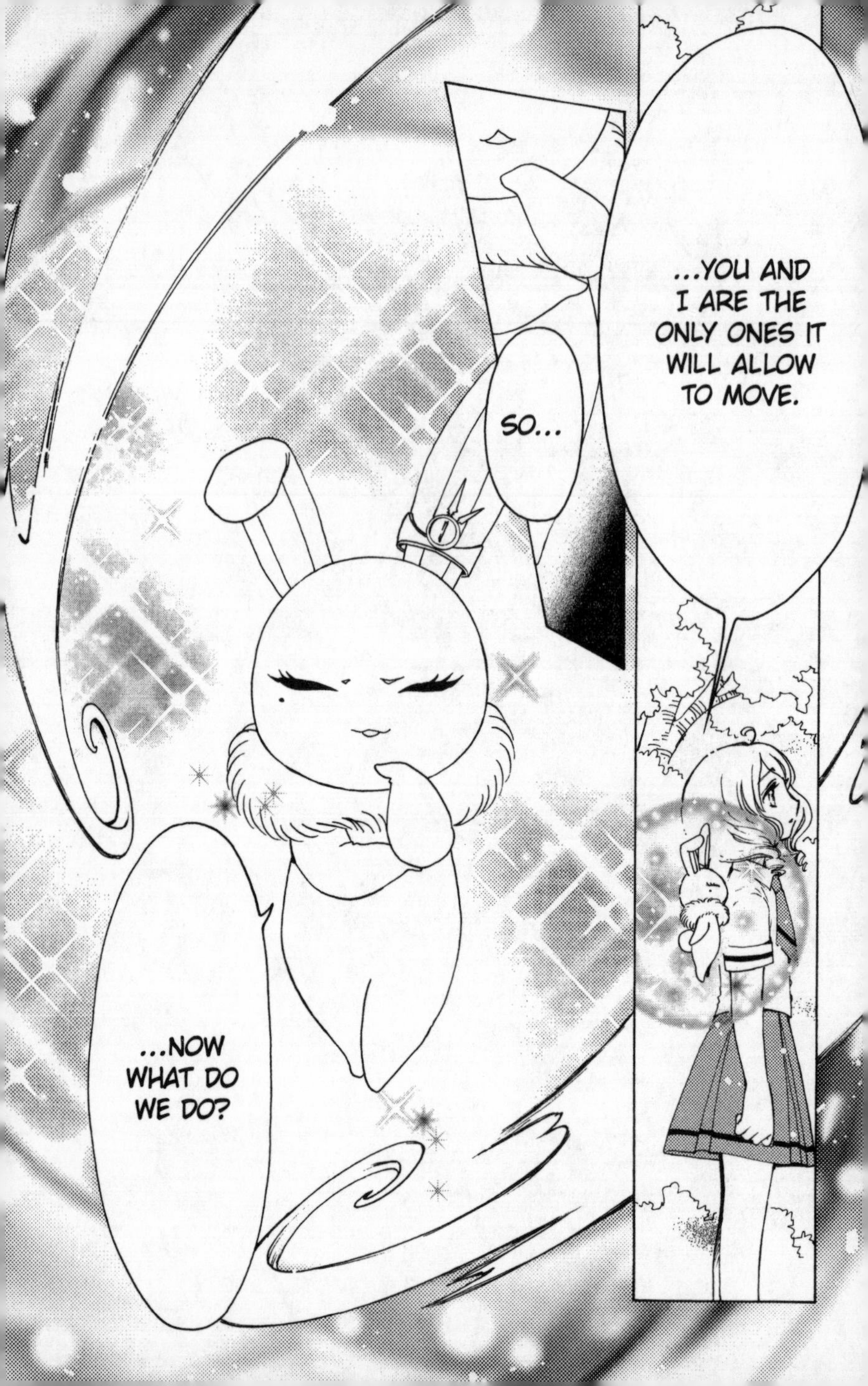
...YOU AND I ARE THE ONLY ONES IT WILL ALLOW TO MOVE.
SO...
...NOW WHAT DO WE DO?

🍀 Continued in Volume 11 🍀

Cardcaptor Sakura

CLEAR CARD

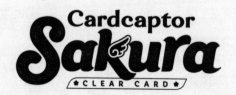

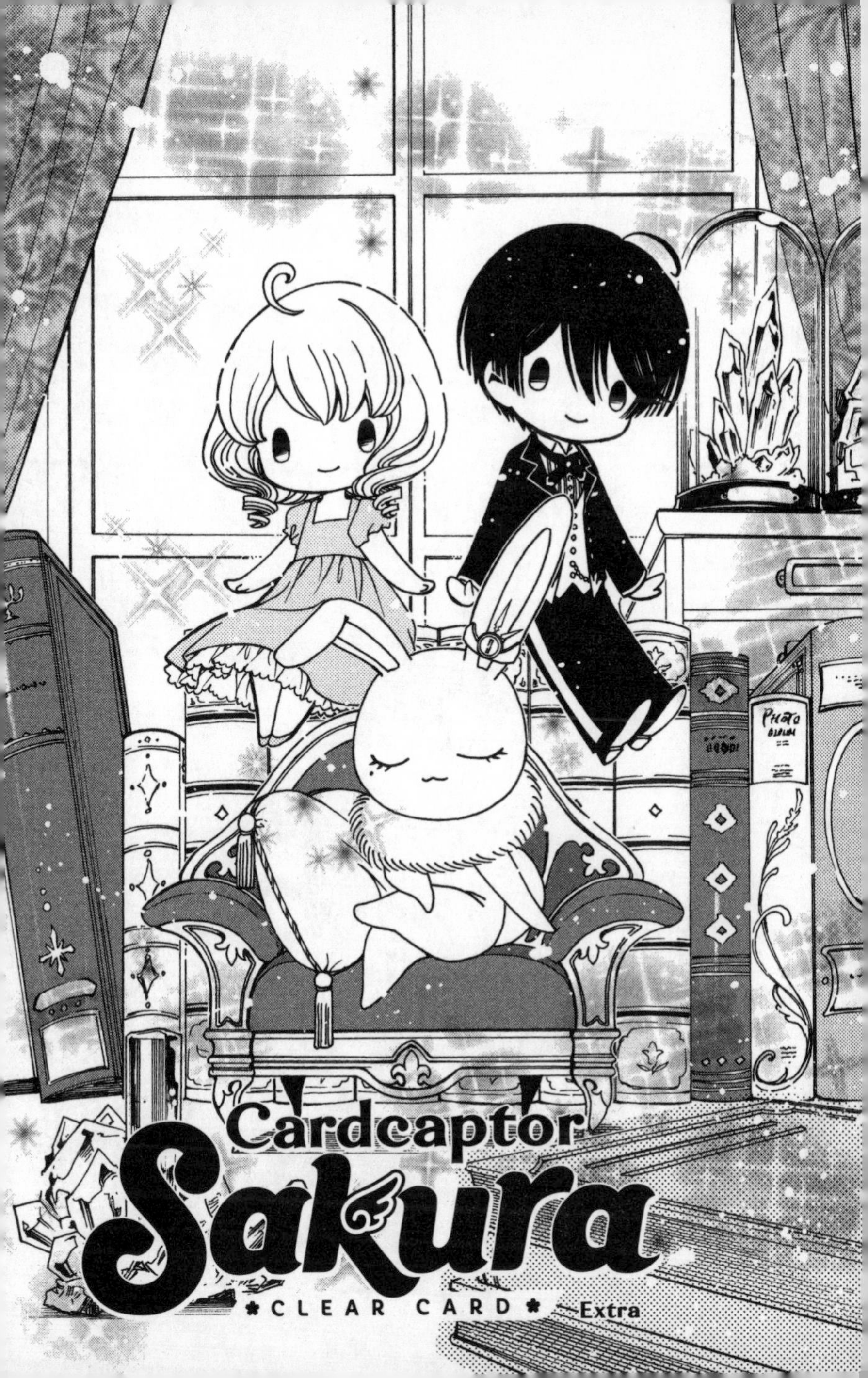
Cardcaptor
Sakura
CLEAR CARD
Extra

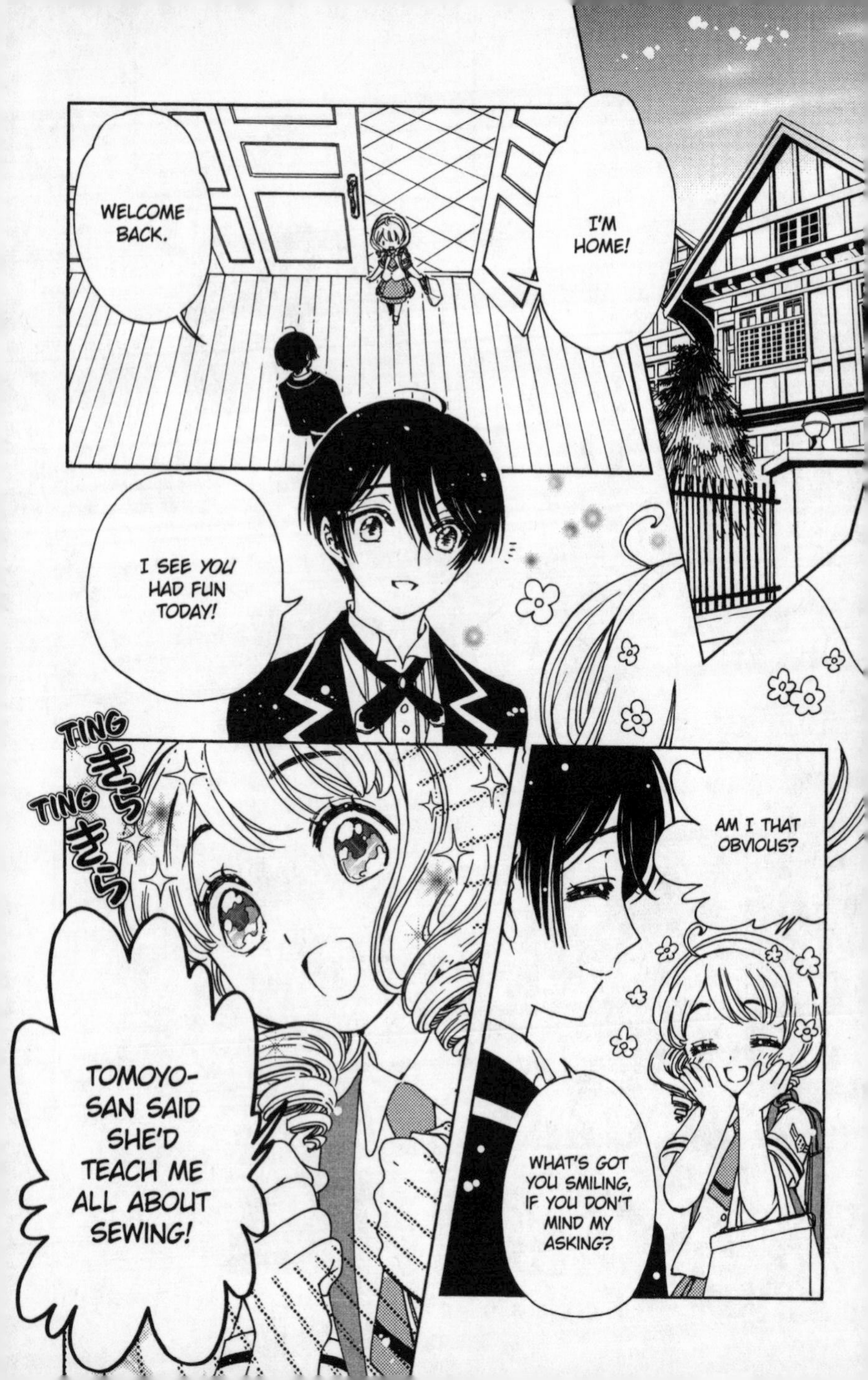
I'M HOME!
WELCOME BACK.
I SEE YOU HAD FUN TODAY!
AM I THAT OBVIOUS?
WHAT'S GOT YOU SMILING, IF YOU DON'T MIND MY ASKING?
TING きら
TING きら
TOMOYO-SAN SAID SHE'D TEACH ME ALL ABOUT SEWING!

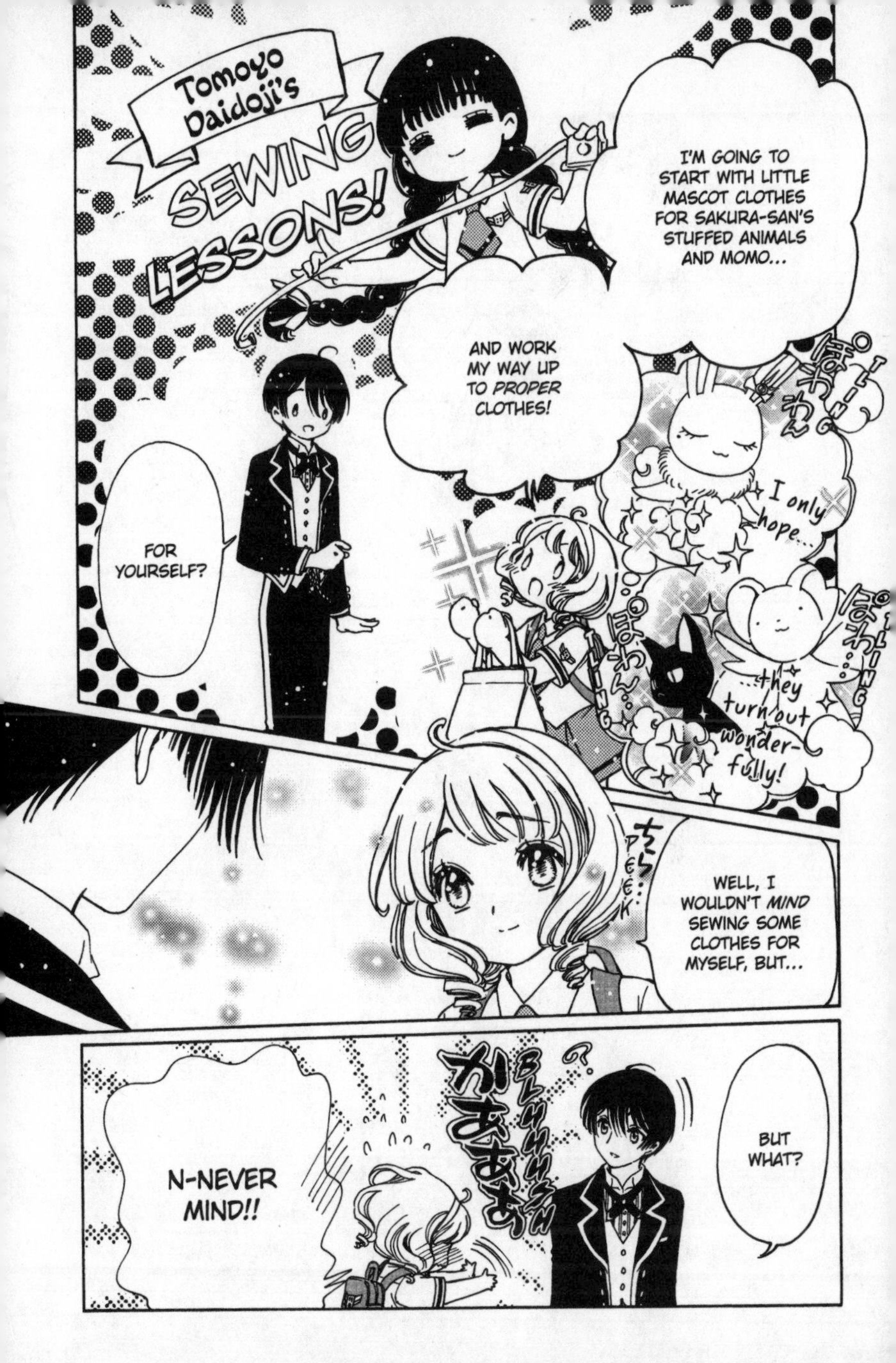
Tomoyo Daidoji's
SEWING LESSONS!
I'M GOING TO START WITH LITTLE MASCOT CLOTHES FOR SAKURA-SAN'S STUFFED ANIMALS AND MOMO...
AND WORK MY WAY UP TO *PROPER* CLOTHES!
I only hope...
...they turn out wonder-fully!
FOR YOURSELF?
ちら PEEK
WELL, I WOULDN'T *MIND* SEWING SOME CLOTHES FOR MYSELF, BUT...
BUT WHAT?
かあああ BLUUUSH
N-NEVER MIND!!

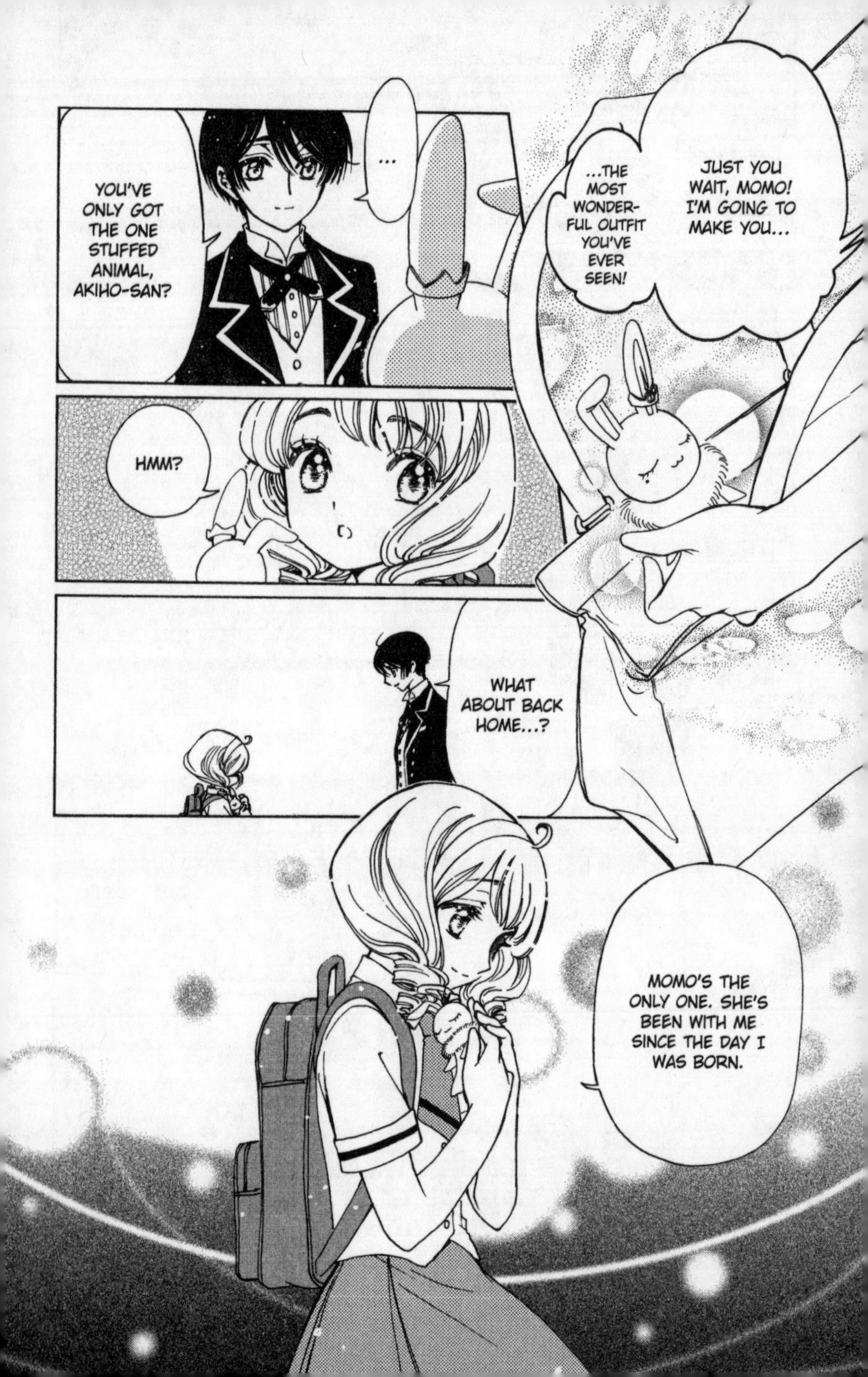

YOU'VE ONLY GOT THE ONE STUFFED ANIMAL, AKIHO-SAN?
...
HMM?
WHAT ABOUT BACK HOME...?
MOMO'S THE ONLY ONE. SHE'S BEEN WITH ME SINCE THE DAY I WAS BORN.
JUST YOU WAIT, MOMO! I'M GOING TO MAKE YOU...
...THE MOST WONDERFUL OUTFIT YOU'VE EVER SEEN!

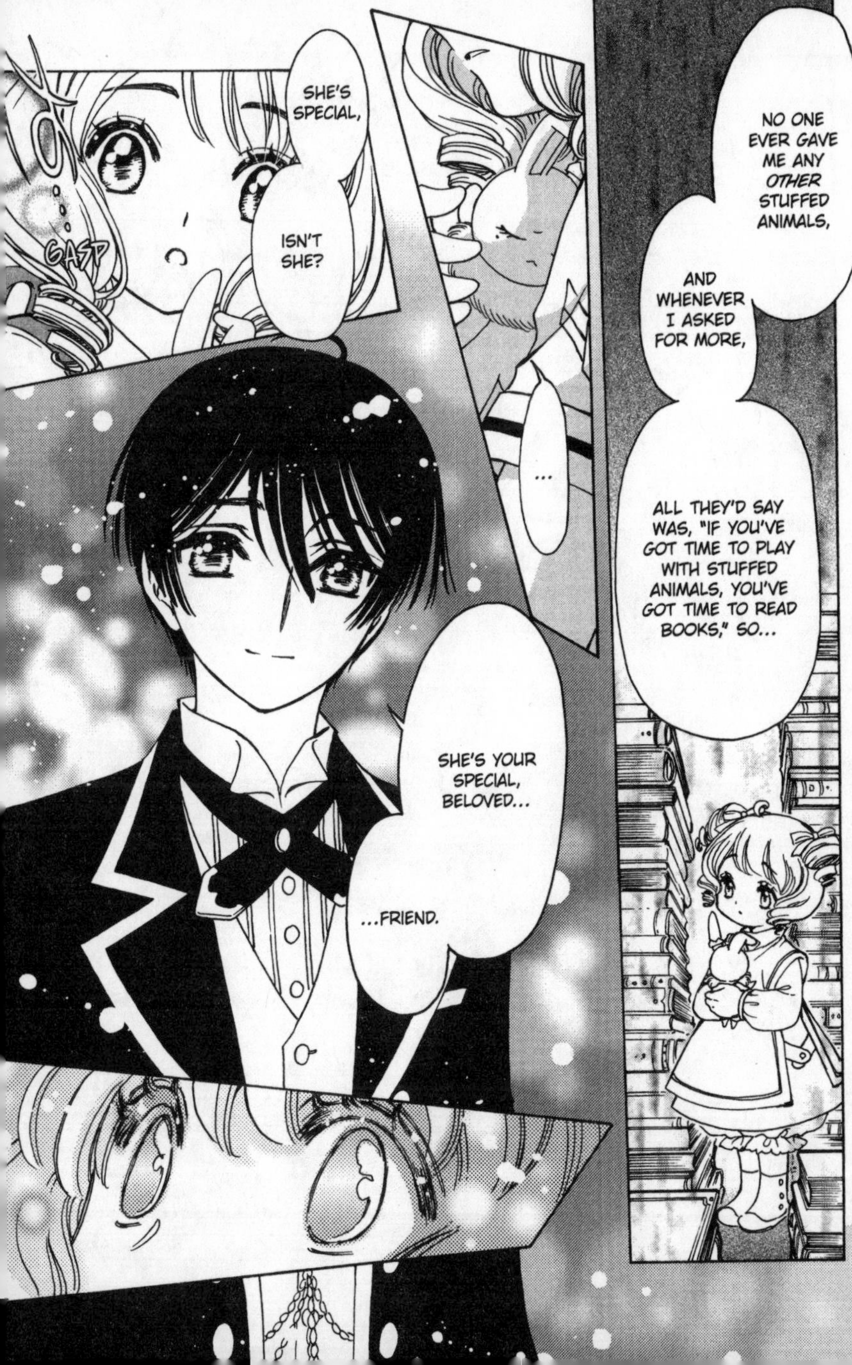
NO ONE EVER GAVE ME ANY *OTHER* STUFFED ANIMALS,
AND WHENEVER I ASKED FOR MORE,
ALL THEY'D SAY WAS, "IF YOU'VE GOT TIME TO PLAY WITH STUFFED ANIMALS, YOU'VE GOT TIME TO READ BOOKS," SO...
SHE'S SPECIAL,
ISN'T SHE?
GASP
...
SHE'S YOUR SPECIAL, BELOVED...
...FRIEND.

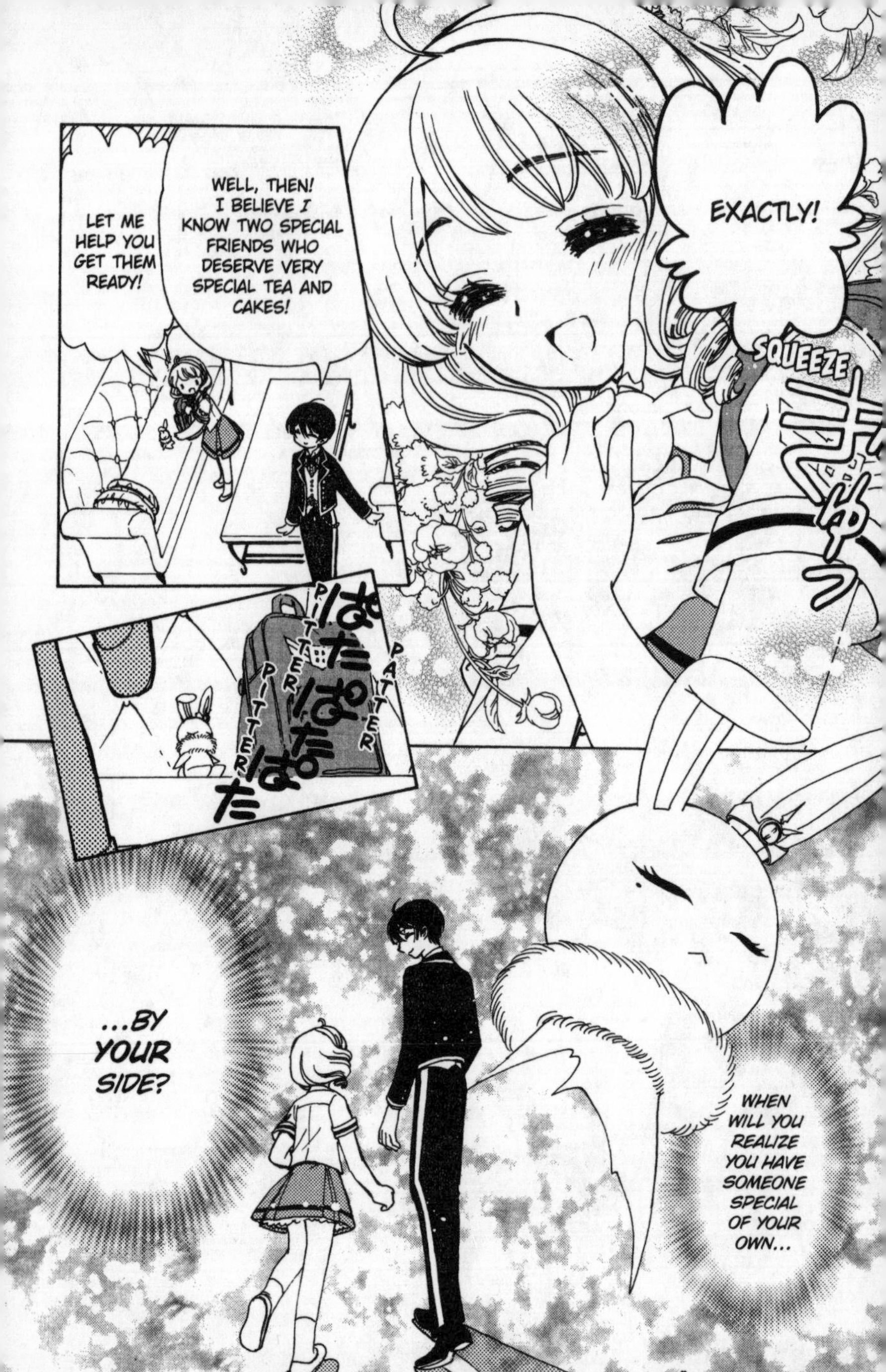
EXACTLY!
SQUEEZE
きゅっ
WELL, THEN! I BELIEVE I KNOW TWO SPECIAL FRIENDS WHO DESERVE VERY SPECIAL TEA AND CAKES!
LET ME HELP YOU GET THEM READY!
PATTER
ぱたぱたぱた
PITTER
PITTER
WHEN WILL YOU REALIZE YOU HAVE SOMEONE SPECIAL OF YOUR OWN...
...BY YOUR SIDE?

✿ The End ✿

Cardcaptor Sakura

CLEAR CARD

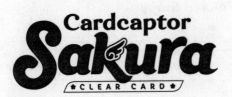

The adorable new odd-couple cat comedy manga from the creator of the beloved *Chi's Sweet Home*, in full color!

Sue & Tai-chan

Konami Kanata

Sue is an aging housecat who's looking forward to living out her life in peace... but her plans change when the mischievous black tomcat Tai-chan enters the picture! Hey! Sue never signed up to be a catsitter! *Sue & Tai-chan* is the latest from the reigning meow-narch of cute kitty comics, Konami Kanata.

KC
KODANSHA
COMICS